## PRAISE FOR *BEYOND THE POLITICS OF CONTEMPT*

"As someone who has long advocated that we elevate our values to sacred status, I was excited to see these authors bring this approach to addressing the national political divide. Living our values is an important first step to better understand how we treat and lead others and how we are being manipulated in unhealthy ways. This book includes practical ways to manage difficult conversations with courage and perseverance and help create a better political environment that can benefit us all. If you want to find ways to feel better about yourself and our country, read this book!"

—Scott Mautz, author of *The Mentally Strong Leader*

"Packed with insight, grounded in facts, and bursting with practical actions, this book hands citizens the keys to take control, step up, and make a difference in their communities. Feeling overwhelmed by the toxic polarization in our country? Tired of the stress, the division, and the urge to retreat? This book is a wake-up call. It doesn't just explain how we got here—it shows what we can do, starting now. No more doom-scrolling. No more sitting on the sidelines. This is a roadmap to bring us out of the chaos—and toward a better way forward for all of us."

—Gary Holland, Braver Angels director of the Office of Field Operations and Connecticut state coordinator

"These are challenging times for our country with declines in trust of both neighbors and democratic institutions. But, as Robert Putnam and I have documented, we faced similar difficulties a century ago. But we overcame them then, and we *can* do it again. The authors of *Beyond the Politics of Contempt* lay out clear steps to help make it happen!"

—Shaylyn Romney Garrett, coauthor of *The Upswing: How America Came Together a Century Ago and How We Can Do It Again*

"During my years in politics, I have witnessed firsthand the decline in voter trust of government and elected officials. This led me to invite Braver Angels to conduct a series of workshops to help legislators work better across the aisle and more constructively manage difficult conversations with constituents. I am excited that Doug Teschner, who led this effort, has stepped up to author this book and take this important work to people across the country. We all need to find better ways to engage respectfully and listen to each other, and this book offers many positive suggestions that can make our lives and politics better."

—Hon. Sherman Packard (R),
Speaker of the NH House of Representatives

"Doug Teschner and Beth Malow bring their formidable experience to bear in this timely and helpful book, including Doug's experience in politics, diplomacy, and consulting; Beth's experience as a physician helping children with complex neurological problems; and their work with Braver Angels. They offer guidance and resources to help people move from intense disagreement and hostility to find common ground and common purpose. Thanks to them for their courage and wisdom."

—The Rt. Rev. Mark Beckwith, retired bishop of Newark (Episcopal), Braver Faith of Braver Angels co-chair, and author of *Seeing the Unseen: Beyond Prejudices, Paradigms, and Party Lines*

"Having served in politics since the 1980s, I have had a front-row seat to the growing polarization and distrust of government. Having served with author Doug Teschner in the NH House of Representatives some years ago, I was not surprised when he stepped up to volunteer with Braver Angels. This included leading workshops to help citizens and elected officials work better together. And now he and his colleagues have authored this book, which is so needed in these challenging times!"

—Hon. David Scanlan, New Hampshire Secretary of State

"Beth and Doug are such model bridge builders. They've inspired me and so many others with their no-nonsense tools and the thoroughly disarming way they share them with divided communities. They've walked the walk, and this book's the map."

—Mónica Guzmán, author of *I Never Thought of It That Way: How to Have Fearlessly Curious Conversations in Dangerously Divided Times*

"In the past 25 years I have had a front row seat as we have witnessed the decline of public discourse in America. It is easy to become discouraged, but the authors of *Beyond the Politics of Contempt* offer a hopeful alternative to this trajectory. The steps they describe are both practical and vital for our country's future. I encourage everyone who cares about the future of politics and governance in the United States to read this book!"

—Steve Driehaus, former state legislator, member of Congress (D-Ohio), and founding partner of Good Government Group LLC

"Teschner, Malow, and Robinson draw from a deep field of researchers, bridge-builders, and democracy reformers to craft a work of clarity and conviction. *Beyond the Politics of Contempt* rejects the notion that division is inevitable and reminds us that it is, in fact, a choice. For those who have chosen to devote their efforts and talent to healing a fractured republic, this book stands as a clear and compelling blueprint."

—Stephen Hawkins, global director of research at More in Common and lead author of *Hidden Tribes: A Study of America's Polarized Landscape*

"This book is both a master class in strengthening personal relationships threatened by political disagreements and a call to citizenship for all of us who want a better society. It's brimming with humane insights and practical wisdom. In these troubled times, it's just what we need."

—David Blankenhorn, founding president of Braver Angels

"All of us are capable of feeding the rancor and division that dominate our politics. The authors point to a brighter alternative. *Beyond the Politics of Contempt* provides a much-needed breath of fresh air to a world often suffocated by anger and animosity. It's a welcome invitation to transcend the forces that paint your fellow citizens as the enemy."

—Seth Gillihan, licensed psychologist and author of *Retrain Your Brain: Cognitive Behavioral Therapy in 7 Weeks*

"Having served in politics, I have witnessed firsthand how division and polarization led to a decline in trust of government and our fellow citizens. This led me to join the citizens' organization Braver Angels where I helped lead a national initiative to bring people together to increase voter confidence in trustworthy elections. People need to find better ways to connect and listen to each other, and this book includes many practical suggestions to do just that!"

—Lenny Mirra, former Republican state legislator, Massachusetts

"In *Beyond the Politics of Contempt*, Teschner, Malow, and Robinson offer nourishment for America's hungry soul. You'll discover, in invitingly bite-sized chunks, a cogent analysis of how we became so polarized. Diverse in their politics and rich in expertise, these authors add in generous dollops of storytelling where they examine their own assumptions and biases, often with surprising outcomes. Then, they challenge us with intriguing exercises to explore our own role in today's political dynamic. Take them up on the challenge. Use this book to get together with colleagues or cousins, neighbors or strangers, friends or frenemies, and explore the art of listening to understand."

—Susan Clark, coauthor of *Slow Democracy: Rediscovering Community, Bringing Decision Making Back Home*

# BEYOND THE POLITICS OF CONTEMPT

Practical Steps to
Build Positive Relationships
in Divided Times

**DOUG TESCHNER**

**BETH MALOW**

**BECKY ROBINSON**

Copyright © 2025 by Doug Teschner, Beth Malow, and Becky Robinson

All rights reserved. No part of this book may be reproduced or retransmitted in any form or by any means without the written permission of the publisher.

Excerpts from pp. xiv, xix, 17, 63, 149, and 163 reprinted with permission of Avid Reader Press, a division of Simon & Schuster LLC from WHY WE'RE POLARIZED by Ezra Klein. Copyright © 2020 by Ezra Klein. All Rights reserved.

Excerpts from pp. xi, xii, 9, 13, 73, 95, 123, 137, 138, and 279 from HIGH CONFLICT: Why we get trapped and how we get out by Amanda Ripley. Copyright © 2021 by Amanda Ripley. Reprinted with the permission of Simon & Schuster, LLC. All rights reserved.

979-8-9990632-0-5 (soft cover)
979-8-9990632-2-9 (e-book)

Together Across Differences, LLC
beyondthepoliticsofcontempt.com

Production Management: Weaving Influence, Inc.
Cover and Interior Design: Rachel Royer
Copyediting: Sydney Spencer
Typesetting: Lori Weidert
Proofreading: Keri Hales

Printed in the United States of America

*For our children, grandchildren, and future generations*

# CONTENTS

Introduction
In This Moment, Why This Book? ................................................................ 1

## SECTION I
### EMBRACING HOPE, DIGNITY, AND RESPECT IN THESE CHALLENGING TIMES
### 13

Chapter 1
Finding Hope Amid Despair ................................................................ 15

Chapter 2
Beyond "Us vs. Them"—Can We Treat Others with Kindness? ......... 27

Chapter 3
Can Politics Coexist with Dignity and Respect? ................................ 39

## SECTION II
### THE ROOTS OF UNHEALTHY CONFLICT
### 51

Chapter 4
Healthy vs. Unhealthy Conflict ............................................................ 53

Chapter 5
How Did We Get Here? Forces Driving the Politics
of Contempt .......................................................................................... 63

Chapter 6
Polarization as a Business Model ....................................................... 77

## SECTION III

## CHANGE IS POSSIBLE, STARTING WITHIN YOU AND ME
### 89

Chapter 7
The Power of the Exhausted Majority ............................................................. 91

Chapter 8
Mind the Gap Between Thoughts and Values ................................................ 101

Chapter 9
Change from the Inside Out ............................................................................ 107

Chapter 10
What Positive Change Can Look Like:
The Promise of Citizen-Led Solutions ............................................................ 119

## SECTION IV

## SKILLS FOR LEADING YOURSELF AND OTHERS
### 131

Chapter 11
Embrace Your Self-Leadership Potential ....................................................... 133

Chapter 12
Skills for Braver Conversations ...................................................................... 145

Chapter 13
Applying Critical Thinking to the Polarization Challenge ............................ 159

Chapter 14
Positive Engagement with Family, Friends, and Colleagues ....................... 171

Chapter 15
Leading Others for a Better America .............................................................. 185

## SECTION V

## YOU WILL MAKE OUR COUNTRY BETTER
### 197

Chapter 16
**Find Your Path—Think Global, Act Local** .................................. 199

Chapter 17
**Embrace the Courage to Change and Grow** ........................................ 213

Appendix
**Additional Resources and Information** ................................................ 229

**Endnotes** ........................................................................................... 243

**Index** .................................................................................................. 263

**Acknowledgments** ............................................................................. 279

**About the Authors** ............................................................................ 285

> "Out beyond ideas of wrongdoing and rightdoing,
> there is a field. I will meet you there."
> —Rumi, 13th century Sufi poet

Introduction

# IN THIS MOMENT, WHY THIS BOOK?

> *"The only policy likely to succeed is to try to make the future."*—Peter Drucker

On November 6, 2024, the morning after Election Day, Americans awoke with an array of emotions, ranging from jubilant and relieved, to despondent and uncertain. Then came the inauguration and subsequent presidential actions that further stirred a range of viewpoints and reactions.

While competing ideas and opinions are vital for democratic governance, disdain and demonization of those with different political views has grown significantly in recent years. Friendships have dissolved and family relationships have become strained. Is politics *really* more important than friends and family? How did this happen? And how do we fix it?

We need to find a way to turn the politics of fear and contempt into the politics of hope.

The fundamental idea of our book is this: In a climate of widespread contempt and even hatred for people who disagree politically, we can each make important contributions to better our lives, our relationships, and our country. We can stand up for what we believe while also building bridges across the political divide. While many fear for our nation's future, there are practical steps we can each take to build hope for a better America.

The view of Mt. Moosilauke in the White Mountains from North Haverhill, NH. Courtesy of Doug Teschner.

## A POST-INAUGURATION REFLECTION BY DOUG

One Saturday, I drove forty miles north to Woodsville, New Hampshire, to attend the wake of a ninety-five-year-old farmer. His antique tractor was idling outside the funeral home, bringing joy to those gathered. I had known this man, who always had a smile on his face, and his son and grandchildren when I lived for thirty-six years in nearby Pike. Both Pike and Woodsville are villages in the town of Haverhill that I represented in the state legislature more than twenty years ago.

With a population of forty-six hundred, Haverhill is wedged between the Connecticut River and White Mountains and has a rich agricultural heritage. When I first moved there in the 1980s, it was the largest dairy-producing town in New Hampshire. While many fields are still mowed for hay, family farms are largely gone, as the economics of agriculture have changed dramatically in recent years.

While celebrating that heritage and beautiful scenery on my drive, I also felt a deep sadness for current and future generations who won't have the opportunity to make a living off the land (and experience the lifestyle and pride that go with it). It is also hard not to notice boarded-up businesses and homes needing repair.

I contrast Haverhill with Lebanon, New Hampshire, where my wife and I moved in 2023 to be closer to our son and grandson. This small city (population fifteen thousand) has a major medical center, prosperous manufacturing businesses, and Dartmouth College in nearby Hanover. There are many good jobs in Lebanon and Hanover, but most people from Haverhill and other towns cannot afford the high-priced housing so they get by with longer commutes.

According to New Hampshire Employment Security, Haverhill's 2022 median household income was $59,000, with 10 percent below the poverty line and 18.5 percent of adults ages twenty-five and up with bachelor's degrees or higher. That compares to Lebanon with a $91,000 median household income, 8.4 percent below the poverty line, and 55.8 percent with college degrees.[1]

In the 2024 Presidential election, Haverhill voters went 60 percent for Donald Trump and 39 percent for Kamala Harris, while Lebanon voted 25 percent for Trump and 74 percent for Harris.

Two communities, so close but so different.

This is a microcosm of the national geographic siloing trend—where people tend to live and primarily interact with others who have the same ideas about politics. I am sure there are some in prosperous communities like Lebanon who think of people in Haverhill as backward rural people who aren't educated or smart enough to know how to vote in a way that best meets their needs. And there are rural folks from places like Haverhill who view people in Lebanon as elitists who look down at working-class people.

Having lived in Haverhill and Lebanon, I know there are many caring, thoughtful people in both. Sadly, there aren't enough opportunities for people to better get to know those from different communities. People easily fall into stereotyping and oversimplification. If we are going to get past this country's division, we need to find ways to facilitate connections so that people better understand those with different life experiences and perspectives.

## IS POLITICS CAUSING YOU PAIN?

Are you losing sleep after watching or listening to the national news? Do you feel helpless at times, not knowing where to turn? Are you noticing that your health and well-being are affected by political events? Are you finding you can't talk with your brother-in-law or other relatives? What about friends and neighbors? Do you want to do something to improve our country, but aren't at all sure what that might be? This book includes many practical suggestions to help you take specific steps to better your life and our country, too.

## WHAT WILL YOU LEARN FROM THIS BOOK?

Many books identify the problems facing our nation. We appreciate the thorough and thoughtful approach these authors bring to the conversation. Our approach is complementary and builds on their ideas. We offer practical steps for addressing the nation's challenges, including:

1. Creating greater self-awareness about how your reactions to political events may impact your health and well-being, and realizing how you can act in ways that can help you feel better and more in control;

2. Finding ways to mend relationships torn apart by politics and ways to empower yourself and others when difficult conversations arise;

3. Understanding how you can stand up for what you believe while also building bridges across the political divide;

4. Identifying actions you can apply to help build a national culture of kindness, dignity, and respect, including citizen-led solutions as antidotes to the nation's unhealthy division.

We will provide many examples of these approaches throughout the book.

## WHO ARE WE, AND WHY DID WE WRITE THIS BOOK?

**From Beth:** I hail from the Northeast (Long Island, New York), born to parents who consistently voted Democratic, and I have lived in the North most of my life. However, I spent twenty-one years in a suburb of Nashville as a neurologist at a large medical center. My husband and I recently relocated to Quechee, a community in the upper valley of Vermont and New Hampshire. The sense of civic engagement in New England is palpable, and although I appreciated the political diversity in Tennessee, I am grateful to be part of this region now. I volunteer with Braver Angels, a grassroots national nonprofit that brings Americans together to bridge the partisan divide and strengthen our democratic republic (see more about this organization in the appendix). I have moderated events, designed workshops, and served as a debate chair. While I identify as a Democrat, I have developed close relationships with many Republicans, and I relish conversations with people who view issues differently than I do. As a physician and medical researcher, I have come to understand the importance of communicating science and health to the public in ways that they can relate to. I recently added that component to my career by earning a graduate certificate in science communication, and my interest in this area was influenced by my work with civil discourse.

**From Becky:** I grew up as an Army brat, but I've spent my entire adult life in the Great Lakes region, with the last fifteen years in Michigan. As a high schooler, not even old enough to vote, I made posters and worked to welcome George H.W. Bush to my small town's square during his 1988 campaign. My parents and grandparents voted Republican, and I voted Republican all the way up until 2020. Raised as a conservative, evangelical Christian, and continuing in those communities as an adult, I experienced some shifts in my perspectives during and after Trump's first term. I joined this book project just after the 2024 election, when I counted myself among those feeling desolate about the election's outcome, especially because of the fear and disappointment I felt about the President's anti-LGBTQ policies and initiatives, which directly affect my family. I am the CEO of a book marketing and production company, Weaving Influence, and the author of *Reach: Create the Biggest Possible Audience for Your Message, Book, or Cause*.[2] I want to use my talents in book production and marketing to get the messages of our book out into the world and reach as many people as possible.

**From Doug** I am grateful to have had the opportunity to serve our nation in various ways, including as an elected Republican member of the New Hampshire House of Representatives. I represented our country overseas in the Peace Corps, as a volunteer in Morocco and country director in Ukraine and several African nations. Now I volunteer with Braver Angels, serving as New England regional leader and helping elected officials to develop the skills and commitment to work together. This initiative, known as Braver Politics, facilitates opportunities to develop the skills and commitment to work together in goodwill across political differences. I'm especially proud of a three-year effort that led to the creation of the Granite Bridge Legislative Alliance, a caucus of Republican and Democratic legislators in New Hampshire working to foster positive relationships. While I could have chosen to enjoy a relaxing retirement, I instead feel called to help address the stark problems of division and polarization facing our nation.

## WHY DID WE CHOOSE TO SELF-PUBLISH?

Doug began this book project in January 2024, and Beth joined him in the summer. We went through multiple drafts together and made the decision to self-publish because we wanted to get our message out to the public as quickly as possible. (Traditional publishers have a long queue of twelve to eighteen months between signing a contract and publishing a book.) We also wanted control over our content and decisions related to elements such as the book cover. We were thrilled when Becky Robinson joined us as an author, adding valuable perspectives and stories while also sharing her book production and marketing expertise. We are also grateful to multiple writers and thought leaders who read our early manuscripts and provided excellent suggestions on style and political balance; they are recognized in the acknowledgments.

## WHAT IS IN THE BOOK?

In Section I, we make the case for why we should embrace hope in these challenging times. Hope is such an important motivator for building bridges that heal division. We emphasize the importance of going beyond an "us versus them" framework and moving toward better ways to think about others with kindness, dignity, and respect. We reflect on how we see friends, family members, neighbors, and strangers with different political perspectives.

In Section II, we explore the roots of unhealthy conflict and the differences between healthy and unhealthy conflict. Healthy conflict is when we debate issues and ideas, and sharpen our policies. Unhealthy conflict is when we move toward demonizing those we disagree with. Then we outline the factors that drive us to engage in unhealthy conflict and the politics of contempt. Finally, we discuss how polarization is perpetuated as a business model via social media algorithms and conflict entrepreneurs.

In Section III, we begin moving toward solutions. We identify the power of the exhausted majority. Coined in a report entitled *Hidden Tribes: A Study of America's Polarized Landscape* by the nonprofit organization More in

Common, the exhausted majority refers to Americans who are fed up with our nation's polarization. "They know we have more in common than that which divides us: our belief in freedom, equality, and the pursuit of the American dream. They share a deep sense of gratitude that they are citizens of the United States. They want to move past our differences."³ We discuss the gap between thoughts and values, and how we can change our mindsets, starting with reflection on core values. We move into how we can work with others to create citizen-led solutions starting at the community level.

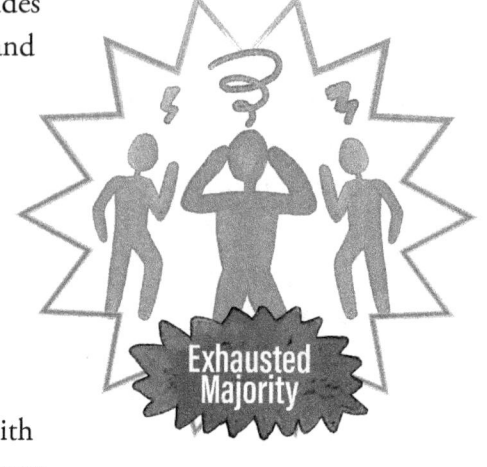

In Section IV, we focus on specific skills, including self-leadership, braver conversations, critical thinking, positive engagement with those with different opinions, and leading others. These are discussed in the context of creating a culture of dignity and respect, which in turn strengthens our politics and empowers us to build positive relationships while also benefiting personal health and well-being. Change can happen by promoting practical steps that begin with Gandhi's insight: "If we could change ourselves, the tendencies in the world would also change."⁴

In Section V, we emphasize the importance of finding your path and embracing the courage to make a difference. This includes analyzing how you can better understand and effectively influence the various factors driving the politics of contempt.

The appendix has a practical checklist to develop a personal plan based on the key ideas shared throughout the book. That section also includes background information on Braver Angels and other organizations working to bridge the political divide.

## WHAT ISN'T IN THE BOOK?

This book is not about kumbaya and compromise. If people engage respectfully, finding common ground is possible and compromise might happen, but that is not the central point of our book. Disagreement and conflict are an inevitable part of democratic governance. People need to advocate and fight for what they believe. The problem is when those disagreements cross over into unhealthy conflict, demonizing people with different views. We need to respect those who disagree with us, to honor each person's humanity. Through engaging together across differences, we can strengthen our nation and ourselves as well.

## QUESTIONS TO CONSIDER

As you work your way through this book, we encourage you to ask yourself a few key questions:

- Do I sometimes view those with different political views as misguided, duped, or maybe even as enemies?
- Can I consider that those with different viewpoints might help me to view contentious issues through a different lens, offering perspectives from which I might learn and possibly even grow?
- What role do silos (also known as tribes, in-groups, and echo chambers) play in my interactions, or lack of interactions, with fellow citizens with different perspectives?
- What actions can I take so that political issues do not affect my health or undermine relationships with family, friends, coworkers, and neighbors?
- How can I be an effective political activist who fights for my beliefs while also reaching out to those on the other side?
- What can I do to help rebuild a national culture of kindness, dignity, and respect?
- What might the answers to these questions help me to understand about myself?

Stepping out of silos and engaging in curious ways with others—rather than demonizing them from a distance—takes patience, humility, and courage. But, as we show throughout this book, it is possible and worth it.

We each have an extraordinary opportunity to make a difference in people's lives, including our own. When enough of us act and demand better, fellow citizens and politicians will follow. Do not underestimate your potential to make a positive impact!

# SECTION 1

# EMBRACING HOPE, DIGNITY, AND RESPECT IN THESE CHALLENGING TIMES

*"The occasion is piled high with difficulty, and we must rise with the occasion."*
—*Abraham Lincoln*

## Chapter 1
# FINDING HOPE AMID DESPAIR

> *"Once you choose hope, anything's possible."*
> —*Christopher Reeve*

Are you discouraged by events in our country and the world? Does consuming the news bring you down and compel you to shut it off? Have you experienced unpleasant incidents and unkind behavior that affect your daily morale—such as drivers riding your bumper or making disparaging gestures?

Have your relationships with friends or family been negatively affected by politics? Do you feel helpless to do anything about it?

We sure feel that way some of the time.

**From Doug** I recall an unpleasant conversation in 2017 at an outdoor community concert where I set up my lawn chair near a couple I had known for many years. One of them had served (like me) as a state legislator. As you might expect, the conversation turned to politics. Sadly, it quickly became a bit nasty as we expressed how we had voted in the 2016 presidential election, with brusque comments exchanged back and forth. Neither of us convinced the other, and I remember being upset and dissatisfied by that conversation, thinking it had been a lose-lose situation. I left that evening disappointed in myself and vowing to do better.

**From Beth** I remember talking with a friend who no longer called her son who had voted differently from her in the 2020 presidential election. They had previously been very close, but they hadn't communicated in more than a year. Falling out with her son meant that my friend hadn't seen her daughter-in-law or grandchildren either. It was sad to see a family separated by politics.

Braver Angels (https://braverangels.org/) provides one model for bridging differences and finding hope amid despair. Founded in 2016, this national organization seeks ways to get beyond what cofounder Bill Doherty describes as making someone's policy positions a fundamental test of their humanity and integrity.

**From Doug** I was introduced to Braver Angels by folksinger Peter Yarrow of Peter, Paul, and Mary fame, whom I had first met in Ukraine in 2010. Peace Corps Volunteers had invited him there because his nonprofit Operation Respect promotes anti-bullying in schools using music—including an incredibly powerful song titled "Don't Laugh at Me." In November 2019, I reconnected with Peter at the Lebanon Opera House in New Hampshire after his concert with long-time partner Noel Paul Stookey. After a big hug, Peter made a pitch for Braver Angels (then called Better

Angels). Given my concerns about where our country was headed, this turned out to be exactly what I was looking for. As we were writing this book, I was sad to learn of the death of my friend Peter.

Author Doug Teschner and Peter Yarrow singing "If I Had a Hammer" in Ukraine in 2010. Photo courtesy of Doug Teschner.

**From Beth** I first became involved with Braver Angels in 2017 after hearing about the organization on NPR. I helped recruit "Blues" (Democrats or left-leaning voters) for workshops they were planning to hold in Nashville that summer that included a mix of "Reds" (Republicans or right-leaning voters) and "Blues," and I attended one of the first "Red/Blue" workshops myself. I found hope through interacting with others who held different political views from mine and realizing how many values we had in common.

In July 2023, Doug and Beth attended the Braver Angels national convention on the sacred ground of Gettysburg, Pennsylvania. Attendees were asked, "Why are you here?" Doug wrote on his 3×5 card: "I am worried that my grandchildren will not experience the benefits of this country that I have." Beth wrote on hers: "I want to engage with other like-minded people who love this country and want to bridge divides."

Others among the nearly seven hundred Braver Angels convention attendees responded with comments including these to the question of why they were attending:

- "We need to trust each other again, and trust begins with communication and relationship."
- "I'm here to dig deeper into my own biases and judgments."
- "For personal inspiration and practical ideas to rebuild unity in our divided and rancorous democratic republic."
- "To build relationships with people with different experiences and perspectives than mine."
- "To leave the world better than I found it."
- "I am deeply concerned about the country I love. My grandkids deserve to inherit a better country."
- "I am here because, if we don't change how our politics is done, we'll see ourselves in another civil war. Except this time, it won't look like Gettysburg—it'll look like Rwanda."

**From Doug** Having worked in Rwanda in the early 2000s, that last comment really caught my attention. I led a US Agency for International Development-funded project to strengthen the parliament in that nation, which was so scarred by the 1994 Hutu genocide against the Tutsis. Neighbors killed neighbors, even people they knew well, just because they were in a different tribe. The killers were emboldened by leaders who exploited difference and fear. I remember feeling grateful that we didn't have political tribalism in the United States.

In 2014, I was working in Guinea during the Ebola epidemic in West Africa that touched many other nations. I recall thinking that Americans, unlike many Guineans, would have faith in our public health system in the event of a national medical emergency.

I was obviously wrong on both counts. We find ourselves today in political tribes, and the COVID pandemic severely tested our ability to communicate with each other and trust what the government was telling us. While that pandemic may be behind us, it has clearly left deep scars.

---

People are being torn apart by politics, often engaging in unpleasant conversations and feeling increasingly suspicious of those with different viewpoints. In *The Age of Grievance,* Frank Bruni describes the potentially devastating erosion of civility, common ground, and compromise that are so necessary for our democracy to survive.[1] And some of us are so hooked on political division and anger that we hold on tight because it makes us feel righteous and safe.[2] Therapists ask this question: When people are angry, what are they protecting?

A 2023 Associated Press–National Opinion Research Center poll found 62 percent of adults felt that the US democracy could be at risk depending on who won the 2024 presidential election.[3] Democrats (72 percent) and Republicans (55 percent) agreed. While this wasn't part of that study, it seems that members of the two parties had very different reasons, with Democrats worrying that we were at risk of electing an authoritarian president and Republicans concerned that a Democrat leader could promote government overreach and threats to fundamental freedoms.

An April 2024 *PBS News Hour*/NPR/Marist Poll survey found that one in five US adults believe Americans may have to resort to violence to get our country back on track.[4] Another study found that 49 percent of

Republicans and 33 percent of Democrats would feel "displeased" if their child married someone outside their party—compared to only 5 percent and 4 percent in 1960.[5]

The old bumper sticker "Question Authority" feels so inadequate to describe where we stand as a nation these days. Once that phrase seemed like a quaint assertion inviting us to ask questions, verify information, and hold leaders accountable. Today, that same message (if anyone chooses to use it) would likely convey total disdain: Throw the bums out, no questions required.

These are difficult times with wide-ranging national (and international) challenges, including these:

- Inflation, taxation, and tariffs
- Economic disparities
- Affordable and accessible health care, childcare, education, and housing
- The national debt
- Climate change
- Immigration
- Racism and antisemitism
- The urban-rural divide
- Distrust of government and other institutions
- War and political unrest in many parts of the world
- Uncertainty about the expanding role of artificial intelligence

In addressing these challenges, we often differ on how to react to the issue. Take, for example, climate change. While most Americans agree that climate change is man-made and accelerating, we differ on perceived urgency, trade-offs (giving up our current way of life for electric cars and vegetarian or meat-reduced diets), and the role of government regulation versus innovations in the private sector. We differ on our language, too; some of us refer to the climate crisis while others talk about clean energy job creation.

In addition to the longer list above, there is also:

- Growing distrust of fellow citizens
- Declines in kindness, respect, humility, and decency in how we treat others
- Political polarization

This is all a lot to be worried about, but we believe that real change can start by focusing on the shorter list: distrust, how we treat each other, and polarization. We can begin with ourselves and how we engage with others, especially with people who might have different perspectives from us. People vote the way they do for any number of reasons, and every person is an individual with their own needs and aspirations. We can resist making assumptions and putting people in boxes.

*Polarization* was selected as Merriam-Webster's 2024 Word of the Year, which was no surprise given how much it has dominated our national culture.[6] Political polarization has two aspects. Disagreements over ideas and policies (called ideological polarization) is one aspect that can be healthy for our society. In contrast, dislike and distrust of people with different views (called affective polarization) is toxic and interferes with healthy disagreement about ideas and policies. It creates an "us versus them" mentality.[7] This latter kind of polarization is what concerns us. Journalist, author, and Senior Fellow for Public Practice at Braver Angels Mónica Guzmán describes this political polarization "as the problem that eats other problems, the monster who convinces us that the monsters are us."[8]

Hope starts with believing that, despite our differences, we can find a way to hold our country together. This is both necessary and possible, despite the obvious challenges. Embrace the idea that hope and despair are connected and that we can hold on to both at the same time.[9] Finding something meaningful to accomplish, often with others, is a critical aspect of hope as well. Take stock of your skills and interests, and find a path forward, however large or small.

Being stressed about politics is increasingly common these days, so it is important to take care of your mental health by focusing on healthy habits, staying socially connected, and doing things that bring you joy.[10] Ongoing self-reflection, including a deep understanding of how your actions and behavior impact others, can be coupled with a commitment to ongoing personal development and relationship building. We each can make a personal investment to earn the trust of others by acting with authenticity and openness. "No one cares what you know until they know that you care!" has often been attributed to Theodore Roosevelt.

The same PBS News Hour/NPR/Marist poll we mentioned earlier that indicated the increased likelihood of violence also struck a positive note, with 81 percent of respondents saying they had friends with different political beliefs than theirs and 68 percent saying they believe the American Dream is still attainable.[11]

Historian Doris Kearns Goodwin offered this hopeful perspective reflecting on her book *An Unfinished Love Story, A Personal History of the 1960s*:

"America has been at odds with itself before. I've been drawn to such turbulent times—the Civil War, the Industrial Revolution, World War II. This is the story of one of those times, of my husband and myself, and our generation shaped by the cataclysms of the 1960s. We see what historic opportunities were seized, what chances were lost, what light those years cast upon our own fractured time. 'The end of our country has loomed many times before,' my husband often reminded me, 'America is not as fragile as it seems.'"[12]

America is not as fragile as it seems. We believe that, but it is up to us to live it and embrace it. If we don't like what we see, it is our responsibility to act with a hopeful spirit.

Author Thomas Friedman writes, "Pessimists are usually right and optimists are usually wrong, but all the great changes have been accomplished by optimists."[13] But hope is possible without being optimistic. Journalist and author Krista Tippett observes that hope is distinct from idealism or optimism and unrelated to wishful thinking.[14] We can look at the world and insist that it doesn't have to be that way.

Yuval Levin, the author of *American Covenant: How the Constitution Unified Our Nation—and Could Again*,[15] commented in an online conversation:

> "I think optimism and pessimism are both dangerous vices, and between them sits a virtue of hope. Hope is different from both of them in that it is not passive. It invites us to act on the potential for good, and it calls on us to be deserving of good, and to be capable of it, to actually take up the work of making it happen. I think looking at America, looking at our history, looking at our people, looking at the world we live in now, we should be hopeful about it. There's no society you'd rather be in this world. And I think in a lot of ways, there's no time you'd rather live in than this time. It's not without its troubles, very serious and grave troubles, but we have a lot to work with in addressing those. And I absolutely am hopeful about the future of this country, because I think we're up to the challenge."

Finding ways to connect with others helps us build hope. We often pass by people, barely noticing them (while often remaining engrossed in our phones). Listening to others is an important skill that has largely been lost in our busy times. This is hard work, but it's so important.

**From Beth** After the 2016 election, I was invited to attend a rally at our city library in Brentwood, Tennessee, focused on bringing down the Trump administration. Flocked by bullhorns, signs, and knitted hats, I didn't feel that I was in my element. I wanted to understand why my neighbors had voted for Trump—what appealed to them and what their values were.

I received one lead for what I should do—a friend of a friend suggested that I visit "Common Ground Nashville." I loved this civil discourse group and ended up co-leading it for five years. We held monthly meetings on national and local topics. One memorable meeting featured a woman who was a gun owner and trainer. When she was growing up in a rural area, her parents were often away at work, and she needed a gun to protect her younger brothers and sisters from trespassers. That story changed my thinking on gun rights—I remember thinking, "I get why she feels guns are important."

I now have a more nuanced position on guns. While it was intellectually rewarding to create a welcoming space where my neighbors could discuss controversial issues, I also felt a *palpable sense of hope* after I left these meetings. We saw humanity in others who were different from us, and we understood—and truly felt—that people who disagreed with us were not necessarily ignorant, misguided, or evil.

---

We know from our volunteer work how, when you bring people together with strong political views (and set ground rules that ensure respectful discussions), they agree on much more than they expect to at the start. This can seem incredibly hopeful. For example, at the end of a Braver Angels workshop focused on finding common ground on promoting trustworthy elections, one participant commented, "We agreed on more things than I would have thought, and people in this room were hungry."

Yes, people are hungry for something better, and we need people—such as *you*—to help build hope and show us the way. Embracing positive change is fundamental to growing as a person, and while growing as a person, you can make our country better, too.

Yes, there is hope, but change is up to us.

This book offers concrete ideas for making valuable changes in yourself, in your family and relationships, in your community, and in our country.

At the end of each chapter, we'll invite you to reflect on how you can apply the book's ideas to your life. You may find it helpful to write down your responses and action steps as you read the book.

## FOR FURTHER THOUGHT

- What concerns do you have about our country's future?
- When have you had unpleasant conversations about politics with family, friends, or work colleagues? What might you want to do differently?
- Would you like to develop ways to better engage with people who might have different ideas from yours?
- What would make you more confident in situations when difficult conversations arise about politics?
- What information and ideas could make you more hopeful about our country's future?

Chapter 2

# BEYOND "US VS. THEM"— CAN WE TREAT OTHERS WITH KINDNESS?

> *"Be kind whenever possible. It is always possible."*
> —Tenzin Gyatso, 14th Dalai Lama

A 2024 *Wall Street Journal* story was headlined "We Are Starting to Enjoy Hatred: The Country Has Long Been Divided, but Estrangement Has Become Alluring in the Age of Biden and Trump."[1] Have we really sunk that far? And for a more personal question—are you enjoying hating Democratic or Republican politicians and the people who support them? Do you find yourself speaking with disdain about "those people" on the other side? Are you contributing to the politics of humiliation and contempt?

If you are, is this really where you want to be? Are you becoming like Dr. Seuss's memorable character The Grinch whose "heart was two sizes too small"? Step back and consider how this is impacting your personal health and relationships. As author Kurt Vonnegut observes, "Hate, in the long run, is about as nourishing as cyanide."

The problem clearly runs deeper than politics. In an article in *The Atlantic,* "How America Got Mean," author David Brooks writes about how our culture has shifted from an emphasis on character and reputation to self-centeredness and narcissism. Fewer Americans are giving to charity, while murder rates are high, gun sales are rising, and social trust is dropping.[2]

## WHATEVER HAPPENED TO KINDNESS?

*"People will forget what you said, people will forget what you did, but people will never forget how you made them feel."—Maya Angelou*

We don't want to exaggerate—there is still a lot of kindness among family, friends, and even strangers. We love the podcast series *My Unsung Hero,* which delivers short segments produced by Hidden Brain Media that often appear on NPR. In these powerful stories, people recall ways that others—most often strangers—did something that touched them profoundly and positively impacted their lives.

For example, Mary Fran Lyons describes being stressed in a mall while wearing a baseball hat after losing her hair to chemotherapy. A passing stranger, who clearly observed her distress, said, "You're going to be OK." More than twenty years later, Lyons recalls that moment: "If that woman were standing in front of me right now, I would say to her, 'You gave me hope at a time when I really needed to hear it.' And I still think of that to this day."[3]

Another example: Samantha Hodge-Williams was twenty years old and terrified as she lay on an operating table worrying that a large ovarian mass might be cancerous. A kind anesthesiologist sensed her unease and engaged in a gentle conversation that led to singing. Hodge-Williams remembers "her reassuring voice, how much it meant to me . . . not just the science of medicine, but the compassion and care to take a few moments to care for me."[4]

Little acts of kindness can touch people in memorable ways, positively influencing our lives.

While kindness is still around, most people would agree that there is less of it than there used to be. We remember television's Mr. Fred Rogers telling children to be kind to one another, but many think it is perfectly OK these days to demean—or even threaten—other people. Disrespect and distrust pervade our whole society, including schools, workplaces, and public spaces. Rudeness on our highways is one example.

**From Doug** I was riding with my wife on an interstate entry ramp when the driver behind us came close to our bumper, clearly suggesting that my wife speed up. As we merged onto the highway, the angry driver quickly passed, giving my wife the finger before speeding off. We have all heard stories of these kinds of situations deteriorating into confrontation and even violence, but I was feeling more sad than angry that day. I was wondering about that driver's personal story. Is he often this angry, or was he just having a bad day? Did he regret his behavior later? Does he treat his family and friends differently than strangers? Sadly, I've seen behavior like this repeated multiple times since.

**From Beth** During COVID, I recall attending a county school board meeting in Tennessee, where I lived at the time, with the intention to speak on the importance of masking in schools. When I arrived, it was more of a political rally than a "boring" school board meeting. There were bullhorns and people holding up signs and chanting "No More Masks." I recall being thankful that I didn't secure a speaking spot because they had all been given out hours before. A medical professional who did speak in support of masks was threatened in the parking lot. CNN covered the event, and I felt embarrassed for my community. For days afterward, I felt a sense of uneasiness—what if I had spoken and had become personally endangered?

Unfortunately, examples of abusive behavior like this are increasingly on public display. News reports recount physical threats against school board members and airline employees getting self-defense training. The New Hampshire legislature felt compelled to act on a bill to protect school sports referees from irate parents and fans.

As reported in the *NH Business Review*, the manager of Bowl-O-Rama in Portsmouth, New Hampshire, felt a need to speak out on Facebook, decrying "rude, belligerent, and frankly abusive behavior" by customers.[5] In a "Miss Manners" column, one letter writer complained about people being "oblivious, uninformed, narcissistic, or just plain rude" on the golf course or in the gym.[6]

We are increasingly numbed by rudeness that is degrading the human experience. What are we teaching our children? Mr. Rogers must be rolling over in his grave.

## AGGRESSIVE BEHAVIOR IN MEDICAL SETTINGS

*"Nothing is so contagious as example, and we never do any great good or great evil which does not produce its like."—François de La Rochefoucauld (17th century French author)*

**From Doug** Since 1996, I have been a patient at an orthopedic medical practice, and I had knee replacements in 2019 and 2020. During a follow-up visit, I noticed a prominent new sign in the reception area: "Our staff and patients have the right to work in and visit a safe and respectful environment. We will not tolerate violence, physical aggression or verbal abuse towards our staff or fellow patients."

I thought this was common sense and wondered if that sign was really needed. In 2024, the sign was still on display. I asked why and was told that aggressive patient behavior accelerated during COVID, and some patients became very belligerent when told they needed to wear a mask. Then, a couple of years later, when COVID was in decline and masks were no longer required, the opposite happened: there were aggressive patients complaining that the medical practice was no longer insisting on masks being worn!

Staff told me they still get nasty comments almost every day, typically related to required paperwork and appointments running late. One person threw a clipboard that hit a receptionist in the chest. A doctor observed that there no longer seem to be social consequences for bad behavior. It used to be unacceptable and embarrassing for the person involved, but that seems to be much less the case today, he added.

Yes, apparently, they still need that sign, although I wonder how much of a difference it makes. Staff now receive training on how to de-escalate difficult situations.

How sad that this has become so necessary. "Violence has become a daily occurrence in our hospitals," an emergency room nurse recently told Vermont lawmakers in the House of Representatives committee on health care.[7]

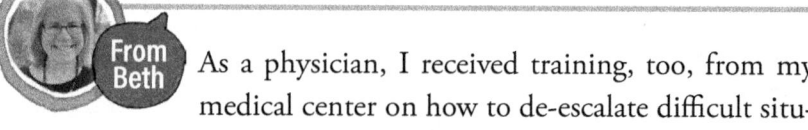 As a physician, I received training, too, from my medical center on how to de-escalate difficult situations, and even "active shooter" training. I learned how to respond to life-threatening situations involving belligerent patients with guns. I've realized how common it has become for people to show aggression toward medical personnel, especially if they are ill or their loved one is hospitalized.

These kinds of events speak to a social problem that clearly runs much deeper than politics.

## WHAT GOOD IS HATE?

*"Holding onto hate will damage your soul."—Karen Salmansohn*

Not only is there less kindness, but thoughts and feelings may evolve into hate and disdain for others. Most therapists will tell you that finding healthy ways to get past contempt is essential for one's own health. Apparently, many people are not hearing that message.

*NH Business Review* columnist Ron Bourque has written that "malaise has spread to just about every facet of our lives. Some formerly close families have separated. And yes, it's found its way into the workplace."[8] He describes the potential impact this can have on businesses and how it has been steadily worsening for many years.

The 1977 Dave Mason song "We Just Disagree" (written by Jim Krueger) offers the idea that neither side is good or bad when two people differ.[9] That tune may be about a romantic breakup, but the thought can be a helpful way to step back when there are strong differences over politics or other topics.

An infectious multiplier effect adds to the problem. When we experience distasteful or unkind behavior, we can find ourselves more inclined to be unkind to others. After all, if they are doing it, I can, too! But that is a dangerous rabbit hole to enter that will only bring us down.

 In 2024, I attended a church service at All Saints by-the-Sea, a summer chapel in Southport, Maine. Mark Beckwith, a retired Episcopal bishop and Braver Angels faith leader, gave a sermon highlighting the difference between humility and humiliation—two very different words with the same root. Acting with humility is important even if it seems out of fashion in these "us versus them" times. Vulnerability is closely related to humility but may put us at increased risk of being talked down to and possibly even feeling humiliated ourselves.

Of course, no one wants to be humiliated, but when we act in ways that humiliate others, we only demean ourselves. Yet so many seem so quick to do it, especially on social media. What price do we pay for mean-spirited behavior? Have we forgotten how to treat others? Are our families, schools, and workplaces doing their jobs?

## HOW TO BE A LITTLE KINDER

*"Be kind to everyone. You never know what they are going through."*
—Ian Maclaren

Making our country kinder might not require that much extra time or effort in your busy day. The key is increased self-awareness of how your actions impact others. Embracing a kindness mindset will help ensure that you don't overreact to difficult situations. You can be a positive role model by making a little extra effort to say thank you to those you encounter in daily life—like retail workers or work colleagues.

**From Beth:** I was traveling home from Florida in February 2025. It was Valentine's Day and the start of the school winter break, so the TSA was a mob scene. Not the usual walk up, show your license, and proceed through. Two women travelers immediately behind me in line, traveling to Asheville and Austin, were anxious about making it to their flights in time. As I had plenty of time, I invited them to go ahead of me. They were so appreciative, even though it didn't seem to save them any time. Waiting for luggage to pass through the security checkpoint, we were back together and started chit-chatting. That's when they shared that it was the kindness I had shown them, rather than the time they saved, that uplifted their spirits. One woman said, "Kindness is so important—right now." The brief encounter with these women put me in a great mood for a long travel day.

---

How each of us touches others, whether positively or negatively, is critically important. These are some simple actions to support a culture of kindness:

- Act in positive ways—it's contagious.
- Encourage others—we all need a kind word sometimes.
- Say "thank you"—a little appreciation goes a long way.
- Be trustworthy and reliable.
- Adopt humility and be more curious about other people.
- Embrace gratitude and respect for others.

These actions are simple. All that is required is self-awareness, stepping back to better understand how our behavior impacts others. Changing your approach and mindset with a little mindfulness can go a long way.

## CAN WE EMBRACE DIGNITY AND RESPECT?

*"Love your enemies, do good to those who hate you."—Luke 6:27*

In his book *Love Your Enemies: How Decent People Can Save America from the Culture of Contempt,* author Arthur Brooks advocates for a higher standard for how we should think and behave:

> "I want something more radical and subversive than civility and tolerance, something that speaks to the heart's desire . . . And not just love for friends and those who agree with me, but rather, love for those who disagree with me as well."[10]

We agree that civility and tolerance are too low a standard. But maybe love is too high, unrealistic for all but the very best of us. Instead, we "settle for"—or maybe "propose" is a better way to say it—dignity and respect.

Dignity and respect for others is not quite love, yet it's still certainly a big reach!

But what does dignity and respect look like in a practical way?

It starts with being more conscious of how we think and talk about others, including people with different political opinions. That sounds simple, but we know it is not always easy.

## BE THE ANGEL

*"He only has the right to criticize who has the heart to help."*
*—Abraham Lincoln*

In an op-ed related to campus demonstrations after the October 2023 Hamas attacks and Israel's response, Dartmouth professor James Heffernan wrote:

> "No matter who gets arrested, we live in a time of zero-sum animosity. Anything good for my side is bad for yours. Anything I say against

your side can be taken to mean that I want to annihilate you. And no matter how much pain and misery and mayhem and death my side inflicts on yours, my side's pain and suffering will always and forever trump yours. Can we somehow find a way to stop this mindless tug of war, stop demonizing each other, and start reaching out across the gulf between us?"[11]

So many of us are quick to criticize others—especially on social media, but also in public settings. What about you? How often do you criticize *with a heart to help?* Changing the country for the better can start with changing how we see and treat others.

This is tough work, but change can happen, beginning with understanding that how we see others is a reflection of ourselves. Back to Dr. Seuss: We can be like the Grinch at the end of the story whose small heart grew three sizes in one day.

As author Mónica Guzmán observes, stepping out of our political silos "can take patience, humility, and a good heap of courage."[12] But, when enough of us act and demand better, politicians will follow, too. The impact can ripple outward.

We loved this takeaway by podcast host Kelly Corrigan, recalling her conversation with director and stand-up comedian Judd Apatow. She said: "Sometimes all it takes is one person, one angel to say, I see what you're doing. It'll work. Keep going."[13]

Be the angel. What better advice can there be?

## FOR FURTHER THOUGHT

- Do you find yourself speaking with disdain about those on the other side of the political divide and, if so, what might you do differently?
- What experiences have you had with people engaging in unkind behavior and how have you reacted or responded in those situations?
- What steps could you take to embrace a kindness mindset?
- Recall situations when you criticized others without a heart to help, and consider what might you want to do differently next time.
- What steps could you take to be the angel who treats others with dignity and respect?

Chapter 3

# CAN POLITICS COEXIST WITH DIGNITY AND RESPECT?

> *"We need to build a politics where one of our aims is the participation and respect we give to each other."*
> —Ezra Klein

Maybe we can each be a little kinder in our daily interactions with others. But what about when it comes to people whose ideas or political views we find deeply offensive?

Derek Black, the godson of former Ku Klux Klan Grand Wizard David Duke and son of Don Black (founder of the Stormfront online community), was a student at New College of Florida. After his white nationalist views became known on campus, a group of Jewish students invited Black to attend their weekly Shabbat dinners. Derek accepted the invitation, and he came back regularly. Eventually, at age twenty-two, Derek wrote an article renouncing white nationalism, published by the Southern Poverty Law Center in 2013.

Why the change in Derek Black? Clearly, it resulted from the relationships he had developed with the Jewish students who welcomed him to eat and socialize with them week after week. They could have denounced

Derek or called him nasty names. Instead, they treated him with dignity and respect and invited him into their lives. This must have been anything but easy, but look at the amazing result! Those students modeled the way to bridge difficult divides.[1]

We can't talk about improving political discord and reducing contempt across the political divide without some discussion of reversing the decline in everyday kindness. We can assume that the driver who gave Doug's wife the finger in the previous chapter didn't know how Doug's wife voted in the previous election. Of course, assumptions are always possible based on the kind of car or the state on the license plate, but our guess is that politics had nothing to do with it.

But we know when we talk about politics and differences in personal beliefs, the conversations get a lot tougher. This is where kindness and empathy need to come in, with a commitment to really listening and being curious about those who have views different from our own.

Most of us spend more and more of our time with those who think like us, reinforcing our sense of being right and our disdain for "those people" on the other side. According to a 2023 poll by the University of Virginia's Center for Politics (before Biden left the presidential race), 70 percent of Biden supporters and 68 percent of Trump voters believed electing officials from the opposite party would result in lasting harm to the United States.[2]

This is a scary trend, and we know that Americans increasingly distrust data and factual information, with a blurring of the lines between truth and opinion. The result? An erosion of civil discourse, contributing to disengagement, political paralysis, and uncertainty.

Consider the people influencing you—whether it's in person, on social media, or in the news. Are they improving your life, or are some of them having the opposite effect? Are there people or information sources you might want to pull back from? Alternatively, are there others you might want to spend more time with?

## EMBRACING DIGNITY AND RESPECT

*"We have to face the fact that either all of us are going to die together or we are going to learn to live together and if we are to live together we have to talk."*—Eleanor Roosevelt

Everyone deserves dignity and respect. We suspect many of us agree with this simple idea, at least in principle. But it is also complicated and challenging. What about someone who hurls a clipboard at a receptionist in a medical office? Does it help to know the person may be sick, experiencing trauma, or have a loved one struggling with a serious illness?

Or what about Vladimir Putin, the leader of Russia?

**From Doug** I lived for more than four years in Ukraine, including when Putin first invaded that nation in 2014. In 2019, I was back there serving as an election observer with the Organization for Security and Co-operation in Europe when Volodymyr Zelenskyy was elected President. I find myself pushing back against my idea of everyone deserving dignity and respect when I think of Putin, given what he has done to a beautiful country and its people.

When thinking about who deserves dignity and respect, we can be quick to cross off people like Putin who we believe behave so badly (for instance, violating democratic norms in Russia and invading Ukraine). Then there are violent criminals who engage in unlawful behavior. And many feel that politicians in general are unworthy of dignity and respect.

Then, of course, there are "those people" who support politicians and policies on the other side of the political divide. Aside from our internal struggle to treat them with dignity and respect, if we drop our personal resistance to this idea, we may elicit confused reactions from our political peer group. They may even accuse us of normalizing anti-democratic behavior.

> **From Beth**
>
> After the 2024 election, many of my friends and family members could not understand how President Trump had won the election, especially the popular vote. They considered anyone who voted for him to be misguided (at best). I saw it differently, with issues such as the economy and immigration playing an important role in the election. While everyone has their reasons for how they voted, I have found that many of the people I know who voted that way are thoughtful, kind, and respectful. When I tried to explain this viewpoint to my friends and family, I often encountered the same reaction as back in 2016: "Beth, it's wonderful that you are so nice, but there are moral issues at play here." I found it very painful to explain my point of view, and felt like an outsider. I recognize that I can't convince others to think like me. Nevertheless, I've kept my relationships both with people who voted for President Trump, and those who did not.

Even if you believe in the principle that everyone deserves kindness, dignity, and respect, it is tempting to carve out exceptions. We are quick to identify people with denigrating labels such as bigot, extremist, racist, elitist, stupid, evil, dangerous, ignorant—and worse. Derogatory terms have become so widespread in public forums that they have reached a level of common usage, even acceptability. (Except, of course, when they are directed at you and your side.)

Once we start making exceptions to the everyone-deserves-dignity-and-respect principle, it becomes harder to decide where to draw the line. So, we think it is better not to have any lines, as hard as that can feel sometimes. Everyone—no exceptions—deserves dignity and respect.

Of course, we need to hold people accountable for their behavior when they violate laws or social norms. But that does not negate treating them with dignity and respect.

**From Doug** It is tempting to make assumptions about people based on how they look and dress, where they live, how they voted, and a variety of other factors. This is human nature, and we all do it, sometimes based on very limited information or impressions. However tempting this may be, it can be dangerous to make judgments that may be inaccurate. Think about this in reverse. What might people making quick assumptions be thinking about you? I have worked hard to train myself to avoid making hasty assumptions, but I don't always measure up. This requires ongoing self-awareness when a negative thought pattern emerges. I remind myself to step back with a spirit of curiosity and respect.

After all, it can be helpful to engage with others you may disagree with. They are not "the enemy," but instead, people who can remind us that we can differ, still get along, and even learn from each other. This will not be appropriate for everyone you meet and every situation. You need to pick and choose the moment and circumstances. Sometimes you don't have the time or energy for this hard work. You especially need to walk away if you feel physically or emotionally threatened. But if we always choose to walk away from hard conversations, we limit our potential for change and growth.

We were fascinated by an interview with New Jersey Senator Andy Kim, a Democrat who was elected to the US Senate in 2024. He had previously served in a congressional district that voted for the Republican candidate for president.

Wondering why he had been elected, Kim held some eighty town halls across the district to find out. Embracing a depth of curiosity and humility that seems unusual for elected officials, he learned that people felt judged and disrespected. Politicians, he came to understand, "are being paternalistic and telling them what they need to do, and what's best for their lives, without listening to them." He adds that we've become a nation addicted to anger and contempt. How we see and treat others matters.[3]

## DOES HATE HAVE A HOME HERE?

*"Resentment is like drinking poison and then hoping it will kill your enemies."—Nelson Mandela*

Some have taken to posting "Hate Has No Home Here" signs, which Mark Beckwith, the retired Episcopal bishop, describes as a statement of misguided self-righteousness. He elaborates:

> "Whenever I see a HATE HAS NO HOME HERE sign, I can't help but think that the owner hates the hater. Which defeats the whole purpose."[4] "The boundary between righteous wrath and venomous hate can be confusing and is often exploited. There are plenty of people who claim to carry the banner of righteousness on a particular issue, but their commitment and actions are fueled by a venom that is personal: they don't so much want to achieve the goal as much as they want to vanquish the other side."[5]

While this thought resonates, we caution that it is best to avoid assuming what people are thinking when they put up these signs. Hopefully some avoid the trap of hating the haters.

We are supporters of workplace practices that emphasize diversity, equity, and inclusion, and we have participated in various trainings during our professional careers. One of the greatest challenges of these efforts is how to engage those who are resistant to being trained, or feel left out, much the way Beckwith described the "Hate Has No Home Here" sign dilemma. How do we integrate inclusive practices and trainings into organizational goals and performance, rather than engaging in a corporate check-the-box exercise? Can we include *both* conservatives and liberal underrepresented minorities? How do we avoid making inclusion only for "us" and not for "them"?

Tribal behavior encourages a sense of belonging and protection, and we tend to build a wall around our side. We attack others to presumably protect ourselves, to achieve some misguided idea of safety that becomes ingrained in our psyche. We can be so quick to embrace our side that we miss seeing the possibility that we might be missing something fundamentally important.

So how *do* we best confront hatred and the practice of pitting people against each other?

The Jewish students at New College who invited Derek Black for Shabbat dinner are modern-day heroes at the highest level—incredible role models for us all. They let down their defenses and opened themselves to their humanity. But sadly, who has even heard of them? Today's media environment focuses a lot more on those who strive to divide us. People who bring us together get much less attention.

**From Beth** I took part in a series of Braver Angels conversations with a journalist who had strong pro-life sentiments. This conversation partner became my friend. I was impressed by her passion for this topic and encouraged her to speak at a Braver Angels debate on abortion. When my friend spoke the words "Abortion is murder," I normally would have left the debate or found some other way to stop listening. But this time was different because I had gotten to know her over several conversations and had built up a friendship. Although I held true to my belief that abortion is not murder, I was able to hear my friend's arguments and understand her point of view.

These kinds of stories seem to be the exceptions. Shaming others is just so much quicker and easier. But what good comes from it?

## SHAMING OTHERS ONLY ADDS TO THE PROBLEM

*"Let no man pull you so low as to hate him."* —Rev. Martin Luther King, Jr.

Rather than working to avoid hatred, these days it is so much easier to condemn others and make derogatory comments about them on social media or in conversations with people in your "tribe." Or, if we are bolder, to make derogatory comments and try to shame those on the other side. Maybe it's just too easy to send nasty anonymous comments via email or social media.

The irony is that we can be quick to criticize others, while holding ourselves to a low standard. Consider this thought from President George W. Bush: "Too often we judge other groups by their worst examples, while judging ourselves by our best intentions."[6]

**From Beth** I previously described wanting to speak at a contentious school board meeting during the COVID pandemic where masking was being discussed. Before that meeting, I had coffee with a woman who didn't believe in mask mandates. While disagreeing on masks, we found common ground on needing experts to communicate clearly about the science and the importance of good ventilation in schools.

After that coffee, I realized that assigning the label of "bad person" to someone who didn't feel masks were appropriate was not the direction I wanted to take in my planned speech for the school board meeting. If I took that direction, I would be shaming people who disagreed with me.

But even more memorable is what happened next. After that school board meeting, I reached out to that same woman again and listened as she strongly condemned the threatened violence aimed at those who spoke in favor of masking at the meeting. This positive connection helped me get over the traumatic experience of that unpleasant school board event.[7]

---

Mónica Guzmán notes that persuasion "cannot work from shame. It cannot work from attack. It can only work from genuine, open, vulnerable conversations."[8] Shaming others for their views is ineffective, argues David Keen, a professor of conflict studies at the London School of Economics and Political Science. He writes in the digital magazine *Psyche* that shaming can entrench divisions and even be manipulated by its targets to reinforce their support base. Shaming comes at the expense of meaningful discourse, perpetuating cycles of blame and division without fostering genuine improvement.[9]

Failing to treat others with dignity and respect might feel good in the short term and generate kudos from your tribe. But it only adds to the divide, reinforcing for those on the other side their own negative views of people on your side. In this climate of contempt, the popular solution seems to be vanquishing the other side. We are reminded of the term "mutually assured destruction" from the Cold War period.

We also reflect on the wisdom of Drs. John and Julie Gottman whose work has demonstrated that showing contempt toward a partner is a clear sign of a troubled marriage and a leading indicator of divorce.[10] A national divorce, however appealing to some, would be both impractical and devastating.

We need to do better.

## FOR FURTHER THOUGHT

- Do you believe that all people are worthy of dignity and respect? Are there exceptions?
- How often do you use the words "those people" (with a negative connotation), and how might you want to change or reword those thoughts?
- Have you found yourself using derogatory terms for people with different political viewpoints than yours or even trying to shame them? How effective was shaming in changing their minds or behavior?
- Are you quick to make assumptions and judge people based on first impressions or limited information, and, if so, how might you want to change?
- How might you be more open or curious about those who have political views different from yours?

# THE ROOTS OF UNHEALTHY CONFLICT

"We build too many walls and not enough bridges." —Isaac Newton

Chapter 4

# HEALTHY VS. UNHEALTHY CONFLICT

*"When conflict escalates past a certain point, the conflict itself takes charge."—Amanda Ripley*

How have we gotten to a point where there is so much conflict and distrust over politics, even among family and longtime friends?

Personal identity has many components, including family, friends, career, schools, sports affiliations, hobbies, geographical connections, and, of course, politics. But for many, politics has seemingly risen to the top with respect to how we view others' identities. For example, several young people interviewed about dating in today's environment commented that different political beliefs were a potential deal-breaker.[1]

Is politics really more important than family and friends? And how is it that people are becoming so disconnected from others? David Brooks cites research that 60 percent of Americans said their neighbors were trustworthy two generations ago, but now only 33 percent think they are trustworthy, adding that this "precipitous decline" threatens the future of our country.[2]

Conflict over politics, it seems, is nearly always present, or at least close by. Should we totally avoid disagreement and conflict? Of course not! But we need to distinguish between conflict that is *necessary and constructive* as opposed to conflict that is *unhealthy and destructive*.

In *healthy* conflict, we value others and believe they are worthy despite differences of opinion on politics or other issues. We are mobilized to discuss ideas. We debate, we advocate, we protest, and we take other actions for causes we think are important. Politicians, political parties, and everyday people must feel welcomed and encouraged to promote policies that they believe are best. This is essential to the success of democratic governance.

The problem comes when we cross a line to engage in *unhealthy* conflict, also called high conflict. Amanda Ripley, journalist and author of *High Conflict: Why We Get Trapped and How We Get Out*, describes intolerance of difference that cultivates "us versus them" thinking. The conflict itself takes charge, and people are dehumanized.[3]

When there is unhealthy conflict, issues become less important, as do relationships. We can even forget how the conflict started. Recall the infamous family feud between the Hatfields and McCoys. At some point, the initial disagreement was largely forgotten as hatred and violence took on a life of their own. When people get caught up in this kind of thinking and behavior, it can become difficult to find a way out.

According to Ripley, you can recognize high conflict when you hear "sweeping, grandiose, or violent language to describe the conflict" with "rumors, myths, or conspiracy theories present."[4] This is because high conflict occurs when there is low trust. Reaching a point where it is difficult to create a consensus about facts, we become suspicious of each other. Enter conflict entrepreneurs who add fuel to the fire, exploiting the situation for their own gain.

Conflict entrepreneurs, a term coined by Amanda Ripley, describes those who exploit conflict for their own ends, which include profit, attention, and power.[5]

When this happens, you may observe some people withdrawing; this can lead to the

You will see this conflict entrepreneur crocodile getting ready to chomp on the American flag throughout the book as we describe ways that conflict entrepreneurs are threatening our country.

appearance of two extremes, when the reality is often much more nuanced. At this point, the conflict may have its own momentum and can be magnetic and hard to resist. Any sense of healthy conflict is lost amid a downward spiral of mistrust and humiliation of those with different perspectives.

In politics, the difference between healthy and unhealthy conflict comes down to advocating for policy positions on their merit versus debasing people who have contrary opinions. This distinction is not always totally clear, and there can be gray areas. But it is very important to be aware of this critical difference as we assess the actions of ourselves and others.

**From Doug** I have observed a major shift in political perspectives over the past twenty-plus years. In 2002, I completed six terms as a Republican member of the New Hampshire state legislature, a challenging—but also very satisfying—experience. I especially loved the constituent work, which sometimes meant getting involved in people's lives in intimate ways. I remember helping foster parents manage a complicated adoption. Another woman wrote a gratifying letter to the editor after I intervened in her elderly mother's insurance problem. I was invited into people's homes where they shared intimate details of personal issues and asked me to intervene to obtain government help. Sometimes I was able to help them, other times not, but my life was enriched by those experiences.

I was also excited about local legislative projects: creating a state park on the pristine Lake Tarleton, a boat launch on the Connecticut River, and upgrades at a state home for the elderly. I recall receiving a shout-out in the Piermont, New Hampshire, town report after asking the state department of transportation to improve visibility at a road intersection where a young college student was tragically killed.

I made a lot of friends, too, among elected officials from across the state and on both sides of the aisle. While there were, of course, disagreements, I found nearly every representative and senator to be motivated by public service and open to the ideas of others. There were tough fights over policy that sometimes left some scars, but the elected officials from both parties mostly got along.

In 2012, ten years after leaving the legislature, I was working overseas and heard a *This American Life* public radio podcast titled "Red State Blue State" that featured the growing divisiveness in the New Hampshire legislature.[6] In the same show, there was a segment on how politics was impacting American families. I was struck by one man's comment that his brother-in-law could still come to a family barbecue, but, because he voted for Obama, he had to bring his own meat for the grill.

My reaction was, *Yikes, are things getting this bad back home? Were politics really having so much impact on the everyday lives of friends and families?* Today, the problem is obviously much worse, and I look back on my reaction to that 2012 story with a kind of lost innocence.

---

We see this playing out more and more in events happening today.

We were saddened by the October 7, 2023, Hamas attack on Israel and the aftermath of Israel's assault on Gaza. In our country, people were quick to pick sides, and "us versus them" dominated the public discourse. So many are suffering on both sides, but where is the nuance? Shouldn't it be possible to embrace the humanity of both the Israeli hostages and their families, as well as the Palestinian people suffering in Gaza—while also condemning the barbaric Hamas attacks on Israeli civilians and the Israeli government's aggressive response impacting Palestinian civilians?

This Middle East conflict has torn apart many Americans, with some media outlets presenting a binary choice between being pro-Palestinian or pro-Israeli, when most everyone in both populations shares a desire for peace. In watching the college protests since October 2023, is there a way to transcend these tensions and move back into healthy conflict? Could universities create innovative programs for students and faculty that provide a space for balanced debate? There are models for these programs across the country, including Dartmouth's Brave Spaces.[7]

How do we move from unhealthy to healthy conflict?

David Blankenhorn, one of the founders of Braver Angels, observes that a big part of the problem is binary thinking, which is overly simplistic. We need to "count higher than two," he says, as we consider how to assess conflict and understand what lies behind it. Generalization is another concern as we put people and problems into categories. We need to be more specific in how we consider what underlies conflict.

Blankenhorn describes three basic stages or approaches to conflict in his book In *Search of Braver Angels*.[8] In the first stage, we subconsciously submit to conflict, ignoring and internalizing it in a way that fails to fully recognize it exists. This can put conflict in charge of us. In the second stage, we manage conflict by assuming good faith in our adversaries. This second stage requires civility in our approach to others and a willingness to find common ground.

In Blankenhorn's third stage, we transform conflict by creating a new framing that is valid and helpful for both sides. It requires seeing dignity in the other side. Achieving this third stage is vital to our well-being and that of others. For example, Utah's Republican Governor Spencer Cox relates how he and his Democratic political opponent were featured together in a 2020 campaign ad. They agreed to disagree without hating each other and to debate issues without degrading each other's character.[9] The Stanford Polarization and Social Change Lab chose their ad as part of a depolarization experiment that was tested on over thirty thousand people. These researchers found that this ad had a measurable depolarization effect, including a reduction in urges toward violence.[10]

Of course, Governor Cox's approach is the exception, not the rule. He elaborated on this principle in "Disagreeing Better," the national campaign he spearheaded as the 2023 to 2024 chair of the National Governors Association. There were four events across the country that attracted thought leaders and people from Braver Angels and other organizations interested in reducing political polarization. Unfortunately, these events got little press coverage, as the present media environment focuses much more on dissension rather than efforts designed to bring Americans together. (In 2025, this initiative that began with the National Governors Association became a new nonprofit, Disagree Better: https://disagreebetter.us/.)

Governor Cox, like all people who run for office, has faced pressure when it comes to following the party line (no matter his values and intentions). He has been criticized by some for his support of President Trump. At the same time, he faced backlash at the Republican state convention in April 2024 for not going far enough. Cox defended his conservative policies and added, "Maybe you're booing me because . . . you hate that I don't hate enough."[11]

A telling line in these divisive times: "Maybe you hate that I don't hate enough."

Congressman Don Bacon (R, Nebraska) wrote an op-ed titled "The Other Party Isn't the Enemy—I support Donald Trump, but I'm an American before I'm a Republican" in *The Wall Street Journal* (September 9, 2024):

> "At a March GOP meeting in my congressional district, I said, 'I am a Christian first, an American second, and then a Republican.' Immediately, an older gentleman yelled out, 'That is why we don't like you!' I wondered what bothered him more, the Christian or the American part. Our politics have become toxic. Too many voters treat their political party as the most important thing in their lives. They consider the other side to be their enemy or, even worse, evil. This phenomenon spans both parties."[12]

Would Americans come together to defend our nation if it were under attack by another country—or would we just squabble and blame "those people" who support the other political party? We need to build relationships across differences to help us see others as more than Republicans or Democrats.

When people become aggressive toward others, it can provide some sense of control and purpose. "We are fighting evil," argues Amanda Ripley, adding ironically, "What could be more meaningful?"[13] But shaming politicians (and others) almost always backfires and rarely has the effect of changing someone's opinions. People are more likely to just dig in. A key to influencing others is to build relationships, as these change us more than facts and make it harder to dismiss and dehumanize people.

In his *A Book, an Idea and a Goat* newsletter, lawyer and Democratic activist Andru Volinsky posed the question of how to engage with Trump supporters. He wrote:

> "The answer is to engage broadly, regularly and respectfully. By this, I don't mean engage politically or through political parties. I mean engage informally and formally. Join organized groups if you are so inclined but also walk in your neighborhood. Help your neighbors. Share work and share joy. Be informed about what is going on around you and don't be afraid to start conversations in the gym, at the grocery store, at your kid's school. Don't treat others as if they're stupid or deplorable. If you need help, ask for it. If they need help, offer it."[14]

It is important to be curious about others, but this is very hard to do when we are angry or upset. By stepping back and understanding that our reactions can get in the way of both our personal health and openness to others, we can create space for meaningful dialogue. And this is vital for successful activism, too!

## WHAT ABOUT ACTIVISM?

*"Dialogue without activism can be like 'navel gazing'—excessive self-contemplation, an intellectual exercise. Yet activism without dialogue? It's 'reckless, uninformed, and doomed to fail.'"—Mónica Guzmán*

Activism is defined by Merriam-Webster as a practice that emphasizes direct vigorous action, especially in support of or opposition to one side of a controversial issue.[15] It's speaking up about causes you believe in and taking action to make a difference.

In writing this book, we have focused on bridge building, emphasizing the importance of dialogue with people on the other side. For many of us, that is plenty to focus on. We also recognize that everyone has their own path. Some find a calling in political activism: organizing for specific causes, demonstrating at peaceful protests, writing opinion pieces for the news, or lobbying legislators. There are many ways to make a difference in this world.

We believe that it is possible to be *both* an activist and a bridge-builder. Might engaging with those we disagree with strengthen activism, just as activism gives meaning to bridge building? Can connecting with others who bring fresh perspectives create a bigger tent for building a more powerful cause? Being open to seeing ideas in new ways may also lead to personal growth.

**From Beth** Over the last six years, I have advocated for a healthy climate. Before I moved to Vermont, I co-led a volunteer lobbying team focused on a conservative legislator. Our team combined activism *and* dialogue. We were passionate about our cause and also knew our audience. We listened to our legislators' concerns. We started each meeting with gratitude for the work they were doing. We didn't *stop* talking about climate, but *started* talking about climate *and* economic growth; climate *and* public health; climate *and* energy national security. Our efforts were successful, and we achieved bipartisan climate legislation.

It is up to you to decide what paths you choose and what works best for your life and situation. But, whatever you decide, we hope that bridge building and healthy conflict will be part of your approach.

## FOR FURTHER THOUGHT

- As you think about conflicts in your life, can you distinguish between healthy and unhealthy conflict?
- What features have characterized your personal conflicts? What has initiated and sustained them, and how did they end (or not)?
- How is unhealthy conflict impacting you and the people you care about?
- How might you connect and become more curious about people who take positions that upset you?
- How can you separate advocating for policy positions from disparaging people who have contrary opinions? Can you be both an activist and a bridge-builder?

Chapter 5

# HOW DID WE GET HERE? FORCES DRIVING THE POLITICS OF CONTEMPT

> *"When a nation loses faith in each other, the nation collapses."* —David Brooks

We are experiencing a perfect storm of unhealthy conflict and polarization in our society today. While we can all see the stresses in our politics and relationships, we may not know what has influenced and created them. As we review some of the key forces driving the politics of contempt in the following pages, think about which of these are most influential in your experience.

## BINARY THINKING AND IDENTITY POLITICS

Politics has increasingly fallen into binary (zero-sum) thinking with distinct political identities. The tendency to see things in oversimplified terms, one way or the other, parallels the "us versus them" thinking we have described previously. Nuance is vital, but often gets lost, as we can become hostile and dehumanize people with alternative beliefs. As noted by social psychologist and author Jonathan Haidt, "People bind themselves into political teams that share moral narratives. Once they accept a particular narrative, they become blind to alternative moral worlds."[1] Knee-jerk reactions and stereotyping can replace seeing others as complex and nuanced.

Journalist and author Ezra Klein offers this perspective: "We are so locked into our political identities that there is virtually no candidate, no information, no condition that can force us to change our minds. We will justify almost anything or anyone so long as it helps our side, and the result is politics devoid of guardrails, standards, persuasion, or accountability."[2]

**From Beth** When I became aware of binary thinking, I was encouraged to see nuance in positions I was taking, which helped me become less polarized toward others. For example, during the COVID pandemic, I could see where people who valued the health of a community might believe in keeping schools and businesses open. We learned later that the average US public school student in grades 3 through 8 lost the equivalent of a half year of learning in math and a quarter of a year in reading during COVID.[3] I felt that it wasn't right to label people who spoke out for keeping schools open as necessarily being against vaccines or masking. That nuance helped me reduce my own polarization.

## POLITICAL AND GOVERNMENT DYSFUNCTION

Political parties are increasingly less accountable to everyday citizens. Largely unregulated political fundraising favors the wealthiest interests without accountability. Congressional dysfunction is fostered by rules and norms that foster party purity. Widespread gerrymandering undermines the will of the people. We used to expect better from our leaders, but in these politically tumultuous times, there can be rewards for bad behavior. Candidates and elected officials can generate headlines and boost name recognition by playing to emotions and division. This kind of negative publicity can aid fundraising, reinforcing this perverse cycle. It clearly doesn't work for every politician, but more than a few have adopted this approach as a career-building strategy.

> **From Doug** — When I served in the New Hampshire state legislature back in the 1990s, my colleagues did not all fall into pure categories. For example, there were pro-choice Republicans and pro-life Democrats. These days, elected officials are much more likely to toe the party line. If you don't, there will likely be a primary opponent with funding support from interests outside your political district. And primary election turnout is quite low compared to general elections, dominated by the most fervent partisans on both sides. People who think independently are less likely to win, or even run for office, leaving general election choices often dominated by candidates on the extremes.

## FINANCIAL INSECURITY AND WEALTH DISPARITIES

Many Americas are struggling because of inflation, high housing costs, and growing wealth disparities. According to a 2024 study by Pew Research Center, the number of Americans in middle-class households has dropped 10 percent since 1971 (from 61 to 51 percent) while upper-income households grew from 11 to 19 percent.[4] A study by the Federal Reserve found that 72 percent of Americans report doing financially OK, down 6 points from 2021.[5]

The middle class and home ownership, long the economic pride of this country, feel unattainable for too many. Americans with a heavy load of college debt find it difficult to meet their other financial needs, such as childcare. At the same time, those without college degrees resent that their taxes may be used to pay off college debt for others when they lack the benefits of higher education themselves. On an annual basis, median earnings for bachelor's degree holders are $79,716 or 62% higher than those whose highest degree is a high school diploma.[6]

**From Beth:** When I was growing up, my parents envisioned that their children would be financially better off than they had been as first-generation college students. And they were right. Now my generation sees our children struggling to find good-paying jobs, even with their college educations, which saddle them with debt. Our children have a lot of stress about their uncertain futures. Many young adults these days are living with parents because they cannot afford to pay rent or buy their own homes.

## EDUCATIONAL DISPARITIES AND DOMINANCE BY ELITES

Only 37.5 percent of people ages twenty-five or older have a bachelor's degree or higher, according to 2020 US Census data, with similar findings in 2022.[7] This minority has always dominated the news, government, and many professions (not to mention having economic advantages as noted earlier). Peggy Noonan, speechwriter for President Reagan and Pulitzer Prize-winning *Wall Street Journal* columnist, characterizes elites as the accomplished, secure, and successful people who have power, make public policy, and "are protected from much of the roughness of the world . . . the world they have created."[8] She linked the rise of President Trump to the frustrations of unprotected Americans who have less access to money, education, and opportunity. The US Department of Education reports that 54 percent of adults (130 million adults) have a literacy level below the sixth-grade level.[9]

## SORTING AND SILOING

Sorting is a powerful force driving us to align with people who think the same way we do. We cling to positions we know best, fearing the loss of identity. Sticking to our group, we sink deeper into storylines that make it more difficult to hear anything else.[10] A quick glance at the 2024 election map shows geographical sorting—a dramatic divide between urban and rural voters. Overwhelmingly, city dwellers cast their votes for Democratic candidates, while rural voters sided with Republicans. Researchers attribute this growing division to deindustrialization and changes in the economy, with urban areas more rapidly adapting and creating new jobs in technology, the service sector, and the knowledge economy.[11]

As observed by author Seth Kaplan, distrust of institutions is "more apparent the farther you get from the dynamic parts of our most dynamic cities—where our leaders live mostly unaware of how most Americans experience life."[12] In 1992, only 36 percent of counties were "landslide counties," where the presidential candidate won by 20 percent or more. By 2016, the number of "landslide counties" had risen to 80 percent.[13] Siloing reinforces sorting as we sink deeper into our groups and stories, making it harder to hear any other perspectives.[14]

## LONELINESS, SOCIAL DISCONNECTION, AND DECLINING SOCIAL CAPITAL

Social capital refers to the networks of relationships we form that enable us to reach our goals and help our society to function effectively. We are increasingly disengaged from our communities and less likely to interact with others, including those who have different perspectives. More people feel more isolated than in past years, and the growth of social media and technology offering easy ways to generate "friends" have, ironically, only aggravated the problem. People have fewer real friends than they did in the past.[15] Former Surgeon General Dr. Vivek H. Murthy says that we're in the midst of a "loneliness epidemic."[16] In his book *Bowling Alone,* Robert Putnam outlines how American disengagement from community involvement in churches, civic organizations, Rotary Clubs, and other groups has undermined community trust and democratic institutions.[17]

We have witnessed a major decline in trust over the past forty years—not just in institutions but also in growing distrust for our fellow citizens. As a result, we've become easy pickings for demagogues of the left and right.[18]

Disconnected people experience a loss of self-worth and meaning. "People need to matter. It's a fundamental requirement for life, like oxygen," writes Amanda Ripley.[19] A recent study conducted in New Hampshire found troubling trends. Only 43 percent of adult residents felt they mattered in their communities, a significant drop from 76 percent in 2019. The share of those who do favors for their neighbors halved, falling from 11 percent in 2019 to 5 percent in 2021.[20]

Seth Kaplan adds that, "America once had the world's most dynamic local associations, giving millions the chance to lead and everyone the feeling that they had a stake in society. Today, most of us live in places with few if any associations. We don't know our neighbors, and we don't have much influence over the institutions we interact with. Too much is nationalized or made distant—shopping, schooling, praying, government, media, etc. And you cannot easily trust something that you feel you have no control over."[21]

> **From Beth:** I am grateful to have had the opportunity to sing in a chorus with a diverse group of women—not just those of different races and religions, but also some of different political leanings than my own. I learned to respect their work ethic around learning the music and being committed to our chorus. This led to my overcoming stereotypes related to their choice of presidential candidates in recent elections.

The COVID pandemic was a gut punch that has left residual impacts of disconnection and mistrust in government, as well as cultural changes that leave many bewildered and untethered. Virtual meetings, while offering some advantages, can also contribute to disconnection.

**From Beth** I co-organized and co-moderated several Braver Angels workshops on public perceptions around the pandemic. I was astonished to learn how much pain "questioners" of the public health response experienced—including losing their jobs and severing relationships with family and friends over their skepticism of pandemic measures related to lockdowns, vaccines, and masking. While I remained overall supportive of the public health response, I gained empathy for "questioners" when I heard their stories, including how they felt isolated and disconnected from friends and relatives. Bringing supporters and questioners of the public health response together to share stories, including how we held similar values (for example, we valued the health of family members and relationships) was heartening.

## DISCOURTEOUS BEHAVIOR AMID DECLINING INTERPERSONAL AND LISTENING SKILLS

We are witnessing a deteriorating social dynamic with declines in basic manners and interpersonal skills. Adults increasingly model rude behaviors, which get passed down to children as normal. Bullying is severely impacting children's mental health. Attitudes of entitlement, arrogance, and narcissism also contribute. Individualism has always been an important part of our country, but it increasingly seems like today's culture is "all about me." Personal responsibility, sacrifice for a greater good, and general regard for others are on the decline.

Stephen Covey's Habit 5 for successful people—"Seek first to understand and then be understood"[22]—has seemingly been lost as we strive to make our points without really listening to what others have to say. The idea that we need to be open to ideas that might contradict our previously established opinions seems almost quaint in these divided times. We all would benefit if schools put as much emphasis on so called "soft skills" of effective communication and relationship building as they do to cognitive learning.

Threatening and canceling are other aspects of this challenge. People who stand up for what they believe—or sometimes just do their job (such as election workers)—are increasingly at risk of being harassed or threatened by telephone, online, or even in person. Jonathan Rauch describes canceling as organizing and manipulating "the social or media environment in order to isolate, deplatform or intimidate ideological opponents."[23]

Cancel culture is increasingly on display in politics and education. Examples include liberal college campuses shutting out conservative voices, and conservatives trying the same toward progressives using terms such as "woke." These trends, in author April Lawson's words, have "seeped into every part of our public rhetoric and political consciousness."[24]

Negative behaviors against people due to race, religion, national origin, sexual identity, disability, or other aspects of their lives used to be considered socially unacceptable. We suppose a positive aspect is that people act with authenticity without hiding their true feelings. But the extent to which people are increasingly open about their prejudices encourages others to do the same, breaking down social norms and fostering division.

## SOCIAL MEDIA ALGORITHMS

Social media is a great way to connect with family and friends, but it clearly has a dark side, reinforcing our beliefs and playing on emotions and fears. Technology giants are exploiting division for profit, tracking our tendencies and exploiting emotions such as anger and outrage. We are often not shown information that challenges our opinions, which reduces the ability to see or consider different perspectives.[25]

New York University researchers argue "that social media is akin to a funhouse mirror, reflecting and warping our collective sense of what is normative. When people stare into the mirror they do not see a true version of reality, but one that has been distorted by a small but vocal minority of extreme outliers—often amplified by design features and algorithms."[26] An extreme minority of just 3 percent of active social media users generate 33 percent of online content. Further, 0.1 percent of users generate 80 percent of the fake news. Social media is intentionally designed to draw you in, waste your time, and distort your thinking.[27]

> **From Beth** I deliberately engage with posts that are outside my liberal bubble and subscribe to groups that I might normally not be part of (like state firearms associations). As a result, I find a variety of opinions in my feed. You might try it sometime. It gives me a sense of control to know I am gaming the algorithms, rather than the algorithms gaming me. I learn some interesting things, too.

## CHANGES IN THE MEDIA ENVIRONMENT AND INFORMATION OVERLOAD

Media has become sorted for the most politically invested, and the more political media you consume, "the more warped your perspective of the other side becomes," according to Ezra Klein.[28] Some of this is the result of declines in traditional media, newspapers especially, due to the loss of advertising revenue as online shopping and marketing dominate. The decline of local news is another concerning trend. Many lament the old days when there were three television networks that dominated the news; there was a sense of national understanding and consensus (although there were also some monopolies).

Viewers are now swamped with choices, and the most effective media sources have learned how to appeal to audiences and advertisers by targeting people with the strongest beliefs, reinforcing their previously determined opinions. "Politics is, first and foremost, driven by the people who pay the most attention and wield the most power—and those people opt in to extraordinarily politicized media. Then they create the political system they perceive. The rest of the country then has to choose from more polarized options," according to Klein.[29] It is increasingly difficult to distinguish fact-based news from opinion.

Processing information too quickly is easy to do given information overload, and this contributes to the politics of contempt. As discussed in psychologist Daniel Kahneman's *Thinking, Fast and Slow*, we often process information in an automatic way, which is efficient but can lead to jumping to the wrong conclusions.[30] Slow thinking is more deliberative and requires our full attention. Fast thinking has its efficiency benefits, but can lead to knee-jerk reactions, stereotyping, and impulsive behavior on social media, including rudeness or reposting false information.

## MISINFORMATION, DISINFORMATION CAMPAIGNS, AND FOREIGN PROPAGANDA

The governments of Russia, Iran, China, and other countries promote misinformation and disinformation to create division and weaken our country.[31] The "firehose of falsehood" is a technique, perfected by the Russian government to confuse people so they cannot tell the difference between truth and fiction. Microsoft claimed that a Russian disinformation campaign targeted the 2024 US election, spreading divisive content, including criticism of the United States' support for Ukraine.[32] China has been accused of fomenting pro-Palestinian support on college campuses.[33] Misinformation and disinformation campaigns can be domestic as well, and foreign influence is nothing new. But modern technologies using AI and social media algorithms can fuel the fire, making these campaigns much more effective.

## CONFLICT ENTREPRENEURS

Conflict entrepreneurs exploit conflict for their own ends, which include profit, attention, and power. The Outrage-Industrial Complex is another term for the same idea, as used by journalist Marc Ambinder, who writes,

"There are people in Washington who have the job of manufacturing outrage; who get paid to take offense, or to find ways to take offense, and to broadcast their outrage to others."[34] These days, conflict entrepreneurs operate far beyond our nation's capital, and it is vital that each of us try to better understand who they are and how we are being manipulated.

## OTHER FORCES DRIVING POLARIZATION

- **Decline of civics education.** We are not preparing young people to become knowledgeable and effective in their future citizenship roles. With states lowering required hours for civics in grade schools, schools have backed off on educating students about history, how our country works, and each person's responsibility in democratic governance. In 2022, only 13 percent of eighth-grade students scored proficient in history, and only 22 percent scored proficient in civics on the National Assessment of Educational Progress.[35] And, as toxic polarization has grown, it is increasingly difficult to come to an agreement on what such a curriculum should be. Some students are complaining that teachers have shied away from discussions of current events, given the various pressures teachers feel from those influencing the education process.

*From Beth* A high school teacher told me that she waits until the grading season is over for her high school seniors before engaging them in debates on political issues. By waiting, students are less worried that their political stance will affect their grade. I would like to see schools encouraging students to think for themselves and express their viewpoints, even if unpopular. Otherwise, we are not fully preparing our children for the basic responsibilities of adulthood.

Even at the college level, many college students are afraid of speaking up in class, with organizations such as the Constructive Dialogue Institute working to address this concern.[36]

- **Citizen apathy.** As the level of vitriol rises, many people tune out, leaving the political stage to those who are most partisan and extreme. In a later chapter, we will talk more about the "exhausted majority" and how people who are turned off can step up and demand better for our country.

- **Historical changes.** The Cold War brought Americans together as we felt threatened, a unifying force now largely forgotten. David Blankenhorn, cofounder of Braver Angels, notes the passing of the Greatest Generation and their "generational values, forged in the trials of the Great Depression and World War II—including a willingness to sacrifice for country . . . and adherence to a shared civic faith—reduced social and political polarization."[37]

- **Fear.** It is human nature to be on alert for things that threaten us. It is natural to be wary in these times of rapid change in our politics, economy, and technologies. We need to avoid the "sense of fear that's untethered from any genuine sense of danger—the kind of fear that cuts us off from the good things in life without making us meaningfully safer."[38]

## FOR FURTHER THOUGHT

- Which of the listed forces do you think are having the most negative influence on our country?
- What forces driving division are influencing your life the most?
- Are there other forces not listed that you think might be important?
- What new insights do you have about yourself after reviewing this list?
- What are some steps you could take so that one or more of these forces could have less impact on your life and relationships?

Chapter 6

# POLARIZATION AS A BUSINESS MODEL

> *"If it screams it streams, but if kind pay no mind."*
> *—Doug Teschner*

Conflict entrepreneurs magnify nearly all other factors driving national division and polarization. From both our country and foreign nations, they amplify conflict for their own ends—sometimes for profit, but also for attention or power. Conflict entrepreneurs exploit social media algorithms and use disinformation and information overload to maximize fear and distrust. Using grandiose language and manipulating emotions with the pursuit of revenge, they deliver "a sense of exhilaration and mission," talking about conflict "like it is a religion unto itself . . . a sacred flame that must never be extinguished," says Amanda Ripley.[1]

Conflict entrepreneurs operate across the political divide. And they would not be as successful if it were not for social media and ubiquitous smartphones. So many of us are constantly online, distracted by messages that could be positive (connections from friends or family) or not (ads and messages designed to exploit us). People spend an average of four and a half hours a day on their phones (less for boomers and more for Gen Z).[2] That represents 25 percent of our waking hours!

**From Doug:** In leadership trainings on prioritizing the use of precious time, I have asked, "Are you a prisoner to your cell phone?" I sometimes find that people don't really want to hear it. Smartphone use (and misuse) has become so ubiquitous that it is an ingrained part of our culture, with notifications at all hours demanding our attention. We can't help ourselves! Constantly checking your phone can be a distraction, reactively diminishing minutes (adding up to hours) that could be applied proactively to more important tasks. Even the mainstream health website WebMD has recognized this problem, offering online suggestions on "How to Break Your Phone Habit."[3]

Combined with social media algorithms, excessive phone use can also push us down rabbit holes of potential false information and polarization. Our family members and friends may even lose meaningful connection with us. I confess to using a flip phone because I know from experience that I lack the discipline to manage the smart kind. The tech giants are so good at drawing us in, so, despite understanding the temptation, I know that I won't be able to help myself! For sure, I miss out on some of the useful aspects of smart phone technology—such as navigating my way through places I haven't been before. But I have decided that not having a smartphone is better for my overall health and well-being.

---

"Polarization has become a business model," argue the authors of a 2018 study, The Hidden Tribes of America, adding, "Media executives have realized that they can drive clicks, likes, and views, and make money for themselves and their shareholders, by providing people with the most strident opinions."[4] They found that only a third of Americans embrace the most extreme politics of the left and right, but those perspectives dominate the national conversation.

We find it sad that platforms that promised to bring us together are fostering so much division. Social media can be beneficial for staying connected with family and friends, but news and political posts on these sites often dehumanize others and foster division. As conflict entrepreneurs exploit this system, people become agitated and act in ways that feed the polarization machine.

"Polarization is profitable now, but someone will pay the price later," a state representative observed at a New Hampshire Braver Angels workshop that brought together legislators from both political parties. At a Boston workshop focused on trustworthy elections, a participant commented, "We trust social media more than our neighbors." Neither of these statements raised an eyebrow among workshop attendees, presumably because they represent a profound recognition of where our country stands today. Can you really trust anyone anymore, and where do you go to find someone or something to believe in?

Social media posts that are more thoughtful and less emotional get fewer views by design. On the other hand, content that invokes fear or makes people angry or upset gets more views. Facebook owner Meta hopes you take the bait and engage, perpetuating the outrage. By keeping you online for as long as possible, they know you will see more advertisements, and they make more money.

As noted in a report by the Carnegie Endowment for International Peace, "Conflict entrepreneurs often mobilize individuals through three general tactics: appeals to ethnic, religious, and/or ideological solidarity; patronage; and positive or negative promises regarding security."[5] There is also the negative aspect of social media on the mental health of young people, especially girls.[6] It is so ironic that social media sites that promote connection can create so much division even among family and friends.

We recall a debate in the early days of the internet in the 1980s and early 90s about whether it was ethical to make money using this new technology. That discussion sure didn't last long! Now, if you happen to view a website selling pants, be prepared for endless jeans ads on your social media feed. Privacy is elusive as tech giants conspire with businesses to inundate us with targeted messages designed to separate us from our hard-earned cash.

And we are also fed information and falsehoods that reinforce our political views and promote division. This system works great for conflict entrepreneurs and social media companies but ultimately harms our nation. Tech giants have mastered how to suck us in and keep us there to our detriment. Their goal may not be polarization or undermining children's mental health, but they surely know that these are byproducts of their financial success.

Jonathan Haidt argues that social media, since 2009, has led to the fractured country we now inhabit. "Something went terribly wrong, very suddenly," he observes. "We are disoriented, unable to speak the same language or recognize the same truth. We are cut off from one another and from the past."[7]

Playing with the human psyche is a great marketing strategy. Think about going to a restaurant and seeing people immersed in their smartphones, devoid of conversation with the person across the table. Many stare at their devices as they walk down the street, oblivious to their surroundings. Texts and emails can be addictive, but the bigger concern is information overload and disinformation.

Despite these concerns, we recognize the potential to fuel a positive use of social media. Amanda Ripley observes that "Platforms like YouTube and Facebook were designed to drain our attention and divide us, but they could be redesigned to reward cooperation and decency. It is not that hard."[8] It would be possible to design social media that is neutral when it comes to conflict. It is just less profitable.

**From Becky** As the owner of a digital marketing agency who wrote a book about how to grow the reach of messages by showing up in online spaces, I work to keep myself (and my clients) focused on the positive difference we can make when we choose to share our thoughts and expertise through social media. Of course, I've had times when I wish I could leave social media channels completely. But I can see the benefits of them. Even apart from my need to stay in online spaces because of my career, I am convinced that social media is a place where people can make a difference. I generally avoid reading or engaging with politicized content, and instead I mute or unfollow people who seem to be stirring up division. I post encouraging, helpful, and useful content. In this way, social media can be more than neutral; it can be a positive influence by promoting respectful interactions and adding valuable content and insights to people's lives.

---

Yes, we are using social media to share the ideas in this book, including our *Together Across Differences* Substack newsletter (https://togethernow.substack.com). Social media can be a positive force if we each use care in how much time and energy we invest in it and maintain a healthy skepticism about information we see online.

## WHO ARE THESE CONFLICT ENTREPRENEURS?

*"Luke! Don't give in to hate. That leads to the dark side."—Obi-Wan Kenobi,* The Empire Strikes Back

So, who are these people, and how impactful are they? We classify conflict entrepreneurs in several categories described below.

**Tech giants.** As described previously, social media platforms, including Meta and X, have a key role in magnifying conflict. They may not be the original source of conflict, but their algorithms exploit, promote, and magnify it. We rate tech giants as the highest level of contributors to unhealthy division and conflict due to the algorithms they employ.

**Political influencers.** Some people use talk radio, podcasts, and social media, often for their personal financial benefit. Alex Jones promoted a message of government conspiracy and threat as advertisers used his show to sell survival gear, financially benefiting them both.[9] Many lesser-known niche influencers target people with powerful and profitable messages. For example, the NPR *No Compromise* podcast series highlighted a pro-gun group, Gun Owners of America, led by three brothers who effectively used social media to generate many more followers than the National Rifle Association, to the apparent financial benefit of its leaders.[10] Political influencers also exist on the left. Environmentalist Mark Lynas spoke out fervently against genetically modified organisms (GMOs) before reversing his position in 2013, recognizing their benefits for producing higher crop yields and requiring less use of pesticides.[11] And foreign governments also perpetuate division and conflict by propaganda campaigns.

**Journalists.** The line between news and opinion used to be clearer, but today's news is often blurred with stories slanted to appeal to certain audiences. The twenty-four-hour national network news shows are well known for this. Traditional journalists are forced to tailor their messages in ways that will attract viewers and increase advertising revenue. This is especially true for those who choose the headlines that often highlight the most sensationalistic aspect of a more complex story.

Think about all the headlines and news stories that evoke some politician's provocative statement or bad behaviors while barely focusing on the actual event where it happened! Even the most venerable news sources play the game by deciding which stories to follow and highlight and downplaying important stories that are less sensational. Some journalists are committed to reducing division, but the changes in the national media environment are pushing many in an unfortunate direction.

**Politicians and candidates.** "All politics is local," is a famous phrase by former House Speaker Tip O'Neill that seems rather antiquated today. Not so long ago, a Member of Congress could be re-elected for providing excellent constituent service and working hard for projects in their district. Those days are largely in the rearview mirror as national politics has increasingly replaced local politics, a trend mastered by politician Newt Gingrich in the 1990s.

To get elected, today's candidates often need to toe the party line and be prepared to make negative comments about their opponents. This approach works well for fundraising, too. If you want to get elected to a national or state office (and to an increasing extent to local offices), you may need to disparage those on the other side. People who don't want to play this game may either lose their election or choose not to run.

Many politicians are rewarded for bad behavior, which helps explain why so many of our elected officials are increasingly divisive and dysfunctional in their roles. The Polarization Research Lab has developed a dashboard on political discourse that identifies members of Congress who spend their time dividing the country and who focus on policy debate and constructive disagreement. They add these details, which include at least some potentially good news:

> "The public hears a lot from a very small number of individuals in Congress who are firebrands. This is problematic, because these clips get replayed over and over and we form misperceptions about Congress. The obvious conflict entrepreneurs stand out because of their focus on building their brand around conflict, but our data reveal that the most problematic members of Congress are still a relatively small group."[12]

The Dignity Index, an eight-point scale that scores speech from politicians along a continuum from contempt to dignity, is an effort to improve public discourse. It focuses on the sound bites, not the politicians behind them.[13]

**Political parties.** The best way to get people to vote for your party is to invoke fear of those on the other side. Negative campaigning is more effective than promoting a positive vision of what your side has to offer. To appeal to a more polarized public, political actors behave in more polarized ways. "As political institutions and actors become more polarized, they further polarize the public," says Ezra Klein.[14]

---

Which people or information sources are playing on your fears and emotions? Which conflict entrepreneurs are influencing you most? Use the critical thinking skills presented in a later chapter to help you regain your agency.

## WHAT ABOUT US? GOING FROM "I" TO "WE"

*"How do I want to be seen today?"*—Ken Blanchard

It's natural to think of this problem as belonging to other people, especially "those people" on the other side of the political divide. But it is vital to also consider our personal actions and behaviors.

After all, when we dehumanize others, we become conflict entrepreneurs, too.

We each absorb many divisive messages in our daily lives and choose how to use this information. If we pass forward divisive and negative energy—even to family and friends—we, too, are part of the problem, whether intended or otherwise. As James Barragan observed, "We have to look in the mirror and say, 'Is it us?'"[15]

Statements referring to "those people" and putting down others are contributing to this national problem, as are posts (and "likes") that go beyond policy viewpoints. Sadly, we have become increasingly accepting of the negative treatment of others. David Brooks has attributed this state of divisiveness to a decline in moral education. Our culture is "all about me," and this is fueling sadness, depression, disconnection, and the growth of meanness and hate crimes.[16]

While it may seem extreme to lump ourselves in with conflict entrepreneurs who exploit conflict for profit, attention, or power, our actions can reinforce and enable the politics of contempt. How do we move from being conflict enablers to "positive change" enablers or civic entrepreneurs?

In *The Upswing: How America Came Together a Century Ago and How We Can Do It Again,* Robert Putnam and Shaylyn Romney Garrett argue that we have been here before as a nation, having had a highly individualistic and polarized culture in the late 1800s. The twentieth century brought positive change; Americans were less inclined to embrace narrow self-interest and became more focused on our responsibilities to one another. Starting in the 1960s, however, we shifted to focusing more on individualism than each other, leading to what we are experiencing today.[17]

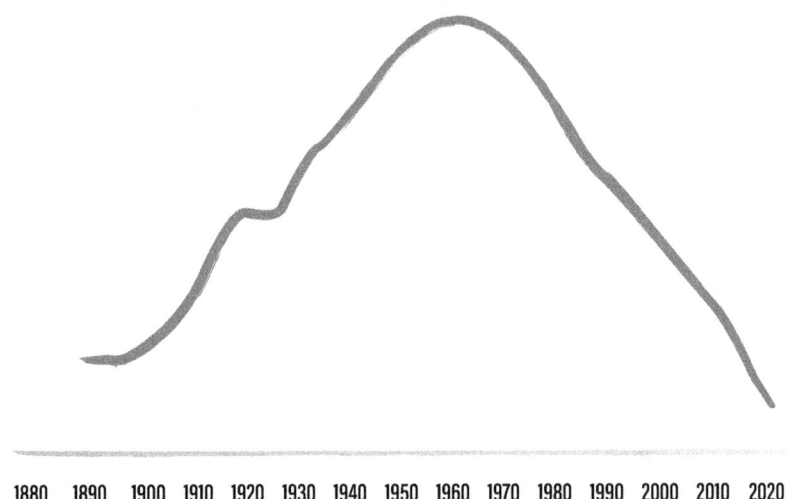

**Graph of Community vs. Individualism in America, 1890–2017**
Reproduced with permission from Robert Putnam and Shaylyn Romney Garrett, *The Upswing: How America Came Together a Century Ago and How We Can Do It Again* (Simon & Schuster, 2020), 13, Fig. 1.2. This inverted U-curve shows a gradual ascent into greater community in the first part of the twentieth century, followed by a steep descent into greater individualism.

On October 8, 2024, Putnam told a packed house in Hanover, New Hampshire, that history shows that positive change is possible. He was there introducing the 2023 documentary film *Join or Die* based on his books.[18]

We can again go from an "I" society to a "We" society, he concluded, but this will require a "moral reawakening." In a June 12, 2024, conversation with the New Hampshire alliance (chapter) of Braver Angels, Shaylyn Romney Garrett implored participants to "Lead with your humanity, rather than your politics."

There are far more of us than there are conflict entrepreneurs. Our individual impact may be small, but collective actions can be powerful. If we are unwittingly enabling conflict, this adds to the national distress and boosts the conflict entrepreneurs. But if we move in a more positive direction, this can attract others and build a movement for change.

Working together, we can collectively blunt the power of conflict entrepreneurs and lead our country past this current state of widespread contempt for those who think differently about politics.

## FOR FURTHER THOUGHT

- What steps could you take to reduce politically negative influences and conflict entrepreneurs in your life?
- Is social media influencing you in any unhealthy ways, and, if so, what might you do differently?
- Are you a prisoner to your cell phone, and, if so, what might you want to change?
- Are you contributing to the polarization problem, and, if so, what might you do differently?
- How might you support a moral reawakening in our country?

# SECTION III

# CHANGE IS POSSIBLE, STARTING WITHIN YOU AND ME

*"The place to improve the world is first in one's own heart and head and hands."*—Robert Pirsig

## Chapter 7

# THE POWER OF THE EXHAUSTED MAJORITY

> *"I speak for the normies. I speak for that vast middle that is tired of the partisanship. I don't want to hate half the country, and I don't hate half the country."*
> —Bill Maher

Like comedian and writer Maher, a lot of Americans are tired of division and contempt.

 I received this email from Todd Miller of North Conway, New Hampshire: "As you know so well, we are living in a very difficult and often scary time. My wife and I frequently become frustrated at the behavior we see on the local and national level, whether it be in Washington, DC, or on the street on our way home at night. I appreciate the fresh outlook and perspective you provide on the issue of bridging differences of perspective and the idea of trying to get back to a place where differences of opinion, or even open debate, can once again be done in a civil manner."

We know a lot of people who feel this way about our country, and Miller's words reminded us of the 2018 report *Hidden Tribes: A Study of America's Polarized Landscape*.[1] Authors Stephen Hawkins, Daniel Yudkin, Míriam Juan-Torres, and Tim Dixon summarized their in-depth research that identified seven segments of Americans (that they call "tribes") distinguished by differences in beliefs and attitudes. The seven tribes are listed in the following graphic from the political left to right.

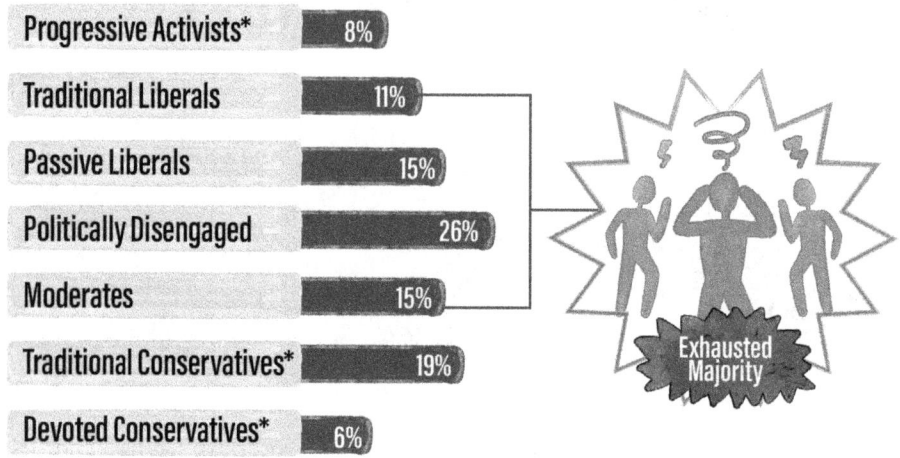

According to these authors, the "wing groups" on the two extremes—progressive activists at 8 percent and two categories of conservatives at 25 percent (marked by asterisks in the graphic)—typically dominate the political conversation even though they only represent 33 percent of the country. And we wonder if that 33 percent number is too high, as we know traditional conservatives whom we would not consider extreme.

The authors combine everyone in the other four categories (67 percent of Americans) into what they call "the exhausted majority." As introduced earlier in the book, these are people who are unhappy with our nation's polarization and who are forgotten in public discourse because their voices are seldom heard. They are flexible in their views, rather than sticking ideologically to a single set of beliefs, and they are willing to find common ground.

September 2024 data from the Polarization Research Lab showed that 56 percent of Americans are polarized (44 percent are not), a view that might seem at odds with there being such a large exhausted majority. They also found that only 3 percent of people support partisan violence.[2] The bottom line, either way, is that there are many Americans who want to see something better than the "us versus them" politics that dominates our news.

The Hidden Tribes authors add this distressing perspective:

"We are long past the point where these differences are contributing to a healthy and robust democracy. The intolerance for the other is a grave threat to our democratic system, as political actors cast off the restraints of convention and even the rule of law, with a ruthless determination to crush the other side no matter the cost."[3]

We are worried about where this may take us. Crushing the other side no matter the cost is not a formula for strengthening our country. At the same time, we believe that there is hope, that those in the exhausted majority can help lead our country to a brighter future.

**From Beth** I've tried to instill hope in myself and others through conversations—not on social media but in one-on-one or group settings with ground rules. My friend Catherine and I started a discussion group in Nashville in 2023 called "Complicating the Narrative" based on the concept that introducing nuance into contentious issues was healthy. We made sure the group was balanced and included both conservative and liberal voices.

When we talked about topics like immigration, we realized that there were many different approaches to how people thought about the southern border. However, we all valued a path to citizenship for people who had legally entered the country. We then complicated the narrative by discussing asylum seekers and where they fit in, and also how our country would pay for vetting processes. We came up with creative solutions such as having small businesses that benefited from hard-working immigrants help finance the vetting processes and paths to citizenship.

While it was exciting to come up with creative solutions as ordinary citizens, what was more profound was the hopeful feeling that we, the exhausted majority, could *work together* to figure out solutions.

---

We know firsthand from our work with Braver Angels that there is far more common ground than what you see from observing our politics. A *Time* magazine article by Karl Vick in 2024 cited evidence that we are less divided than many of us think.[4]

## PERSPECTIVES ON THE EXHAUSTED MAJORITY

*"People are mysteries, not puzzles. This means we can never be sure about them. But we can always be curious."—Mónica Guzmán*

Where do you fall on the Hidden Tribes spectrum? In which segment do you best fit? Maybe if you fall into one of the wing groups, you are not interested in our message, although we hope you might at least be curious.

**From Doug:** After I summarized the Hidden Tribes report in one of my *Growing Leadership* newsletters, I received some interesting feedback. One reader wrote, "This ray of hope is refreshing, especially as the news is quite grim. Thank you for sharing these words of encouragement."

But there were also some negative reactions, including from an old friend who felt it was "unproductive to attempt discourse with folks who are unwilling to accept as factual any facts not comporting with their own prejudices. I think you give these folks too much credit by calling them 'conservatives'; I can't fathom anything they're trying to conserve other than their own ill-gotten privilege. Though I commend your continually striving to bring folks together, I believe there are definite limitations to rapprochement."

And a friend on the other side called the Hidden Tribes study "disturbing" and thought the authors "show a prejudice that we conservatives are distressed by and find unfair. The authors apparently hold the view that everybody on the Right, just by virtue of holding views different from theirs (positions that have stood the test of 2,000 years of western civilization), is a right-wing extremist! Have we really sunk this far in the United States that people who hold conservative views are extremists?"

---

The Hidden Tribes report authors seem to have struck a nerve, but they are not alone in the perspective that many Americans would like to see a different kind of politics. A New Hampshire poll found that 92 percent of New Hampshire citizens thought it was important (67 percent very important and 25 percent somewhat important) to reduce extreme partisanship and political polarization, and 91 percent say political polarization is threatening our way of life.[5]

New Hampshire state representative Tom Cormen campaigned door-to-door at some one thousand homes in Lebanon, New Hampshire, before the 2024 election and asked an open-ended question: "What's on your mind?" Cormen, who has been active in the Braver Angels-inspired Granite Bridge Legislative Alliance, told us that many people expressed concern about polarization with comments such as, "I don't like the way politicians are talking to each other."

Political scientist Yanna Krupnikov believes that the most polarized among us skew opinion, that people who are "deeply involved" in politics think differently from the majority of people and are more likely to see those on the other side in negative ways.[6] Ezra Klein adds, "Politics is driven by the most committed activists with the most intense opinions."[7]

Our view of the exhausted majority is not that this group is politically moderate. Rather, we believe that they may have strong opinions about politics and specific policies, but wish to approach others in a more civil way. People can have strong political opinions without feeling a need to demonize those who disagree with them.

We were fascinated by newspaper columnist Wayne Gerson's cross-country journey during which he observed a great deal of venom on the political TV news shows he saw airing when he visited homes along his route. But then he added, in his June 2024 *Valley News* column, that the people he met didn't reflect this:

> "The world we witnessed in our travels was hardly toxic, rancorous or divided. It was full of mutual respect, genuine kindness and levelheadedness, qualities that I failed to witness in my small, random sample of news watching and that I seldom read about online. American voters undeniably have many differences in outlooks and attitudes when it comes to politics, but I came away from our travels with the sense that the great majority of Americans want to find common ground with each other."[8]

In his book, author Francis Barry similarly described a cross-country road trip during which he and his wife engaged many Americans who shared their experiences in ways that humanized political divisions.[9]

In a 2024 interview, Dr. Francis Collins, former National Institutes of Health director, said: "I have a lot of hope for our future. There are a lot of us, the majority of us, we've even been called 'the exhausted majority,' who are not endorsing all of this vitriol and polarization but are trying to figure out how to get us back on track. I think we can do that."[10]

Of course, conflict entrepreneurs know how to exploit small differences, making common ground seem even more distant. So, it makes total sense that we would seem further apart than we really are! The Hidden Tribes authors argue that we are all being affected by this national division.

"One of the most striking findings from our conversations with Americans from all tribes is not only how often they speak of division as being the country's most pressing problem, but how profoundly it now affects them in their own lives. These discussions provoke strong emotions and sometimes even a sense of despair."[11]

We are all paying for this unhealthy division now, and, if we don't act sooner rather than later, the price will surely be higher. While it's tempting to wait to reconcile with others until after "their side" is defeated, that approach seems unrealistic and can take a toll on our relationships and mental health.

When we hear people attacking those on the other side, we ask, "What is your goal?" If it's to influence others, recognize that you cannot win people over to your side by shaming or putting them down. Short-term gains may be possible in all-out "us versus them" battles, but we believe that engaging others in a healthy manner is the only long-term solution to move our country forward.

*From Becky* While Doug and Beth have been actively involved in Braver Angels for many years, I have been part of the politically disengaged segment of the exhausted majority, and I have not been active in volunteering or participating in civic organizations. In the wake of the 2024 election, I'm still looking for the best ways I can speak out about the topics that concern me, listen to others to understand them better, and get involved to contribute to positive change in our nation. I'm also still learning how to be open to understanding and connecting with those people with whom I disagree.

We believe that actions by the exhausted majority are the best antidotes to the conflict entrepreneurs who are trying to tear us apart. We especially hope to influence people who are politically disengaged by helping those in this group to see the potential for joy that can come from interacting together across differences.

## OVERCOMING A DIFFERENT DIVIDE: A PATH FORWARD FOR THE EXHAUSTED MAJORITY

*"Few will have the greatness to bend history itself; but each of us can work to change a small portion of events, and in the total of all those acts will be written the history of this generation."*—Robert Kennedy

One way forward for the exhausted majority is to consider a different divide from left and right. In the *Hopeful Majority* podcast led by Manu Meel,[12] CEO of BridgeUSA,[13] Tim Urban talks about "high rung" thinking where people are positively engaged in conversations and share their viewpoints freely. It's healthy discourse and you love the debate. You go out for a beer afterward with your friends from the opposite political side.

**From Beth:** This high rung thinking is what we try to create at Braver Angels and other organizations. It's palpable. I've felt it in the "Common Ground Nashville" and "Complicating the Narrative" discussion groups that I have co-led. I've felt it over a meal with young conservative Christian friends, discussing why I feel abortion should be permissible in specific situations related to the health and well-being of a mother.

The good news, say the Hidden Tribes authors, is that most of us want to see something better: "To bring Americans back together, we need to focus first on those things that we share, and this starts with our identity as

Americans. This can create the space for sometimes difficult but necessary conversations."[14]

If we each decide to step up as individuals—even in small ways—there is enormous potential to make meaningful change, as there are so many of us, and our power lies in our numbers. We love our country, we are all patriots, and, like family, we need to figure out how to get along. No, we don't need to agree on everything—that is unrealistic. But we do need to find ways to disagree better, including having meaningful conversations and really listening to those with different perspectives.

In a *Newsweek* article, "How Positive Engagement Can Bring the Exhausted Majority Back Into Politics," authors Sami Sage and Emily Amick add that action is the antidote to despair with these important observations:

> "We can reverse a hopelessness spiral through the compounding and life-affirming effects of empathy, togetherness and community. . . . Silence on politics is also a contributing factor to our polarized political landscape—and having conversations about it is a part of the solution."[15]

Braver Angels volunteer Courtenay Budd told us: "Toxic polarization is not like the weather, like something happening to us. We all play a part and can all be part of the solution. But it takes putting ourselves in uncomfortable places, talking with people who smell bad, who make us look bad to our friends just by listening to them."

To make our country better, we each need to put ourselves in uncomfortable places. We are not so worried about people smelling bad, but we do need to be ready for pushback, including from our own group. Abraham Lincoln once said, "To sin by silence when they should protest makes cowards out of men." Coward is perhaps too strong of a word. But we can each go beyond silence, acting in ways that will have a significant impact.

Our country needs us to step up, to lend our voices, even if only in a very small way, to help our nation overcome this problem of polarization.

## FOR FURTHER THOUGHT

- Does it make sense to you that the people on the extremes are the ones most driving political division? Why or why not?
- Do you think that a majority of Americans would like to see a better form of politics and less division? And how might this be accomplished?
- Would you consider yourself part of the exhausted majority? Why and which segment are you?
- Are you willing to lend your voice, even in a small way, to help our country overcome this problem? How might you want to step up first?
- If you are reluctant to engage, what tools or support would help you be more confident about doing so?

## Chapter 8

# MIND THE GAP BETWEEN THOUGHTS AND VALUES

> *"One may only demand heroism of one person, and that person is oneself."*—Viktor E. Frankl

We hope this is making sense and you are contemplating taking some personal action. But before you do anything, it's helpful to start with some inward reflection.

This is the hard part. We are not going to sugarcoat it. But if you want to improve our country, this inner reflection is essential—a key building block for each of us to help end this unhealthy conflict and toxic polarization. We propose these three steps.

1. **Make a list of your most important values**. If you aren't clear about your values, you won't be clear about the decisions and the actions you take. Your fundamental values and beliefs represent the core of who you are.[1]

In *Dare to Lead,* author and public speaker Brené Brown adds that value clarity "is an essential support, a North Star in times of darkness."[2] Brown lists one hundred values and encourages the reader to add more and eventually narrow their personal list down to the top two. Selecting too many, she argues, diminishes usefulness and clarity of purpose. To get started, you can use the list in Brown's book (available publicly at no charge here: https://brenebrown.com/resources/living-into-our-values/), do an internet search, or just come up with your own list from scratch.

**From Doug** When I went through this process, eighteen values made my initial list. I whittled them down to two top values: growing and grace. Growing with grace defines what is most important to me; it describes how I want to show up and what I want to try to model in daily life. Growing speaks to a willingness to improve and stretch myself and includes my secondary values of courage, connection, curiosity, and leadership. Grace speaks to my Christian faith and the importance of embracing family, gratitude, joy, love, and authenticity. Other important values included hope, respect, positive energy, vision, teamwork, and trust. Defining these values has helped me focus on what I want to do in my life and how to go about it. Writing this book is one example.

**From Beth** I identified twenty-two values from Brown's list and added one more not on that list—diplomacy. I picked authenticity and connection as my top two values. I added diplomacy and kindness. I recognize that practicing diplomacy gives me the courage to be fully authentic. Similarly, kindness fosters connections with others.

**From Becky**: As a business owner, values have been critical to how I've shaped my company. Many of the core values for my business are also my personal values, including generosity and integrity. My other most important personal values are family, faith, gratitude, making a difference, and service.

What about you?

We encourage you to go through this exercise. There is no magic number, but if you have a hard time getting your list of top values down to two, settle for three or five—whatever works for you. You can keep things simple or add an additional layer of complexity by considering how some values contribute to other values, as Doug and Beth did.

2. **Picture the supporters of a politician you dislike (not the politician but their supporters).** *Write down a list of words you would use to describe them.* We suggest you write eight to ten words that come to mind. Yes, this can be a bit painful, but stick with it.

3. **Compare the two lists.** Is there a disconnect? Are you living your values? If, like Doug, connection is high on your list, can you truly see yourself connecting with politicians' supporters with joy—or any other values you named? Can you see yourself being curious about their actions or viewpoints? If, like Beth, authenticity is high on your values list, can you be honest in telling others where you differ from them and, at the same time, inject some diplomacy into the situation? If, like Becky, you embrace generosity, can you see yourself extending that to people with different political views from yours?

How did you find this exercise? Did you see a disconnect between your values and how you would describe supporters of a politician you dislike?

We obviously don't know what you listed. But, given that most people aspire to high values and there is such a strong political divide in our country, we are guessing that most who do this exercise will see a gap—maybe even a big one—between their values and their views of at least some people with different political views. Maybe the gap will be smaller for those in the exhausted majority than it will be for people on the political wings, but we are all impacted by events, social media, and news. Some degree of a gap is pretty common.

It took us a while (and some hard thinking) to see the disconnect between our personal thoughts and our values, but this is where we come down in the end. This is where the rubber hits the road. This is what we aspire to live up to, even if sometimes we don't quite measure up with respect to the difference between our values and the words we use to describe the supporters of politicians we dislike.

Maybe you don't agree and prefer to think that "those people" on the other side are evil, stupid, misinformed, selfish, unpatriotic, or some other negative characteristics. Well, we tend to go there, too, at times. But we have learned that regarding people on the other side of politics as evil or stupid (or fill-in-the-blank with some other negative terms) is hurting our country—and is not good for us either. How we see others is a reflection of ourselves, and our relationships with others reflect back on us, too.

We try to embrace the perspective of the well-known Christian Serenity Prayer: "God grant me the serenity to accept the things I cannot change, courage to change the things I can, and wisdom to know the difference." By focusing on what we can control, we are usually more effective—and it is great for our health, too! We usually sleep better and feel more in control when we can let go of those things we simply can't control.

We each have the power to choose our response to events, but sometimes we forget that. We act in ways that we might think are inevitable or preordained. When things aren't going well in life or work or our country, it is easy to fall into a pattern of blaming others, gossiping, or playing the victim. But even when frustration is justified, these are usually self-defeating strategies.

Author Scott Mautz suggests that you "elevate your values to sacred status. Do you consistently live by these values and let them guide you? Do you hold your values sacred? Living by your values turns guesses into good decisions. When we go astray from our values, regrets pile up."³

In his 2024 Brandeis University graduation speech, Ken Burns reflected on his career as a documentary filmmaker, observing: "If I have learned anything, it's that there is only *us*. There is no *them*. And whenever someone suggests to you . . . that there's a them, run away. It's the surest way to your own self-imprisonment."⁴

In *Man's Search for Meaning,* based on his experiences in a Nazi death camp, neurologist and psychologist Viktor Frankl embraced an extraordinary calling to view those who persecuted him in the most humane way. He believed that doing otherwise would be self-defeating. Frankl understood that, whatever situation we find ourselves in, we have the power "to choose one's attitude in any given set of circumstances, to choose one's own way."⁵

In an interview with podcaster Kelly Corrigan, journalist Judy Woodruff said that she has seen plenty of division, but the 2024 election was the first time the two sides seemed to be looking at each other as mortal enemies.⁶ Are you looking at people on the other side in such terms?

We suggest that you take a step back to focus on your values—and ultimately your heart—and how you think and act. What is in your heart extends to what is in your mind. But everything starts in your heart. If you are thinking negative things about the people who support politicians you dislike, you may be expressing that to others in some way, at least to people on your side. This kind of echo chamber is self-perpetuating and reinforces the politics of contempt.

The bottom line is that if you are thinking and acting this way, you are most likely a contributor to the toxic polarization problem, or in other words, a conflict enabler.

This is painful to write, and we suspect it may be painful to read. We are pretty sure you don't want to think of yourself in this way. We would all prefer to blame others and not ourselves. But internalizing this concept on a personal level is a starting place for making our lives, relationships, and country better.

What is in your heart and what you think about really do matter. Your influence touches others who in turn touch others. You have a lot more power than you might think. Yes, there are conflict entrepreneurs and tech giants who play division to the max, but that only works if we let them. Change and moral reawakening can start with us.

## FOR FURTHER THOUGHT

- What values are most important for you? How do you apply them in daily life?
- Where might there be a disconnect between your values and how you see people who support politicians with views different from yours?
- What might you want to do differently to narrow any gap between your values and your thoughts about others?
- How is the political divide affecting your personal health and well-being?
- Do you think you are contributing to political polarization, and, if so, how might you want to change?

## Chapter 9
# CHANGE FROM THE INSIDE OUT

> *"How wonderful it is that nobody need wait a single moment before starting to improve the world"*
> *—Anne Frank*

The 1985 film *Back to the Future* is one of our favorites. Beyond the great acting and script, there is a powerful and hopeful message: Actions today can change the future. When we first meet the parents of the Michael J. Fox character Marty McFly, they are timid and uncertain. Going back in time, Marty meets them as teenagers and encourages his future father to stand up to the bully, Biff. At the end of the film, when we encounter Marty's parents again, they are confident and successful adults. The implication is clear: Marty's father dramatically changed their lives for the better by one key act of standing up to his high school nemesis.

*It's a Wonderful Life,* released back in 1946, is another cinematic favorite with a hopeful message. When the Jimmy Stewart character George Bailey contemplates suicide, angel Clarence arrives to take George back in time to show how many people benefited from his lifetime of support and assistance. As George Bailey takes the message to heart, angel Clarence observes, "Strange, isn't it? Each man's life touches so many other lives."

In the 2000 film *Gladiator,* Russell Crowe plays Maximus, a Roman general forced into slavery who seeks revenge for the murders of his family and emperor Marcus Aurelius. In a memorable scene, he proclaims, "What we do in life echoes in eternity."

Small actions can lead to big changes. Each life touches so many others, and what we do in life echoes in eternity. These are great examples of how hopeful actions can create a better future.

*Wait a minute,* you say, *this is Hollywood.* Fair enough, but actions that change the future have occurred many times in real life. We tend to think of historical events as if they were destined to happen. But what if George Washington had failed to cross the Delaware? Or if Abraham Lincoln had conceded to the secession of the southern states? Or if the Allied Normandy invasion in World War II had been repelled by Nazi Germany?

Those examples are big historical events, but think of actions that shaped your life.

In the last chapter, we shared our most important values and asked you to identify yours. If you haven't done so already, we encourage you to find time to go through this process. Next, ponder the key decisions that shaped your life and how they relate to your values. Also, which of your actions and behaviors have most significantly influenced others?

We'll start with our own answers to these questions.

## DOUG: REFLECTING ON DECISIONS THAT SHAPED MY LIFE AND VALUES

*"Life is either a daring adventure, or nothing."—Helen Keller*

I wonder how much my life would be different today if my parents had not sent me to summer camp as a child. Among many benefits, camp resulted in my first backpacking trip to New Hampshire's White Mountains at age 13 and eventually to the Appalachian Mountain Club Worcester Chapter. This led to a lifetime of hiking, skiing, and mountaineering.

Of course, it was my parents who made the decision to send me to camp, but I strongly advocated to keep going back! Growing older, I had plenty of opportunities to shape and change my life, building on a special upbringing in a loving and caring family. These are seven of my decisions that had a major impact on who I am today:

1. In 1966, as a senior in high school, deciding to no longer play football and focus more time and energy on hiking mountains
2. In 1971, joining the Peace Corps and going to live and work in Morocco for two years
3. In 1974, committing to becoming a better rock climber despite a major setback
4. In 1981, getting married
5. In the 1980s, deciding with my wife to have children
6. In 1988, running for the state legislature
7. In 2001, pursuing an overseas position in Rwanda
8. The 2019 decision to go all-in with Braver Angels and eventually write this book

Doug hanging precariously on Cannon Cliff, New Hampshire, in 1974, an event that spurred resilience and personal growth. (Photo courtesy of the author.)

While some of these choices might seem obvious as to how they changed my life, I offer some thoughts on the first and third that might seem more obscure.

The mention of quitting high school football in 1966 was about stepping into early adulthood with a realization that I had the power to make decisions for myself. That was a defining life moment in so many ways, a hopeful wake-up call that I could change my life and grow in new ways.

In 1974, a poor performance on a major cliff face led to a stark realization that my rock-climbing skills did not measure up to what I perceived. This affected my self-confidence and identity, requiring a new level of resilience and growth that carried me forward in ways that went far beyond climbing. This event is closely aligned with other values I had on my list, like faith and courage.

Of course, this list is from an internal perspective: reflecting on how my life was changed by decisions I made. Then there are external impacts, such as how my actions influenced others, hopefully in ways that were mostly more positive than negative.

A list of external impacts is a harder list to put together, in part, because you never fully know your impact on other people. Sometimes big efforts don't have as much effect as we hope, while other times little things we do can have enormous influences that we may not even recognize. But just because we aren't fully sure of how our actions influence others, that doesn't mean we shouldn't take time to reflect and consider our impact. This is one important way that the value of grace has been reflected in my life journey.

A list of my external influences starts with the actions I took and impact I had as a husband, father, grandfather, brother, cousin, uncle, and son, which is tied to my value of family.

My approach to leadership is tied to values of connection, vision, trust, and teamwork. My formal leadership roles include serving as Peace Corps country director, engaging with two hundred and thirty staff members and fifteen hundred American volunteers in programs I managed in Ukraine and several African nations. In my volunteer role as New England Regional Leader with Braver Angels, I strive to be a supporter and cheerleader for the other volunteers—acknowledging and hopefully inspiring their various efforts in positive, hopeful ways that improve relationships and political discourse.

Then there are those who have been touched by my writings in the *Appalachia* journal and the "Growing Leadership" column in the *NH Business Review*. These align with my values of joy and gratitude. Using the word *growing* in the column title was clearly no accident!

I strive to consciously apply positive energy and authenticity to honoring friendships, some of which go back many years. I reach out from time to time, especially focusing on life moments that might seem especially important.

I try to interact positively with strangers and be aware of my behaviors during everyday encounters in convenience stores and restaurants, including acknowledging a person who exhibits a smile or extra attention to detail. Applying the values of connection, respect, and positive energy are important for me.

In addition, I try to be aware of when my behavior may have had a negative impact on others and quickly offer an apology. For sure, there have been some missed opportunities, and I try to learn from those, which is tied to the value of authenticity.

Authenticity is sometimes misunderstood as always saying what you think, no matter what the circumstances. For me, it is much more about my internal understanding of who I am and acting in sincere ways consistent with my core beliefs and without pretensions.

Thinking about how we influence other people, I go back to those wonderful *My Unsung Hero* podcasts with special stories of how someone (usually a stranger) touched a person's life in a meaningful way. As I listen to these stories, I wonder sometimes how the person who was so helpful would remember the incident—or if they might not remember it at all!

How might my life experience and values build positive relationships across politics and help our country overcome polarization? I go back to life experiences that helped me embrace growing with grace, being open to others, and doing so in an authentic way. I strive to avoid belittling others or reducing them to stereotypes. I believe this approach is vital for building relationships across politics and trying to influence others in a positive way that can benefit our country.

My writing this book is infused with the spirit of love, faith, vision, and hope that our lives and country can get better. We each have an extraordinary opportunity to make a difference in people's lives, including our own. Don't underestimate your impact!

## BETH: REFLECTING ON DECISIONS THAT SHAPED MY LIFE AND VALUES

*"Perhaps this is the moment for which you have been created."—based on Esther 4:14*

My big life decisions included:

1. In 1980, deciding I wanted to become a physician, to combine my aptitude for science with my interest in people
2. In 1991, getting married to a supportive husband who has always given me the freedom to pursue my passions, and in 1998 and 2001, becoming a mother
3. In 2015, pursuing advocacy and civil discourse (engaging with others across political differences)
4. In 2021, shifting my medical career to include science and health communication infused with advocacy and civil discourse
5. In 2024, moving from Tennessee to Vermont

Thinking about how I applied my values of authenticity, connection, diplomacy, and kindness to these decisions, I have many thoughts. In spring 2023, I became an adult bat mitzvah. A bat mitzvah is a "coming of age" ritual in Judaism, in which we recite prayers and read from the Hebrew Torah (Old Testament). Most girls take part in this ritual around age twelve. But some of us wait until adulthood, for a variety of reasons. I was one of those who waited until I had accumulated enough life experiences to make the experience meaningful. I joined a group adult bat mitzvah class at my synagogue, Congregation Micah, in Nashville, Tennessee.

I took the Hebrew name Esther because I admired how this biblical heroine, who had become royalty, demonstrated the authenticity and courage to speak up and reveal her identity to save the Jewish people. I've felt that sometimes as a Braver Angel moderating workshops I've needed authenticity and courage to help people come together across political differences. I agree with Doug's definition of authenticity as being related to an internal understanding of who we are and acting in sincere ways consistent with our core beliefs.

Albert Einstein is said to have remarked that, "The most important decision we make is whether we believe we live in a friendly or hostile universe."[1] I believe it's a friendly one. I have deep optimism that our country will get through these challenging times if we can learn to talk with each other in authentic and respectful ways. We can build relationships rather than break them down. When I think about how these values have significantly affected others and also contributed to positive change in our country's politics, I hear my friends and colleagues saying they appreciate my outlook and respect my approach.

It wasn't always this way for me, though.

I spent my childhood and much of my adult life as a cautious perfectionist, looking before I leapt, making sure I considered my words and actions carefully. This mindset was shaped by experiences in which my speaking up for what I believed did not often go over well. One of my bosses at work was threatened by my new ideas, and others felt I came on too strong. It was challenging to want to make a difference in the world while feeling like people weren't grasping what I was trying to get across. Fortunately, my supportive and perceptive husband helped me figure out when to step back, listen, and get "the lay of the land." I became more diplomatic, which includes being sensitive to the needs of others and seeking out ways to help them. As I learned these things, I was able to speak up more because the reactions from others were more positive.

I ask myself now why it took me so long to get involved in advocacy and civil discourse. I think the answers were that I needed to be in a position in my career where I felt secure and also where I could speak in a way that encouraged people to listen.

Supporting my two sons helped me move in the direction of advocacy. I needed to speak up and object when well-meaning, but wrong, counselors told me we needed to put my son on strong medications to correct certain behaviors like when he would lash out (sometimes appropriately) at those who ridiculed him. Instead of medications, we got him into a social group with like-minded kids who excelled at design tasks. This approach boosted his confidence and improved his "behaviors" and also set him on a path for a successful career in engineering.

After seeing how speaking up helped my son, and being in a secure position as a tenured professor, I became more of a "leap before I look" person. I haven't excelled at mountain climbing, like Doug, or anything else that involves physical risk (skydiving isn't on my list of preferred activities). But I love novelty: meeting new people, living in new places, and traveling around the world. That novelty found its place in my civil discourse work and propelled me to do some brave things. These included moderating workshops and discussions locally with Common Ground Nashville and nationally with Braver Angels. I also pursued graduate studies in science and health communication to better understand how to advocate effectively and respectfully about public health issues, including climate change and later school start times for teens.

Finally, my move to Vermont has been life-changing. My husband suggested we move to Vermont as he had lived here previously and loves outdoor activities. I decided to leap before I looked again, and stepped down as division chief of sleep medicine after twenty-one years, because I wanted to pursue new challenges. While I miss many aspects of Tennessee, I enjoy the emphasis on civic engagement in New England and having the opportunity to take part in local initiatives, like town meetings and town committees. This includes participating in the incredibly rewarding bridge-building work Doug and his colleagues are pursuing with the New Hampshire state legislature. I'm their token Vermonter!

## BECKY: REFLECTING ON DECISIONS THAT SHAPED MY LIFE AND VALUES

Life decisions that have shaped my journey:

1. While growing up in the church, making a personal commitment to following the ways of Jesus at a young age
2. Studying English and writing in college
3. Marrying Eric before my twenty-second birthday
4. Our decision and experience associated with starting a church in the late 1990s
5. My choice to stay at home with my children through their early years
6. Founding my company in 2012 and deciding to build an organization to be larger than myself

In thinking about who I am today and what matters to me, my love of reading and writing began at an early age as did a desire to make a difference in the world. As a college student, I felt drawn to majoring in writing, even though I didn't have a career vision. While adults in my life encouraged me to choose a major with a clear career path, I resisted. Those early studies, while not related to digital marketing (a field that didn't exist yet), fueled my writing skills and love of books.

My experiences with starting a church with my husband in the late 1990s prepared me for my entrepreneurial journey as well, as I gained many skills and experiences needed to start something new: team building, clarifying a vision and values, and dealing with setbacks.

My current vocation of supporting authors seems like the perfect culmination of all my past experiences, interests, and opportunities. My personal values have shaped my decisions as a business owner, especially my value of generosity, which influences my choices daily.

While decisions and values have shaped my life, I'm aware of how seemingly mundane conversations have had a powerful influence on my life. One happened in 2009 when a friend encouraged me to create a Facebook profile, which led to freelance opportunities, learning digital marketing, and then eventually starting my company.

In 2020, when my oldest child returned from college during the pandemic, I had a Zoom call with a client, David Taylor-Klaus. As we introduced ourselves, I noted the proud and affirming way David shared about his children, including his oldest, Bex, who is nonbinary. Until this time, I hadn't interacted with many parents of queer kids or understood what nonbinary was, and my conversation with David supported me in two ways. First, my oldest child overheard the conversation and appreciated that I had exposure to David's way of being with his children. Next, when this same child came out to me later that year, David's gentle acceptance and fervent allyship with his children served as a powerful example of the parent I wanted to be.

## WHAT ABOUT YOU?

*"Where there is no vision, the people perish."—Proverbs 29:18*

We encourage you to reflect on your life—on the decisions that shaped who you are today and actions you took that impacted others. Consider how those decisions connect with the personal values you identified in the last chapter—how your day-to-day behavior lives up to your beliefs. Think about how your actions have significantly affected others and whether you may have contributed in some way, whether positively or negatively, to our nation's division. And then consider how you might apply your life experiences to build relationships across politics and support positive change in our country.

This kind of self-reflection is an important aspect of both growing as a person and helping make change happen. We tend to think of social or political change as bigger than ourselves, but it can start with us. It is easy to feel overwhelmed by events and to feel like throwing up our hands. Bad things can happen to us or around us, but events are not what change us as

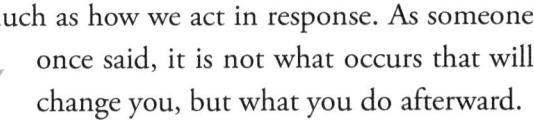

much as how we act in response. As someone once said, it is not what occurs that will change you, but what you do afterward.

If you believe that there is an exhausted majority that wants something better for our country, then you probably also believe that conditions are ripe for change. You may not be able to change our country alone, but don't underestimate how much you might influence others and create momentum for civic renewal. Yes, there are many forces working against us, but we can all be unleashed to create hope and make a difference. You can help make it happen!

## FOR FURTHER THOUGHT

- What are the key decisions that shaped your life?
- How did those decisions shape your values?
- Which of your actions and behaviors have most significantly influenced others?
- How can you best embrace the idea that changing our country can start with you?
- How might you apply your life experiences and values in hopeful ways that build relationships across the political divide?

Chapter 10

# WHAT POSITIVE CHANGE CAN LOOK LIKE: THE PROMISE OF CITIZEN-LED SOLUTIONS

> *"Never doubt that a small group of thoughtful, committed citizens can change the world; indeed, it's the only thing that ever has."*—Margaret Mead

OK, we've taken time for some personal reflection, including examining values and decisions that shaped our lives. How can we use this information to contribute to positive change and a national moral awakening? What specific steps can we take to connect with others and move our nation "from I to we"?

Beginning to get involved in changing our country for the better can feel overwhelming, especially when the problems seem too big to influence. It's helpful for me to consider small steps for moving from me to we: moving outward from personal growth to an expanding circle of influence. First, from myself to my family. Then, from my family to my neighborhood or close community. Next, from my community to my region or state, from my state to our nation, and from our nation to the world. Any small step to engage outside of my own interests is a step toward others.

---

Depolarizing ourselves is a key first step to improving our lives and relationships amid this national political dysfunction. What do we mean by depolarizing ourselves? We look inward to understand how we think and feel about people with different political views as discussed in the previous chapters. At the same time, we can become more aware of the ways we are manipulated by politicians, conflict entrepreneurs, and the media.

Once we understand our biases and triggers, we are much better positioned to build positive relationships and drive positive change through example and advocacy. We can work effectively with other Americans to solve problems at multiple levels. In the spirit of "from I to we," we can work together to develop citizen-led solutions that benefit our local community, our state, and our country.

The Hidden Tribes report lists these positive changes that could help move our country forward:[1]

- Political candidates can speak to the values that unify the nation, instead of mobilizing their base while polarizing the country.
- Activists and advocates can broaden their appeals to the underlying values of those they don't usually reach.

- Philanthropists can invest creatively in the thousand points of light that can show us a way forward to counter polarization and develop robust evaluation measures to prove impact.
- Creative artists and media can spotlight the extraordinary ways in which Americans in local communities build bridges and not walls, every day.
- Technology companies can turn their vast resources and analytical tools to create platforms and systems that help do the hard work of bringing people together, rather than the easy work of magnifying outrage in echo chambers and filter bubbles.

We find all these ideas potentially impactful, but we also see limitations. Political candidates will only change when enough of us demand better. We are less optimistic about the media, given the way that negativity drives viewership. We feel the same about technology companies, given how their algorithms drive division to maximize engagement. Artists and activists can be impactful if they include bridge building in their initiatives.

**From Beth** I volunteered with Citizens' Climate Lobby (CCL) to help climate activists, including myself, become less polarized. I first had to manage my own frustration that progress on global warming was moving too slowly. I channeled my angst into working with a conservative climate champion to create the Braver Angels Action Team within CCL. We developed a new workshop and trained more than two thousand volunteers across the country on communicating across political differences.[2]

Philanthropists have an important role to play. The Carnegie Foundation is working with Braver Angels to strengthen bipartisan relationships in state legislatures. This effort expands on our efforts in New Hampshire,

Doug, Beth, and colleagues with members of the New Hampshire State Legislature. (Photo courtesy of Paul Catsos.)

where Doug, Beth and other volunteers, including former Democratic Representative Patricia Higgins, supported the creation of the Braver Angels-inspired caucus known as the Granite Bridge Legislative Alliance.

Many have suggested political reforms, including ranked choice voting, open and nonpartisan primaries, doing away with the electoral college, campaign finance reform, and ending the filibuster. The People's New Hampshire Together citizens' assembly proposed improving voter awareness, instituting a single ballot primary ballot, improving civics education, and creating an independent redistricting commission.[3] In an upcoming book, Ted Getschman will outline the case to end political division by instituting MaxVoting—voting methods in which each candidate is independently evaluated by every voter.

Various kinds of reforms such as these need to be fully vetted and debated. We believe, however, that structural reforms are less likely to happen (and may be insufficient for driving positive change) unless everyday citizens develop meaningful connections and trust.

This is why the focus of this book is on people as individuals: how we think and behave. Before we can change the country, we need to start with ourselves and build positive relationships with others. Skipping these steps to focus exclusively on political or legislative reforms is unlikely to end distrust and national polarization. When many citizens lead with respectful conversations and thoughtful discussion, politicians will follow, making political reforms more possible

National identity is one theme we believe could foster hopeful discussions and help us to better connect with and appreciate others.

## WHAT DOES IT MEAN TO BE AN AMERICAN? EMBRACING NATIONAL IDENTITY

*"America today needs a renewed sense of national identity, one that fosters a common vision for a future in which every American can feel that they belong and are respected." —Hidden Tribes authors*[4]

While the least-engaged voters tend to look at politics from the perspective of material self-interest, the most active voters view politics through the lens of identity, which drives division.[5] We clearly need to find ways to get past identity politics. Otherwise, we fear for the future of our great nation.

But the concept of identity could also offer a promising way to expand our thinking through meaningful conversations about what it means to be an American. We agree that national identity could be a force that unifies people to overcome polarization.[6] A 2024 Associated Press–National Opinion Research Center poll found that "most Americans share many core beliefs about what it means to be American."[7]

We can build a sense of national identity that transcends partisan identities and polarization. Arthur Brooks describes gratitude as a key to national unity, based on a recognition that we need others, including those with whom we disagree.[8] Conversations about what it means to be American could be very impactful.

Another area that offers great potential is civic renewal—for citizens to come together at the local level to address community concerns.

## CITIZEN-LED SOLUTIONS: SOLVING COMMUNITY PROBLEMS WHILE BUILDING RELATIONSHIPS

*"Reversing the decline in trust requires ensuring every locale matters and that everyone has the chance to participate in improving their place."—Seth Kaplan*

Harry Boyte writes about citizens assuming responsibility and authority for the basic resources and public goods of a community. He defines commonwealth as "a self-governing community of equals concerned about the general welfare—a republican or democratic government, where citizens remained active throughout the year, not simply on Election Day."[9]

Authors Susan Clark and Woden Teachout refer to "slow democracy" as local politics that are inclusive, deliberative, and empowered. In addition to voting for elected officials, residents discuss and decide on issues that impact the community. The authors offer many examples of slow democracy where citizens have direct, bottom-up participation in local decisions rather than consolidating power from the top down in the name of greater efficiency.[10]

Citizen-led solutions is an approach that binds these themes together and has the potential to create positive change in the spirit of "from I to we." What do we mean by citizen-led solutions, also referred to as civic renewal? We like Peter Levine's definition: "Efforts to increase the prevalence, equity, quality and impact of civic engagement." He provides the example that attending a public meeting is civic engagement, but making meetings work better for the whole community is civic renewal.[11]

Braver Angels has been working to promote civic renewal, going beyond talking and listening to include an action component: doing things together to solve community problems. An important outcome of this is activation of the exhausted majority who may not be excited about participating in politics but who want to make a difference in solving problems at the local level.

The "secret sauce" of civic engagement and renewal is for this group of people to be diverse—not just racially and ethnically diverse, but also politically diverse. This means bringing together liberals, conservatives, libertarians, progressives, moderates—you name it! Working on the problem together minimizes divisiveness and promotes common ground.

## THREE CORE ELEMENTS OF CIVIC RENEWAL

*If there is a clear challenge/issue* → **Develop Common Ground** → **Take Action** → **Build Relationships** ← *If there is no obvious starting issue*

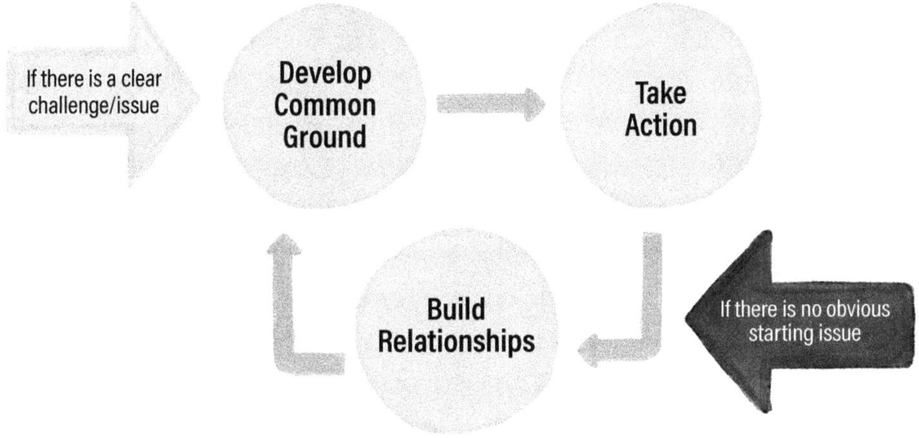

Reproduced by permission from Charles Heckscher, Steven E. Saltwick, Barbara Farmer, Harry Boyte, and David Eisner, *Citizen-Led Solutions Playbook,* Copyright 2024 by Braver Angels.

In the Braver Angels *Citizen-Led Solutions Playbook,* three core elements of civic renewal are identified: [12]

1. Relationship building
2. Developing common ground
3. Action implementation

Starting small is key. Then, as progress is made, a group of volunteers can move on to larger projects. As demonstrated in the diagram above, relationship building, developing common ground, and action implementation is a circular process that continues toward building relationships and trust in a community.

For example, Braver Angels volunteers became involved in a New York state community where there was widespread disagreement and hostility regarding a road intersection and the need for better safety. After a series of meetings that applied listening and communication skills, they reached a consensus about putting up a new stop sign in a way that solved the traffic problem. In addition to enjoying their solution's impact on increasing public safety, community members experienced goodwill from working together, which set them up to tackle bigger challenges in the future.

As this example illustrates, action is a core component of civic renewal. Another core component is building relationships of understanding and trust across all parts of a community. Anthony Simon Laden refers to this component as civic engagement, and, at its heart, it is about how we interact with each other: "To engage with others requires that we hear what they have to say, that we make space in our interaction for them to respond fully and genuinely, and that we are fully responsive to their responses and proposals."[13]

Does this sound familiar? We believe that civic engagement builds upon ideas we shared earlier in this book related to treating others with dignity, kindness, and respect; honing our listening skills; and being fully present to others.

*From Beth*

My team in Williamson County, Tennessee, led an effort to move school bell times ahead, to start school later for teens. Many teens struggle to get to bed at a healthy hour and wake up for school due to changes in their sleep-wake patterns as they get older. Many teens sleep through first period at school. Tragically, some have car accidents driving to school. California and Florida have passed laws requiring school start times for middle school of 8:00 a.m. or later and high school of 8:30 a.m. or later.[14,15]

But before the Williamson school board was ready to change school bell times, which would mean adjusting bus and teacher schedules, they wanted to make sure the community wanted these changes. They feared that responding to a small group of sleep experts and parents would alienate others in the community. Some people in the county were against the proposed change. They believed that teens were struggling to go to bed on time and wake up due to other reasons, such as too much homework, after-school band practice, or excessive use of cell phones in the evening.

We learned that, while educating the community on the biology of teen sleep was important, it was equally important to hear the concerns of these community members and incorporate their feedback into the proposed solution. The school board placed our initiative for later school start times within the larger context of teen physical and mental health (for example, reducing overscheduling of teens). When the initiative did pass the school board, it had support from the community. This was partly because community voices were heard and included in the solution.

---

Consider the impact of a "Skills for Bridging the Divide" workshop at the library in Brentwood, New Hampshire that Braver Angels volunteers organized at the request of Representative Eric Turer. Afterward, Turer wrote:

> "There were pairs of people in that room who were having engaging conversations who likely have never spoken to each other (or haven't in years) and would not ever have imagined doing so. Your efforts will likely set the stage for ongoing community dialogues that everyone has said should happen, but nobody had the right context for."[16]

When we followed up six months later, Turer affirmed that the workshop "left a lasting mark on Brentwood" and shared a video of a community discussion on decreased animosity in town that referenced the Braver Angels workshop.

Here is another story about empowering respected community members to work with others within their circles to create positive results.

**From Doug** The Ebola pandemic started in the West African country of Guinea where I served as Peace Corps country director from 2014 to 2016. While the Peace Corps volunteers were sent home for their safety, I stayed behind with our mostly Guinean staff to support the US Centers for Disease Control and Prevention (CDC) effort to contain this highly infectious disease. Guineans were skeptical about Ebola, and my staff trained trusted community members to go back to their villages and talk about the disease and the precautions required. We trained homemakers, teachers, students, youth leaders, and others about common rumors and how to overcome fear and resistance back home. Furthermore, we didn't mandate how they should act. Instead, each person we trained developed a personal action plan to reach family members and others they knew and then move outward into their community from there. The initiative was estimated to reach 3.2 million people, one quarter of Guinea's population, and Ebola was largely eradicated.[17]

Positive change and civic renewal sound so easy, but we all know that nothing is easy in these challenging times. We need to approach problems in the spirit of being open to opposing viewpoints and actively welcoming everyone to the table. Through this process, we create goodwill and citizens who open their hearts to others. We can become civic entrepreneurs.

We know we can each do more to build positive change in our community. How about you?

## FOR FURTHER THOUGHT

- How might depolarizing yourself help you build relationships and solve community problems?
- How can we build a national identity that transcends identity politics?
- How can people working together in the spirit of "from I to we" promote common ground?
- What steps can you take to promote civic renewal and become a civic entrepreneur in your community?
- Can you think of a project that is important to your community that might excite you to get involved with? (Then take a look at the Braver Angels *Citizen-Led Solutions Playbook* to think about how to implement your idea!)[18]

# SKILLS FOR LEADING YOURSELF AND OTHERS

*"Don't expect things from other people that you yourself can't deliver."* —Kelly Corrigan

## Chapter 11

# EMBRACE YOUR SELF-LEADERSHIP POTENTIAL

> *"In a world crying out for effective leadership, you need to begin with the most obvious source . . . yourself."*—Susan Fowler

When we talk of leadership, thoughts quickly turn to people with titles and defined authority: CEOs, managers, and bosses, as well as elected officials. Our opinions of those in leadership roles are often not very high. In fact, the Hidden Tribes report authors found that Americans rank poor leadership as the country's greatest problem.[1]

We presume that survey was about political leaders and others with formal titles, but there are far more informal leaders around—people without formal titles who act in ways that influence others. This includes everyday leadership by people like you!

Most of us think of leaders as "other people." In a powerful TEDx Talk, author and speaker Drew Dudley asks the audience who considers themselves to be a leader. When few raise their hands, he asks why. He goes on to tell a story of an interaction he had forgotten that resurfaced when a young woman sought Dudley out four years later to say that he had made a profound impact on her life when he took a certain action.[2] Leadership gurus

Jim Kouzes and Barry Posner add that every one of us has the necessary material to become a leader: "You have to go find it inside of you and bring it out."[3]

In short, leadership goes way beyond what we sometimes think. And we each need to recognize our leadership actions and potential, including how we use our time and talents to impact others. Whether you think of yourself as a leader or not, you have the power to influence others in ways that can build positive relationships and help strengthen our nation, too.

> **From Beth** I led a sleep division at my medical center for over twenty years and oversaw multiple clinical and research teams. I learned to cultivate leadership skills, recognizing that being an excellent leader was not only satisfying and meaningful but added to the productivity of the team. One key skill was noticing when someone on the team was supporting their colleagues. I thanked them publicly. It was contagious. Others started supporting each other more. I also notice that in my work to reduce polarization. Just a small comment recognizing how a colleague is helping support others on the team goes a long way. It's easy to get stuck in our echo chambers and disparage others who may have supported a political candidate we don't like. While it seems harder, it's also much more satisfying to commend our colleagues who challenge us to see those others in a different light. That's contagious, too!

You may not think of yourself as a leader, but if you are influencing others, you most certainly are.

> **From Doug** — In my work and business, I have focused a lot of energy on understanding what it means to be an effective leader. I have come to appreciate how much people exhibit leadership traits every day, often without thinking of themselves as leaders. Think of the parent who models positive behavior for her children. Or the coworker you admire who makes helpful work suggestions. Or a friend who encourages you to assist with a volunteer project in your community. Or just someone with good ideas that you decide to embrace in your life. And, of course, the person who steps up to be a positive role model, applying empathy and curiosity to connect with someone on the other side of politics. In my volunteer work with Braver Angels, I strive to give quick email thank-yous and shout-outs when I see good things happening in my region. It is so quick and easy to show appreciation for the positive actions of others.

Some of our most impactful leaders don't have titles, nor do they supervise others. Informal leaders are all around us, and we need to take the time to notice how they use their skills to engage and motivate us, and how we, too, influence others. Of course, we can be negative leaders when our actions impact others in less positive ways, which is why self-awareness is so important.

## UNDERSTANDING SELF-LEADERSHIP

*"I was always looking outside myself for strength and confidence, but it comes from within. It is there all the time."*—Anna Freud

Before any of us can be fully effective as leaders of others, we need to recognize and develop our capacity for self-leadership. What do we mean by self-leadership? Andrew Bryant defines it as "having a developed sense of who you are, what you can do, where you are going coupled with the ability to influence your communication, emotions and behaviors on the way to getting there."[4]

Who do you want to be? Where do you want to go in life? What gives you meaning and purpose? There is only one person who can answer these questions and define what is most important in your life. Of course, that would be you. To find that one person who can change your life and better our country, please look in the mirror!

Sorting this out is an important part of life's journey, and it requires ongoing time and effort. Too often in our busy lives, we skim along life's surface without being fully aware whether we are investing our time and energy in what is most important. We are all busy—who has time for self-development? Author Stephen Covey advises us to not be so busy sawing that we don't take time to "sharpen the saw."[5]

If we fail to dedicate time in an ongoing self-development process—including periodic reviews and adjustments—we quickly lose our way. Over time, frustration and regret are likely outcomes. Devoting time and energy for continuous self-improvement is a recipe for long-term success. And you can help change our country too!

Self-leadership, as defined above, focuses on this internal work, but also includes aspects that strengthen us with respect to our relationships with others who differ politically. We offer some areas to consider for upping your self-leadership game. As you read through this list, please don't be intimidated. Few of us live up to them all. Think of one or two areas where you might want to focus some time and energy to grow. Consider how that might benefit your personal growth, well-being, and relationships.

First, consider some inner areas to focus on for self-improvement. We previously suggested some key steps that we won't revisit here: clarify and model your values, and review your life story. The following paragraphs discuss some additional areas for growth.

**Believe in yourself.** When interviewed by television host and producer Oprah Winfrey, Tom Brady said of his football successes: "I think the greatest thing for you is to believe in yourself, because if you don't believe in yourself, who's going to believe in you?" You are unique and worthy of love, dignity, and respect! Of course, you might say, *But even the most effective among us have moments of doubt.*[6]

> **From Doug** I am a strong advocate for therapy, which has helped me through some difficult times and provided valuable insights in better times as well. For example, when I expressed fatigue and malaise while writing this book, my therapist Kristen asked, "What is wrong with malaise?" She added that I could pause and step back as an observer. Be more curious about dark moments, lean in, and don't think of them as gloom. Don't rush to the answer, sit with the question, and there might be some useful information, she added. Another point relevant to this book is her assertion that "My truth doesn't cancel out your truth." I recommend that everyone have a therapist, or someone they can talk with, to work through life's challenges.

**Live with meaning and purpose.** In *Happier: Learn the Secrets to Daily Joy and Lasting Fulfillment,* Tal Ben-Shahar observes that we are often taught to strive to achieve some future goal (even if we are miserable in the present).[7] Adopting this approach can be self-defeating. Instead, live fully today, embracing a self-determined purpose. And what greater purpose could there be than using your talents to build positive relationships and help make our country better?

**Embrace gratitude as a key to happiness.** The pursuit of happiness is well ingrained in our national psyche, exemplified by that memorable phrase in our Declaration of Independence. To a degree, however, our economy feeds off dissatisfaction, as marketers work to convince us that if we purchase this or that toy or experience we will be happier. WebMD reminds us that true happiness is aligned with our sense of purpose, and the satisfaction of pursuing our goals creates more than just momentary pleasure.[8] Brené Brown observes: "I don't have to chase extraordinary moments to find happiness—it's right in front of me if I'm paying attention and practicing gratitude."[9]

> **From Beth** Each day, I write down three things I am grateful for. Even if I can't think of anything that has happened, I think of what *hasn't* happened—like I haven't caught the flu or injured a body part working out at the gym. Items that align with my sense of purpose, such as repairing a relationship with a family member or friend torn apart by politics, always make the list.

**Embrace hope and a growth mindset.** There is so much to be discouraged about these days, but holding on to hope sustains positive energy. This is essential for learning and growing, not to mention helping us navigate our way through national division. Embrace the idea that life is a journey with countless opportunities for self-improvement and personal change. When we are growing, we feel alive.[10]

**Exhibit authenticity and self-awareness.** Be true to yourself and clear about who you are and what you believe, and communicate that to others in both words and actions. Also, be on the lookout for areas where your actions might not measure up to your stated values. This is a mistake we all make from time to time, and ongoing check-ins and reflection can help us stay on track. Not one of us is perfect! Authenticity is closely aligned with trust—it is hard to be trusted by others if you are not open and honest with them.

**Cultivate empathy, curiosity, and humility.** Striving to understand another's perspective might seem like a lost art, but its importance cannot be emphasized enough. Empathy doesn't necessarily mean agreeing with another person's point of view. Rather, it's about striving to understand and connect with others. In our depolarization work, we get pushback that it is impossible to connect with people who embrace falsehoods. We disagree. If we show we are listening, we can make a connection. If we make a connection, we may be able to influence their thinking. Instead of judging or labeling others, work hard to see things through their eyes.[11] Jonathan Haidt calls empathy an antidote to righteousness.[12]

Humility is closely related to empathy and curiosity, requiring us to be open to the ideas and perspectives of others. Of course, empathy and curiosity are about more than connecting with people who disagree with your politics. Engagement with family, friends, neighbors, coworkers, and employees who are suffering from loss, health issues, or regular day-to-day problems can be much more meaningful if we embrace these qualities.

**Using time wisely.** Time is limited, and Stephen Covey reminds us to put first things first. The urgent/important matrix he describes is a useful way to approach this challenge. Most of us typically find ourselves spending a lot of time in Quadrant I (urgent/important) and Quadrant III (urgent/not important), reactively responding to the needs of the moment.[13]

Quadrant II (not urgent/important) is typically underutilized, even though it includes many important activities, including clarifying priorities, reflecting on your life and making improvements, setting goals, and building positive relationships.

Of course, large segments of our lives are tied up in urgent obligations and responsibilities, but ensuring there is time for important (but not immediately urgent) activities is essential for creating a meaningful life.

> **From Beth:** Quadrant II is where I aim to spend most of my time. My energy level is highest in the morning, and that's when I write or plan presentations, with my email turned off and my phone on silent. Occasionally, a pressing deadline (Quadrant I) will spoil my plans, but most days I can accomplish a lot during this time. Using time effectively in the morning sets me up for handling whatever life throws at me later in the day.

Beyond these internal factors, these are some specific actions you can take to engage more effectively with others.

**Resist making assumptions and judging others.** We all know the tendency to make assumptions based on first impressions, especially in these times of political polarization. We can be quick to judge others and to lump people into categories. But each person's life story is unique, and we do best if we resist the temptation to judge without knowing more.

**Be trustworthy.** Start by trusting yourself, which requires a high level of self-awareness and a willingness to identify strengths and address areas that need more development. Achieving trust with others requires ongoing self-reflection, including understanding how your actions and behaviors impact others. Stephen Covey writes, "It simply makes no difference how good the rhetoric is or even how good the intentions are; if there is little or no trust, there is no foundation for permanent success."[14] (Unfortunately, many workplace leaders are not doing so well: Research shows that only 21 percent of US employees strongly agree that they trust the leadership of their organization.[15]) Jim Collins, author of *Good to Great,* described the concept of the trust wager: There is far more upside to opening relationships with trust rather than waiting for people to earn it.[16]

**From Beth** I became a Braver Angels moderator because I wanted to learn communication skills that foster dialogue, and through this position I realized that the best way to learn something well was to teach it to others. How we listen to others and convey our viewpoints is critical for gaining trust.

**Think win-win.** It's easy to embrace "us versus them" and win-lose thinking when we relate to others. What if we started with curiosity and focused on win-win options in our discussions and disagreements? The authors of *Getting to Yes* describe negotiation skills that separate personalities and emotions from issues in order to focus on underlying issues.[17] This approach is critical to address the national divide where the most strident on each side see their way as the only possible solution.

**From Beth** I love the win-win story in *Getting to Yes* of the two children fighting over an orange. If they could realize they wanted different things—one wanted the orange peel for baking and the other fruit to eat—then they could stop fighting and share the orange.[18] What if we could apply that lesson to the debate over funding for police versus social services? Could we agree to have a stronger police force *and* support social workers and city or town agencies to strengthen communities and reduce crime?

**Be mindful and present.** Living in the present and taking in all that is happening around us is an invaluable internal life skill. And when engaging with others, we show them we care by giving our undivided attention. Being mindful—in the present—also helps our mental health by promoting decreased stress, anxiety, and depression.[19]

## WHERE TO START?

*"The journey is the reward"—Taoist proverb*

*Wow,* you say. *That is quite a list—an awful lot to live up to! It seems a bit overwhelming.* We agree and admit that we don't consistently measure up to this list ourselves. Some days we feel on track, but on others we fall behind, questioning our mindset and commitment.

---

**From Doug:** As I was writing this chapter, my wife said something important to me that I completely missed. I was so busy writing about living my values and being a good listener that I failed to listen! This is a reminder that we can aspire to high goals, but we shouldn't be surprised when we fall short. The important thing is to recognize a mistake and try to do better next time.

---

Yes, working toward self-leadership can sometimes seem like too much, but please don't be discouraged or throw up your hands! Pick one or two areas you want to work on and focus first on those. And then later, when you are ready, add something else.

This is a lifelong journey that transcends politics, ultimately benefiting both you and those you touch. By moving forward—one step at a time—we each have the power to make positive personal changes in our lives and relationships while also building our capacity to make powerful contributions to our country.

## FOR FURTHER THOUGHT

- Do you think of yourself as a leader? If not, why not?
- How do your actions and behaviors influence the actions and behaviors of others?
- What steps could you take to improve your self-leadership skills?
- What could you do more to integrate empathy, authenticity, curiosity, and gratitude in your daily life?
- How will investing time and energy in self-development benefit your life, your relationships, and our country?

# Chapter 12
# SKILLS FOR BRAVER CONVERSATIONS

> *"When people talk, listen completely. Don't be thinking what you're going to say. Most people never listen."* —Ernest Hemingway

Conversations seem more difficult than in the past, whether it's with family members, work colleagues, employees, or strangers. This is especially true, of course, when the discussion veers into politics.

I've struggled in recent years to avoid talking to my parents, avid Fox News watchers, about anything related to politics. Usually, I'll say, "Mom, I don't think you want to talk to me about this," and I can usually steer the conversation to something else. At work, I find that many people who are upset about the current administration will come out and say it boldly, assuming that I'm aligned with them. What's more difficult is when I'm not sure where people stand or when people express opinions that are in conflict with what I believe. I try to stay curious and ask questions, like I did recently when a client mentioned that a loved one is "giddy" about the changes in our government post-election.

When we know that the person we are talking to is on "our side," political conversations may flow more easily. But sometimes political allies go beyond agreeing on policies to putting down those on the other side. When that happens, we suggest pushing back using statements like, "I agree with you on the immigration issue, *and* I believe it is important to respect those who see things differently," or "Even though I believe those on the other side are wrong about this issue, I think it is important to treat people who oppose our position with dignity and respect."

This approach can be difficult. When applying it, we sometimes feel that our credibility is questioned by people who agree with our politics. You might feel cast out by fervent partisans who believe it is downright wrong for people (such as you!) to respect those with different political views. They may accuse you of normalizing behavior that they believe is anti-democratic. In these "us versus them" times, anything that seems like nuance may not be welcome. This can be painful when a person you thought of as your ally suddenly turns against you.

If you find yourself in such a situation, you might feel inclined to back off or just be quiet. We have all felt that way at times, and sometimes backing off is best. You might want to consider another way, though, using the conversation skills described later in this chapter. While often used for challenging conversations with those who have different political views, these skills can also apply to difficult conversations with those on your own side.

## BEYOND FIGHT, FLIGHT, OR AVOIDANCE

*"What lies behind us and what lies before us are but tiny matters compared to what lies within us."—Henry Stanley Haskins*

When we get into conversations with people on the other political side, we tend to apply one of three common modes. These are fight, flight, and avoidance.

*Fight* is one option, which may involve getting into a back-and-forth conflict like Doug described earlier when he discussed the 2016 presidential election with another former legislator and his wife. Conversations can get hot, with angry accusations thrown back and forth, and, in the very worst cases, may even lead to violence (for example, road rage).

Reverend Mark Beckwith has written that anger "shows up whenever the ego is threatened. This can happen—and is happening, when people feel that someone is taking over their turf, their agency, their language, their principles. . . . one faction fighting another, often with disastrous results."[1]

Writer and Braver Angels volunteer Peggy Prichard adds:

"A wise friend once told me, 'When the name-calling starts, the argument has been lost.' That's because there is no interest in listening to learn. Using slurs or insults is an attempt to discredit or shut down those with opposing views. But at what cost? Does winning an argument by shaming the other person do anything to solve the problems we are facing?"[2]

Another indication you are in fight mode is when you hear grandiose language, for example, "disgraceful, "atrocity," "barbaric behavior," or "unprecedented disaster." Be careful when using or hearing words that may appear disproportionate to the issue.

In sum, the fight option is usually a lose-lose situation where no one leaves feeling happy or better understood. If you are convinced you are "right," how is it helpful to attack those who are "wrong," but expect those who are "wrong" to say no such things to you? How does that win them over to your perspective?

*Flight* is another option. We may choose to exit the space where the conversation is happening, perhaps making up a phony reason why we need to leave. This is a good strategy when we feel physically or emotionally threatened, but it is rarely constructive and often leads to frustration.

*Avoidance* is a third option—like flight, but we stay where the conversation is happening and keep our mouth shut. You listen to someone talk in ways you find unsatisfactory. Yet, for any number of reasons, you feel too uncomfortable to engage.

In a family or workplace setting, avoidance may seem better than conflict. For sure, sometimes it is the right decision. However, ongoing avoidance can foster an environment where people who need to live or work together may steer clear and experience the loss of otherwise valuable relationships. Having an elephant (or donkey) in the room can be pretty unsatisfying.

Fear is one of the reasons for flight or avoidance. Fear might not mean that we feel physically threatened; it could just be that we lack confidence in how to proceed and worry that the outcome will be unsatisfying. This is natural when we find ourselves in situations where we are unsure what to say or do. This fear can be overcome when we dig deeper to better understand it and practice the skills described later. "Fear is real and powerful. But in exploring fear, in all its dimensions—in ourselves and in others, we can go a long way in taming it," explains Beckwith.[3]

Fight, flight, or avoidance: None of these three options typically lead to a positive result for you or for the other person. Fortunately, there is a fourth alternative.

## A BETTER WAY: BRAVER CONVERSATIONS

*"I don't like that man. I must get to know him better."*—Abraham Lincoln

Braver conversations, the focus of the rest of this chapter, incorporate practical skills you can use to constructively engage others in ways that will make you feel empowered and listened to. You can offer your ideas in a style that will hopefully be a win-win situation for both you and the other person.

Are courage, curiosity, vulnerability, empathy, and authenticity on your list of important values—or are these areas where you want to boost your self-leadership skills? These values are very helpful in braver conversations as we adopt a mindset of striving to stay open to other viewpoints and treating people with kindness and respect—even if we disagree with their opinions.

Even the best among us struggle to consistently embrace these values. But we cannot successfully engage in braver conversations through skills alone. Our values and mindset are critical, including a willingness to listen

CHAPTER 12: SKILLS FOR BRAVER CONVERSATIONS ✦ 149

and be open to having our own ideas changed, or at least modified in a small way. To be successful, it cannot be just about "me."

**From Doug** Striving to be curious can lead to worthwhile experiences. A few days after the November 2024 election, I traveled to California for a funeral and was on an airport shuttle train to the rental car location. I happened to sit down next to a fifty-ish-aged white man with a hat that read "We the People Are Pissed Off." I asked about the hat and was told he rarely voted because he saw little difference between the political parties. He mentioned Ross Perot as the last candidate that really interested him. But this time, he voted for Donald Trump because he thought the country needed a businessman, even though he was concerned about Trump's language.

The man also expressed concerns about the Democratic Party support for DEI efforts. "They only want to include people who agree with them," he said. He also mentioned abortion, saying he was Catholic and that the Democrats supported killing babies. I mentioned my volunteer work with Braver Angels, and this man agreed that the vitriol across the political divide was destructive. The rental car stop came quickly, so this interesting conversation ended sooner than I would have liked.

Through volunteer work with Braver Angels, we have learned many key ideas and skills related to holding braver conversations, using materials developed by Braver Angels cofounder and professor Bill Doherty. A specialist in family therapy, Bill has a deep understanding of how to apply key practices for engaging others. These skills are not unique to Braver Angels and have been used in disciplines such as motivational interviewing and nonviolent communication.[4] Braver Angels has distilled these skills into a format that is easy to learn and teach others.

For example, these are the goals from the "Managing Difficult Conversations with Colleagues" workshop Doherty led for New Hampshire state legislators. First, show colleagues who disagree with you that you have accurately heard them. Second, express your views in a way that colleagues can hear even if they disagree. Then find areas of agreement or shared interest whenever possible.

These key principles apply to braver conversations with family members, friends, neighbors, and even strangers:

- Connect first, then share your view.
- Aim for "accurate disagreement" based on factual information rather than "distorted disagreement" that twists points in an exaggerated or misleading way.
- Focus on policy and not underlying motives (assume good intentions unless proven otherwise).
- Strive to be consistent.

Another Braver Angels workshop, "Skills for Disagreeing Better," helps participants understand the values and concerns of people who differ from them politically. Attendees listen in a way that makes other people feel heard and share perspectives that other people might hear, even if they disagree. There are four key implementation steps: Listen, Acknowledge, Pivot, and Perspective (LAPP). LAPP is easy to remember and highly useful.

1. **Listen**. Listening skills are critical. Key ideas are:
    - Focus both on the other's viewpoint and their underlying values and concerns.
    - Turn off your inner debater and don't prepare your response yet.
    - Look for something to agree with if at all possible.

The key idea is to focus on understanding what the other is saying rather than thinking about how you will respond. It is critically important that the other person believes that you are *really* listening to their ideas. Asking open-ended questions in the spirit of curiosity is a key part of this process.

These kinds of questions invite the other person to share more, facilitating meaningful conversations and building positive relationships.[5] Your intention is obviously critical—without it, success will be fleeting at best. Give 100 percent attention (including putting down your phone), resist the urge to interrupt, avoid jumping to conclusions, refrain from offering solutions, ask questions that benefit the other person, and (afterward) reflect on what you might have done differently.[6]

2. **Acknowledge.** Before sharing your own ideas, it is important to acknowledge the other person's perspective and connect first before you disagree.
   - Let the other person know that you heard their viewpoint and the strength of their feelings, values, and concerns.
   - Summarize what you heard without just parroting back their words.
   - If possible, mention something you agree with that the other person said.

3. **Pivot.** A pivot signals that you are about to offer your own viewpoint. It's like your turn signal while driving; the actual turn comes later.
   - For example: "Can I offer my thoughts on this?"
   - Look for a verbal "OK, sure," or a nonverbal nod.

   If the other person just repeats their point, ignores your pivot, or shows wariness about you taking your turn (verbally or nonverbally), then consider backing up to repeat the Acknowledge step.

4. **Perspective.** If the other person seems open to listening to what you have to say, this is (finally!) your opportunity to share your ideas:
   - Use I-statements (such as "This is how I see it" and "This is why I see it this way") as opposed to truth-statements ("This is how it absolutely is!").

- Name your sources.
- Share a life experience or personal story behind your viewpoint.
- Avoid negative labels and "You Democrats/Republicans" language.

Pay attention to your body language and tone of voice. We need to be sincerely and genuinely curious about engaging with others when we use these skills.

Using these LAPP skills requires practice. Try using them in less contentious situations first and move on from there. The more you use them, the more confident you will become. They can significantly up your game in managing difficult conversations.

This can take time. Sometimes it is OK to remain in the listen and acknowledge modes for several conversations (even over several weeks or months) before moving on to the pivot and sharing perspective steps. This is not avoidance; it is *building a relationship* with someone so that they feel you trust them. Only after they trust you and feel you aren't judging them will they be open to hearing your perspective. Also, not every conversation needs to be about politics. Strive to find common interests, such as being in the outdoors, playing or watching sports, cooking, traveling, playing or listening to music, doing photography, creating or viewing art, and more. In her essay "The Protest Trap," Amanda Ripley writes:

> "If I had to distill the research into one word I'd have to say (get ready to be disappointed . . .): Relationships. That is the brutal truth. Relationships make it harder for humans to humiliate, dismiss and degrade each other. Relationships are how we hold each other accountable. Relationships are not enough, on their own, but it's hard to find humans living in peace and dignity without them."[7]

It's hard to find humans living in peace and dignity without relationships.

If we are going to get past conflict, we need to develop meaningful relationships with those who disagree with us.

## IS THIS POSSIBLE ON SOCIAL MEDIA... AND WHAT ABOUT BOUNDARIES?

*"The enemy is fear. We think it is hate but it is fear."*—Mahatma Gandhi

Braver conversations are clearly best in face-to-face situations with no one else present. But are they possible in other situations? Perhaps on Zoom and maybe on the telephone (although it is a lot harder to navigate conversations without visual clues). We have learned that using social media for braver conversations is pretty much impossible. Perhaps it could work as a series of back-and-forth private messages on social media (or via text or emails), but rarely in a public post.

**From Doug** I go on Facebook for about fifteen minutes a day and like seeing news of friends and family activities. I usually skip over political posts, especially ones where people put down those on the other side. I find that commenting on these posts often just adds fuel to the fire, whether intended or not. I usually avoid making political posts, although I occasionally post something about Braver Angels and the ideas in this book. While those posts get mostly favorable comments, people sometimes belittle my ideas and even use the comment section to get into arguments with other people they barely know. It is frustrating to see nasty comments aimed at others on my posts, and I rarely add even positive comments, as this often leads to a response that keeps the nastiness alive.

Social media can encourage mean-spirited behavior, which is precisely the opposite of braver conversations. Somehow, people often feel they are not accountable for social media posts or comments, no matter how crass; most would not say these things in personal conversations. Sure, we all sometimes need to vent, but is there a more constructive alternative than doing so in a public way that feeds division?

We each have the power to set boundaries that help us manage what we see and do and how to respond (or not) to the words or actions of others. Social media can be useful in many ways, but it is not a good forum for braver conversations on difficult topics.

## TO CHANGE OTHERS, YOU NEED TO BE OPEN TO CHANGING YOURSELF

*"Everything that irritates us about others can lead to an understanding of ourselves."—Carl Jung*

Consider the *Harvard Business Review* article "The Power of Listening in Helping People Change," especially that last part of the title: helping people change.[8] An important goal when engaged in braver conversations is to express our views in a way that the other person hears us. Perhaps we hope the other person changes their ideas, at least in some small way.

Somewhat ironically, if we truly want to engage with another in a way that might encourage that person to change their ideas and opinions, then we must be open to changing what we think as well. Psychologist and author Adam Grant encourages us to say to ourselves, "This is an interesting opportunity to learn something from someone who sees things differently from me, and I wonder if they know something I don't."[9]

We all get stuck in our beliefs. Our deep-seated convictions shape our perceptions and behaviors in response to the world around us. We hold on tightly to control our world. But holding on too tightly can hold us back from growth and personal transformation.[10]

Keeping our minds open to new ideas and different ways of thinking can be challenging, but there is no shortcut, no easy way. Of course, you can bypass this by choosing fight, flight, or avoidance—but what good do those ultimately do for you or our country? We each need to dig deeper, in the spirit of these words from author Scott Mautz: "Life shrinks or expands in proportion to your courage and perseverance."[11]

**From Beth** I recall a series of conversations with a friend who felt that climate change was happening but did not feel that it should be interfered with. While my first instinct was to inundate her with data, I took a step back and listened with genuine curiosity to what my friend had to say. I asked questions of clarification and learned that she valued religion and believed that God was in control of all things. For my friend, climate change was evidence that portended the second coming of Christ and it should not be interfered with. After this discussion, I was able to understand how she came to this viewpoint.

Only after this exchange could she listen to my perspective—that God was a force that we work through to heal the world, including preventing and minimizing the effects of climate change. I reflected that I might not be able to change my friend's mind, but that perhaps she would be open to different perspectives and less apt to criticize climate change initiatives on social media because of our conversation. Plus, I appreciated being able to understand a new perspective.

---

We need to think bigger than ourselves, in the spirit of this thought from leadership author Jim Kouzes: "What can I do in this moment to make this other person feel more powerful, competent and able to do more than they think they can?"[12] We elevate our skills and influence to new heights when we help our enemies become more capable and feel more effective. We might even stop seeing them as enemies and, instead, as partners we can work with to accomplish mutual goals.

## APPLYING BRAVER CONVERSATION SKILLS IN DAILY LIFE

*"The dangers of life are infinite, and among them is safety."*—Johann Wolfgang von Goethe

An important aspect of this book is helping people to develop and grow in ways that strengthen their lives far beyond just improving our politics. These braver conversation skills also apply to nonpolitical conversations—such as family or workplace disagreements. For example, when someone acts in a disrespectful or unprofessional way in a workplace setting, we have these action choices.

### OPTIONS AND CONSEQUENCES FOR DIFFICULT WORKPLACE CONVERSATIONS

| Action | Possible Consequences |
| --- | --- |
| React with anger | Undermines your professionalism and reputation |
| Internalize anger | Bad for your health and the poor behavior may repeat |
| Gossip | Undermines your reputation, infects others, and poor behavior may repeat |
| Quit | You will need to find a new job! |
| Braver conversation | Requires that you be vulnerable, but can potentially prevent future problems and also be empowering |

Consider this potential scenario: My coworker knows I voted for President Trump and, even though we are supposed to work closely to ensure that sales are processed on time, she is increasingly avoiding me. When we pass in the hallway, she avoids eye contact. This is stressing me out, and I worry that my work and reputation in the company are suffering.

Scott Mautz suggests starting a difficult conversation with something like, "I need to have a difficult conversation with you about_____. I want to acknowledge that I've contributed to this situation by _____, and I want you to know that having this discussion doesn't come easy to me because _____."[13]

Consider this response to the coworker: "I know you and I disagree about politics, but it is important for both of us that we work together for the benefit of this company and to keep our jobs. Let's find a way to respect each other and communicate better despite our differences."

When navigating a difficult conversation, it helps to plan what you will say ahead of time whenever possible. Try to carefully craft your message while keeping the other person's feelings and opinions in mind. Some common mistakes to avoid include the following:

- Don't assume your viewpoint is obvious.
- Don't exaggerate.
- Don't tell others what they should do.
- Don't blame others for your feelings.
- Don't challenge someone's character or integrity.[14]

Politically related conversations often go off the rails due to these mistakes. Doing our best to treat everyone with dignity and respect is a more productive path.

## FOR FURTHER THOUGHT

- When conversations become difficult, are you inclined to resort to fight, flight, or avoidance? What moves you in that direction?
- What steps could you take to strengthen your capacity and mindset to implement braver conversations with kindness, empathy, and authenticity?
- How can you better apply effective listening skills with questions that communicate curiosity?
- What would help you be more open to the ideas of others during challenging conversations?
- How much does fear hold you back, and how might you overcome that?

## Chapter 13
# APPLYING CRITICAL THINKING TO THE POLARIZATION CHALLENGE

> *"A great many people think they are thinking when they are merely rearranging their prejudices."*
> —William James

In this chapter, we will provide guidelines for how to process the mounds of information you are likely bombarded with and how to become a more discerning consumer. Critical thinking is an important skill to master. By critical thinking, we don't mean being critical of people or viewpoints, but instead we are referring to a process of objective analysis and evaluation that helps you reach judgments. We believe this is something that all of us can learn to do better.

During the COVID pandemic, I was invited to write scripts for videos as part of a grant to increase vaccine uptake among people with disabilities. I immediately thought of one of my patients and her family. She was a Hispanic teenager on the autism spectrum, living in a multigenerational household. Her mom had a lot of anxiety about vaccinating her daughter, and yet she was also concerned about protecting the older adults living in the home, given how active her daughter was at school and in the community. She didn't want her daughter to be exposed to the disease and have it spread to her elderly grandparents. This mom felt barraged with conflicting information on social media and from state and federal agencies. I realized how hard it was for her to make decisions about her neurodivergent child, and I considered how other families might also be struggling with this decision-making process in a time of uncertainty.

To write an informative script, I watched many existing videos and decided that the approach I preferred to take with our team was not the Dolly Parton one (even though I'm a big fan of Dolly and country music). In her video clip, Dolly takes the vaccine while singing to the tune of the hit "Jolene": "Vaccine, vaccine, vaccine, vaccine, I'm begging of you, please don't hesitate. Vaccine, vaccine, vaccine, vaccine, because once you're dead, then that's a bit too late."[1] The message of this video didn't resonate with me as one that would be helpful to the mother of my teenage patient.

Instead, I was drawn to the very few videos that used words like "hesitant" and "uncertain." I included these words in our video script, along with a scene where a mom was researching facts about the COVID vaccine on her laptop. In another scene, the video mom is shown discussing the vaccine with her daughter's doctor with whom she has built a trusting relationship. The video mom and her daughter made the decision to get vaccinated, but only after a thoughtful process.[2]

---

Two of the most common buzzwords in the news these days are "misinformation" and "disinformation." Misinformation has been defined as false information: getting the facts wrong. Disinformation is more sinister—false information deliberately intended to mislead.[3] Like many words these days, these terms have become politicized. Audrey Nguyen, a doctoral candidate at the University of Washington, suggests opting instead for "rumors" or "misleading content."[4]

Whatever you call it, no one is immune, says Briony Swire-Thompson, director of the Psychology of Misinformation Lab at Northeastern University. "We just don't have the time, the cognitive resources or even the motivation to literally fact-check every piece of information that comes our way."[5]

But who gets to decide which facts are false? You may be thinking, *I'm no expert. Trying to identify false content on Facebook is like figuring out how to fix my car on my own.* But you might also feel strongly that it's up to yourself to decide rather than an expert who may be biased. We support that position with the understanding that we each need to recognize our own biases and be aware that conflicts entrepreneurs are trying to mislead us. It is best to consider any information with some skepticism.

## BETH RECALLS THE COVID PANDEMIC

*"Nothing is at last sacred but the integrity of your own mind."*
—Ralph Waldo Emerson

I recall that when the pandemic emerged in spring 2020, I went immediately to the position of "trust the science" and putting all faith in quarantining, masking, and hoping for the rapid development of a vaccine.

I read scientific articles and listened to podcasts to learn more about what the data were showing. But looking back on the sequence of my actions, I first believed what the experts were saying and then processed the articles to support what I heard. And I didn't understand why people questioned the experts. I thought that if only my colleagues and I could explain health to the public in a clear way, they would see the merits of following the science. They would see things the way we did.

I was beyond grateful to the hard-working scientists who were working tirelessly to develop a vaccine and to the public health officials on the front lines trying to keep people safe. And yet, I saw room for improvement. For example, in 2020, my dad was in an assisted living facility with (thankfully) strict guidelines for visitors. I was reluctant to participate in a vaccine trial because I might develop a fever or other side effects from the vaccine that would keep me from visiting him. The physician researcher leading the trial spent an hour with me going over my concerns, and encouraged me to take Tylenol around the time of getting vaccinated to prevent these side effects. It worked.

My friends were told by their doctors, nurses, and mainstream media not to take drugs when getting vaccinated. They were informed that if the vaccine caused a fever, it was a good thing because it showed that their immune system was reacting to the vaccine as it should. That type of contrasting information bothered me. I wonder how many people might have gotten vaccinated against COVID if they knew they could prevent some side effects by taking Tylenol?

To get better at communicating with the public, I pursued a graduate certificate in science communication through the Alda Center for Communicating Science in Stony Brook, New York. Through those studies, my attitude toward communicating science to the public was transformed. I learned about the importance of storytelling and theater-based techniques to communicate effectively (actor Alan Alda has had a strong influence on the center). Of equal importance, I understood how necessary it is for scientists and doctors to be receptive to hearing from the public and know what they are experiencing.

Effective communication is a two-way street, a foundational concept in Braver Angels, where we don't seek to change minds but to open hearts. David Blankenhorn, Braver Angels cofounder, talks about allowing change to happen freely rather than forcing it.[6]

I also was selected to give a TEDx talk through Vanderbilt University on "The Art of Communicating Science."[7] In this talk, I described the conversations I had with a friend who was trying to decide whether she should get the COVID vaccine. She didn't want to get caught up in the "political football" of her friends advocating for or against vaccination.

In my TEDx talk, I explained how I supported her in the decision-making process and emphasized that facts are critical, yet not sufficient, when talking with others. It is important to tap into the wisdom of what Aristotle described as logos (facts), ethos (credibility), and pathos (emotional stories).[8] There is also a fourth element that Aristotle didn't mention—agency—that encourages people to make decisions on their own rather being told what to do.

This kind of self-reliance is a key American value. No one likes being manipulated by conflict entrepreneurs or being told what to do by distant government bureaucrats. When I tell people what to think, or express disdain when they don't agree with me, they are less likely to trust me.

In community workshops we carried out through our Braver Angels Truth and Trust Project, both supporters and questioners of the COVID public health response stated that they examined the science—while also admitting that they differed in their sources.[9] Questioners were naturally frustrated when they were called derogatory terms such as anti-vaxxers or conspiracy theorists.

What I learned from this experience is that directives often backfire when they come from those in authority outside someone's inner circle. Giving people space to ask questions and make their own decisions is often more effective. My mind opened to the idea that talking with others needs to be about more than just sharing facts. I realized that I can change my mind, too. Now, I am more inclined to question experts and try to engage in critical thinking rather than accepting the results of a scientific study based on the reputation of the author, or trusting that the review process for studies is perfect.

## BARRIERS TO CRITICAL THINKING

*"We think we believe what we know, but we only truly believe what we feel."—Laurence Gonzales*

Shouldn't we be able to teach people how to identify false information that's present in social media posts, news articles, and podcasts? Does being able to read scientific studies make a difference? Not necessarily, in either case! Even people with high levels of science literacy are prone to cognitive bias. Being skilled at reasoning allows you to reach the conclusions you want, based on your worldview.[10]

Experienced scientists admit to cognitive biases, including Dr. Francis Collins, a geneticist who headed the National Institutes of Health. He wrote that he finds it unusually hard to accept information that attacks a scientific conclusion he has been part of, "even though intellectually I recognize that the very nature of science requires consideration of alternative perspectives based on evidence—and that's how science progresses!"[11]

How do we become critical thinkers? To begin with, humility goes a long way. Keep in mind that it's OK to be ambivalent or uncertain about a position. That can be a strength, rather than a weakness, when engaging in critical thinking.

According to Daryl Van Tongeren, four main aspects of intellectual humility include being:

- Open-minded: avoiding dogmatism and being willing to revise your beliefs;
- Curious: seeking new ideas, ways to expand and grow, and changing your mind to align with strong evidence;
- Realistic: owning and admitting your flaws and limitations and seeing the world as it is rather than as you wish it to be;
- Teachable: responding nondefensively and changing your behavior to align with new knowledge.

Intellectual humility is often hard work, especially when the stakes are high.[12]

Dr. Collins recommends asking people whose positions differ from ours to share what about their backgrounds contributes to their stated positions, and to ask ourselves the same question. Compare notes regarding our sources with those with whom we differ. Be honest about the weaknesses underlying these sources. Dr. Collins and *Derate the Hate* podcast host Wilk Wilkinson became friends during the pandemic and developed trust despite strong disagreements. This pair appeared together on *PBS News Hour*.[13]

## WAYS TO PRACTICE CRITICAL THINKING, IN RELATION TO POLARIZATION

*"What we hope ever to do with ease, we must learn first to do with diligence."*—Samuel Johnson

Start with a framework, rather than getting caught up in focusing on my facts representing truth and yours being falsehoods. Jonathan Rauch, in *The Constitution of Knowledge,* describes two core rules.[14]

1. Hunt for your own and others' errors, even if you are confident that you are right.

2. No one has personal authority. No one proposing a hypothesis gets a free pass because of what group they belong to. The rules apply to everybody, not just your in-group or people who believe as you do.

Once these rules are accepted, you can evaluate a policy and engage in fact-checking.

We like to refer to easy-to-remember acronyms. There are lots of them, and you can take a look at the "Tools to Evaluate Media" blog post Beth wrote on *Medium* as part of her graduate studies in science communication.[15] One of our favorites is ESCAPE—Evidence, Source, Context, Audience, Purpose, and Execution.[16] As we go through this example, keep in mind that you don't have to apply all the letters of ESCAPE to every situation. Focusing on even one will hone your critical thinking skills.

Let's consider the debate over mask-wearing to prevent COVID or other infectious diseases. Pretend that you are reading a social media post from a friend who is sharing this blog post, "New Medical Study: Your Face Mask is Not Protecting You."[17] Published on November 18, 2020, by the Ron Paul Institute for Peace and Prosperity, it reads:

"The long-awaited medical study from Denmark examining the ability of face masks to protect people from coronavirus was finally published on Wednesday. Providing good news for people suffering through wearing masks, and bad news for the politicians and businesses pushing the uncomfortable, dangerous, and dehumanizing dress code, the newly released medical study indicates face masks are not protecting people from coronavirus."

**E = Evidence.** Look for facts you can verify: names, stats, places, quotes. Ask yourself: Do the facts hold up? Is the blog post, social media post, or whatever source you are reading several years old and no longer current? If the blog or post makes a claim about another blog or post, follow that trail. Make sure that the other blog post or article relates back to that claim.

This November 2020 blog post above references an op-ed by Daniel Horowitz in *Blaze News*.[18] By going to the Horowitz article, you can find the original paper published in a scientific journal.[19] The abstract is understandable, even if you aren't a scientist.

The original paper notes that wearing a mask outside the home did not reduce the risk of being infected, although there were shortcomings to the study. For example, people often wear their masks incorrectly (think about those masks drifting down off the nose and into the mouth area, leaving the nose area open to spread infection to others and pick up infection from others). So it may be that masks work just fine, as long as they are properly worn.

**S = Source.** Dig deep to figure out who wrote the blog post or other type of post—who were the authors, publishers, and funders. If a funder, does the article's (or post's) message connect at all to any funding source? Who is behind the article or post? Can you find a different article or post about the same topic? Does it agree with the one you are reading?

As we've mentioned, if you look at the source of the *Blaze News* blog post, it's the Ron Paul Institute for Peace and Prosperity. Ron Paul is a retired libertarian politician. Therefore, it's important to read this blog post recognizing it is coming from the perspective of personal freedom. This is OK—as long as you consider other perspectives.

To balance out the Peace and Prosperity information, you might look at sources like FactCheck.org, a project of the Annenberg Public Policy Center of the University of Pennsylvania. In their post, FactCheck.org explained that the conclusion of the study was not that masks didn't work, but that face mask intervention didn't have a significant protective effect for wearers.[20] FactCheck.org states on its site that it does not accept advertising, only grants and individual donations, and provides a link on its page to funding resources: https://www.factcheck.org/our-funding/.

**C = Context.** What's the big picture? How does it fit in with current events? Are you getting the whole story? Is there another side to what is being presented in the blog post or article you are reading?

When considering all sources and FactCheck.org, a discerning reader will have the complete story, whereas the Peace and Prosperity and *Blaze* posts only presented one side of the argument (that masks don't work). This should raise suspicion that there is another side of the story that you aren't reading about in the Peace and Prosperity and *Blaze* posts.

**A = Audience.** Who is the blog post or article appealing to? Look at image choices and words used.

There is a lot of rhetoric in the Peace and Prosperity and *Blaze* posts. Here is one example: "Fortunately, there are still some cracks through which information challenging the 'follow the pseudoscience torrent' can emerge"[21] and "For such an unconstitutional invasion of personal liberty, they are responsible to show us some amazing degree of effectiveness of this cultish ritual."[22]

**P = Purpose.** Why was this made? What is the purpose of the person who created it? Are they trying to get you to do something or believe in their cause?

Given the text above, the purpose appears to be to appeal to personal liberty and to challenge science. Again, this is fine—the key is to recognize it and realize that there can be other viewpoints.

**E = Execution.** How is the information presented? Flashy layout? Bold colors? These can appeal to a different part of your brain than the part that focuses on facts.

The Peace and Prosperity post shows a photo of a young woman taking off her mask and smiling, with the caption: "Your Face Mask Is Not Protecting You." It looks enticing to take off a mask!

Using ESCAPE, you might conclude that masks still may work in certain instances, even if they may not have a huge effect in preventing COVID, and that the benefits of mask-wearing may outweigh the risks. Going through this analytical exercise also reveals that how we communicate or how we balance the relative annoyances and benefits of mask-wearing is often at play rather than a difference of facts among sources.

Granted, this takes time and energy. But we believe it is best to be careful about jumping to conclusions and to avoid passing on false information. To be informed citizens, we each need to make an effort to analyze some of the key issues and controversies that cross our path. You might not have time to go through the full ESCAPE framework all the time, but use care, especially when you decide to share information that you have not examined.

One shortcut is to consume media from sources that present both sides of the story. Sources that can help with this include *All Sides*,[23] *The Flip Side*,[24] *Tangle*,[25] and *Ground News*.[26] *Ground News* includes a feature called "Blindspot," which contains stories disproportionately reported by the left or the right (which you may not even see in your newsfeed). *The Flip Side* provides the left and right sides, with community comments. *Tangle* presents angles from the left and right, as well as the founder's take on the news. In contrast, Fox News and MSNBC report more one-sided views.[27]

## SHARING YOUR CRITICAL THINKING PROCESS WITH OTHERS

*"Critical thinking is not an option. It's a necessity."—Robert Lutz*

Having applied these principles and the ESCAPE steps to a particular situation, you can next decide if you want to share what you learned with others. We recommend that a good place to start is not on social media, but instead in one-on-one conversations with others. You can gently share your opinion using the Braver Angels skills reviewed earlier: Listening, Acknowledging, Pivoting, and sharing your Perspective. Using the LAPP approach offers an opportunity to communicate what you have learned while also demonstrating how you applied critical thinking skills.

First, listen to the other person and acknowledge what they said, even if you don't agree. For example, with respect to masking, you might say, "I can see how you came to the conclusion that masks don't work."

Then pivot with a statement like, "I read a recent news article on the issue, and I have done some digging into news sources. Can I share with you what I learned?" Only after they say "Yes," "Sure," or otherwise give permission to hear your perspective should you move ahead. When you do, include some of the steps you followed. You don't have to explain every part of ESCAPE (or whatever other method you are using). Just share enough to provide a sliver of your critical thinking process.

For example, you might say:

"When I first saw that post in my Facebook feed about masks not working, I forced myself to dig deeper. I learned some interesting things, including how the study didn't capture how a person was actually wearing their mask. That is probably contributing to the conclusion the authors came to and our difference of opinion. Remember seeing masks under people's noses? That can contribute to a mask not working."

Be prepared for this possible response (and be open to understanding and perhaps agreeing):

"Okay, but I'm focused on how it is impacting my life, like having to mask in the restaurant between taking bites of my meal. Or not being able to take my mask off when I'm outside in a public park, trying to relax and recharge in nature."

In sum, applying critical thinking skills to the polarization challenge starts with a commitment to hunting for errors, including your own and those of people on your side. Next, go through a process, such as ESCAPE. Finally, share what you have learned with others in a humble way that increases the chances you will be heard. This approach takes discipline, time, and patience, yet it is so important for the future of our country.

## FOR FURTHER THOUGHT

- What barriers could be undermining your critical thinking process?
- Are you quick to accept information that confirms what you believe and reject anything that is contrary?
- What steps could you take to access and evaluate information in a more balanced and rigorous way?
- How often do you pause before sharing a post on social media that you think could have questionable validity?
- Do you fall into a pattern of telling people what to think and feeling disdain when they don't agree with your opinion? How could you better listen to different views with humility and curiosity?

## Chapter 14

# POSITIVE ENGAGEMENT WITH FAMILY, FRIENDS, AND COLLEAGUES

> *"I never considered a difference of opinion in politics, in religion, in philosophy, as cause for withdrawing from a friend."—Thomas Jefferson*

Have you disconnected or distanced yourself from friends or family members over political issues? Of course, politics is one of many topics we discuss with others, but it should not dominate to the exclusion of shared history, values, hobbies, personal interests, and so many other dimensions of life. It's critical to learn how to fuel positive connections with our closest relationships, even when we disagree.

David Brooks observes in *How to Know a Person:*

"There is one skill that lies at the heart of any healthy person, family, school, community organization, or society: the ability to see someone else deeply and make them feel seen—to accurately know another person, to let them feel valued, heard, and understood."[1]

Doug's brother Jim adds, "I think what's key is that we do NOT have to agree, at all . . . but what's important is to see the humanity in the other person no matter how much we may reject (or even detest) their ideas."

So simple in one respect, but so hard to fully achieve in these divisive times.

It is unrealistic to think that we can have open, braver conversations with everyone we differ with over politics. We have choices along a continuum. On one end of the spectrum is shutting people out of our lives completely. On the other end is choosing to talk openly, applying braver conversation skills to create greater connection and understanding (even as you continue to disagree).

Somewhere in the middle, but closer to the first option, is distancing ourselves from selected people: interacting superficially and not engaging on topics where we expect conflict or difference. A better option might be to openly acknowledge you have differences and mutually agree to set boundaries, such as not talking about politics while still discussing other topics.

Most of us will become stronger by attempting to move at least some of our interactions toward braver conversations. When people from different sides really listen to each other, they often find much more in common than they previously believed.

## MANAGING RELATIONSHIPS ON SOCIAL MEDIA

*"Social media erodes the mortar that holds the moral community together."—Jonathan Haidt*

Posting about politics on social media can undermine relationships and promote unhealthy behavior. Consider this observation from the *Hidden Brain* podcast: "It's the paradox of our times: We have access to an endless amount of content to keep us engaged, yet the more of it we consume, the less engaged we feel."[2]

Social media is designed to encourage quick (and not always well-thought-out) comments. Not stepping back to ponder a thoughtful response can lead to rapid back and forth that may quickly become nasty. Or, depending on your contact list, responses may fall into an echo chamber of smug comments that reinforce a we-are-better-than-them mentality.

There is a difference between political posts that focus on policy as opposed to posts that contain attacks against people on the other side. But both of these often lead to comments by social media friends that can foster a chain of comments that demean those on the other side.

Of course, people *need* to have conversations about politics. After all, our democratic governance depends on it! We simply believe that social media is not a great venue for this, that the potential for positive discussion and healthy conflict is much greater when these conversations happen offline. And we find it ironic how the term *friend* has taken on such a new meaning. This term can feed into a myth that we are all so connected, when the reality is widespread loneliness.

**From Doug:** I confess to having 726 Facebook "friends," most of whom requested that status. Encouraging me to expand my network is exactly the sort of thing that Meta loves, as it encourages increased usage. I increasingly have come to realize, however, that the way the algorithms work, I only see occasional posts from most friends.

How many of Doug's connections are friends in the traditional sense of being someone who shares valued history, reaches out to provide support, and really cares about him (and vice versa)? Of course, most are acquaintances, maybe friends of friends—or someone who slipped in trying to sell something. Of course, social media has many advantages, but it brings together a group of people who you don't necessarily know that well. Care is required when discussing politics in such an open forum!

There is also the issue of siloing: segregating among people on "our side" of politics. You would think that having so many friends would make us see more different opinions, but social media algorithms tend to keep us in our bubbles.

## FAMILY POLITICAL CONFLICT

*"It used to be, the land of us and them was made for you and me."*
—Jud Caswell

**From Doug:** Jud Caswell is a Maine singer-songwriter I've come to know at the Sea Gull Shop. He has a beautiful song titled "The Great Divide" that opens with a description of his grandparents who were registered in different political parties and would "cancel out their votes," but "You never heard a word of anger pass between that husband and his wife." He goes on: "We get kind of stupid when we're angry," and "It seems to me, you've forgotten who's a friend or enemy." "We are all losing," and "There was a time we could agree to disagree, before the slide to the great divide."[3]

We recall this observation by Amanda Ripley: "No one will change in the ways you want them to until they believe you understand and accept them for who they are right now. (And sometimes not even then.)"[4] What people want most is to be accepted, but of course these issues can be very challenging.

**From Becky:** When my son came out to our immediate family as transgender a few years ago, he chose to keep that decision private from most of our extended family, who do not live nearby. When he realized a family wedding would make his transition public, I really struggled with how to best support him, especially since I wasn't sure how some family members might respond. Unfortunately, due to some negative comments, I have needed to distance myself from some family members, but this is necessary because my support of my son is most important to me.

---

Although we believe that embracing braver conversations is usually a better approach than fight, flight, or avoidance, there are times we need to establish healthy boundaries. Hopefully, this can be done with dignity and respect while allowing for the possibility of future reconciliation.

## SKILLS FOR NAVIGATING FAMILY AND POLITICS

*"We're scared to have hard conversations because we can't control the path or outcome."—Brené Brown*

"Family and Politics" is one of the workshops developed by Bill Doherty, the Braver Angels cofounder and University of Minnesota professor of family social science. The workshop includes powerful and practical ideas on how to preserve family bonds over Thanksgiving dinner or in daily interactions while staying true to our values and political beliefs.

Many of us are upset (even terrified) when family and politics collide, but it helps to anticipate situations that may arise and consider how to respond effectively. One aspect is recognizing the various roles people choose to play. In group situations, such as a family dinner, these include the gladiator (who initiates battles against "wrong-headed" relatives); the defender (who counterattacks unfairly when others go first); the sniper (who uses digs to get a rise); the peacekeeper (who tries to prevent all political conversations); the bystander (who avoids participating); and the engager (who tries to have respectful conversations across differences).

While every situation is different, we advise having respectful conversations whenever possible. Take, for example, if a relative makes a dig about how you voted when you are swallowing a mouthful of turkey and cranberry sauce. After you pause and swallow, you could say something like, "I think it is important to engage in political conversations, but I would prefer to do it after dinner."

Or you can say, "Family is so important to me and I don't want to see politics get in the way of our relationship, so I prefer not to go there right now." Then perhaps quickly change the subject with a question like, "And how is your cousin in Indianapolis doing these days?"

Fortunately, there are positive and healthy ways to engage in these kinds of situations. Some preparation ahead of time (including practicing with sympathetic friends or in Braver Angels workshops) can significantly increase your readiness for satisfying conversations. With a little planning and practice, you might even leave a family dinner with a smile on your face as opposed to grumbling with your partner on the way home over the upsetting comment by Uncle Fred.

## WHAT ABOUT CHILDREN?

*"Those who choose, even on a small scale, to love in the midst of hatred and fear are the people who offer true hope to our world."*
—Henri Nouwen

With adults so quick to go at each other over politics, it is easy to see how children are also affected. This is perhaps the most painful part of our nation's polarization crisis. Future generations are being influenced. Children can come to believe that the bad behavior they are witnessing—be it in person, online, or on radio or television—is perfectly "normal." Or they are learning that certain people and types of people are "bad," when there is another side to every story. Whether intended or not, children are learning unhealthy behaviors.

We must do better. We know that adults influence children in positive ways if we do so consciously and deliberately. A long-term study demonstrated sustained effects when parents actively modeled empathy in their involvement with their children. The research showed that these children tended to show more empathy toward their friends in their teen years, and it even extended to their own parenting skills later in life. Empathy was passed on to the next generation![5]

Key skills parents can employ include:

- Being present and attentive
- Reflecting back feelings
- Acknowledging challenges and helping children work through them
- Recognizing distress
- Offering warmth and understanding

What could be more important work than demonstrating for young people positive ways to engage with others? When we model kindness and treat others with dignity and respect, our children will follow. And our children can teach us about this as well.

**From Becky** One overlooked aspect of parenting is a willingness to be influenced by our children, especially through their teenage years and into adulthood. My kids have modeled acceptance of others and sensitivity to differences, which has exposed me to new ways of thinking, believing, and behaving. If we are open to and listen to our children, we will discover that they can be our teachers. My youngest child, who is autistic, has taught me about ableism (discrimination, prejudice, and bias against people with disabilities, including harmful stereotypes) and seeing and identifying ableist comments and behaviors.

## SKILLS FOR MANAGING CONFLICTS WITH FRIENDS

*"Choose to be optimistic, it feels better."*—Dalai Lama

The skills and approaches used with family also work with friends—and by friends we mean the term in its traditional sense of those we truly care about. The big difference between family and friends, of course, is that we get to choose our friends. Yes, we can choose when and how much to engage with certain family members. And there may even be very good reasons (such as abusive behavior) for pushing family members far away. But, as much as we might try, it can be difficult to 100 percent disown them.

With friends, there is much more freedom to pick and choose.

Of course, friends come and go in our lives for any number of reasons. But we are saddened when someone with a longtime friendship decides to back away from their buddy based on politics. This can be such a personal loss for both sides and leave holes in our hearts. We push back on the idea that politics is more important than friendships!

When we choose to only engage with people on our side, we can end up in a bubble. It is so much better—for us and our country—to have friendships that cross political lines. When you find that your friendship ties are being pushed apart by politics, a similar open and honest opening like that we shared for family could be a great way to break the ice and start a discussion:

> "I know we have some differences when it comes to politics. I want you to know that our relationship is important to me, and I don't want political differences to get in the way, no matter how much we might disagree."

Hopefully, the other person will respond positively to this idea and your friendship will be sustained in a way that will make you both more comfortable moving forward. You will also be demonstrating how to have a positive conversation and be doing your part to model constructive engagement.

Maybe your friend will do the same with someone else, passing it forward. If the response isn't so positive and the person chooses to pull back, you will at least know that you tried in good faith.

Politics may get in the way of potential new friendships, too. It can be sad when we meet someone with whom we feel a connection and the potential for a meaningful friendship, but, when we learn their politics are different from ours, we choose to back away. We encourage you to stay engaged, at least for a while, in the spirit of curiosity. When you show that you care, you might find that you have a new friend. And that person might even be willing to be curious about your political ideas! You could try a statement like this:

> "I see that we have some differences when it comes to politics. I want you to know that friendships are very important to me, and I don't want politics to get in the way of getting to know you better."

## MANAGING POLITICAL CONFLICT AT WORK

*"Example is not the main thing in influencing others. It is the only thing."—Albert Schweitzer*

What about political conflicts and conversations in the workplace? The most common view is to avoid political discussions on the job, and this is certainly better than employee conflicts that undermine morale and productivity. A higher value, though, would be fostering respectful conversations that include good listening skills, curiosity, and humility.

**From Becky:** My company is made up of about twenty-five people, some contractors and some employees, most working remotely. Throughout my years in business, I have mostly stayed away from political conversations with team members and clients. This has been tricky during elections or other major events.

What I've noticed is that whoever I'm talking to usually assumes that I believe the same as they do, which can become uncomfortable.

On January 6, 2021, our company chat filled with comments about what was happening that day at the US Capitol. While many people were distressed about the events, others seemed bothered by the entry of politics into our workplace interactions. In the aftermath of January 6, we had to come together as a company to reinforce our core values and to discuss how we could talk about politics and hot-button issues at work in respectful ways.

In a message to my team, I wrote, "We want to hear what you're experiencing and listen to your ideas for how we can continue to create a workplace that embodies our core values. Every single person on this team is welcome to their own perspectives, beliefs, and ideas. We each bring unique nuance to our opinions and perspectives. There are no sides here, only individuals. I don't want us to take sides or create false polarities."

One colleague pushed back that it was inappropriate to "sweep such issues under the rug. . . . we need to be able to come together and decompress and acknowledge how it's affecting our brain and heart spaces." These issues can be so challenging for companies as we strive to meet our business goals and keep our team connected and fully engaged.

---

A Gallup study found that nearly half of US workers said they had discussed political issues with a coworker in the past month and that workplace political discussions appear to have both positive and negative effects on employees.[6] Aside from politics, 63 percent of employees do not feel they are treated with respect at work, which adds another challenging dimension to the workplace.[7] If workers are not feeling respected, what might happen if a political topic is broached?

Another Gallup study found that a majority of US adults (57 percent) say they have at times avoided sharing their political views because of fear of harassment or poor treatment. Nearly a third (31 percent) say they have been treated poorly or harassed in the past year because of their political views. More Republicans than Independents or Democrats report being treated poorly because of their political perspectives.[8]

How much is political conflict impacting your work environment? The authors of *We Can't Talk about That at Work! How to Talk about Race, Religion, Politics, and Other Polarizing Topics* argue that conversations on difficult topics are happening all the time in workplaces. If they aren't handled effectively, they can negatively impact productivity, employee engagement and retention, teamwork, and employees' sense of safety in the workplace.[9] And Becky's story reminds us that we should resist making assumptions about others.

As a business leader (or employee) are you ignoring the problem or acting in ways that add to the issue? What might you want to do differently? When business leaders (and colleagues, too) model positive behavior, others will follow. Embracing respect, humility, and empathy goes a long way toward establishing a positive workplace culture. Most organizations have mission statements; if you are a business leader, review yours to ensure it incorporates values such as dignity and respect and that these are consistently communicated and followed.

Consider this example from the perspective of a workplace manager. Two of your best employees had always worked well together, but more recently their political differences have led to diminished cooperation. You notice them having heated discussions about the election or, alternatively, avoiding each other altogether. You realize that this behavior is cutting into their productivity and diminishing the bottom line.

What is a business leader to do? *Wait a minute,* a manager might say, *I am trying to run a business; I don't have time to deal with this stuff!* But these situations are going to happen, so it is better to have a plan. Intervene when necessary. These are challenging conversations, but when you have set clear expectations and model positive behavior, they are easier and ultimately more effective.

In sum, business owners and managers can have a big impact by creating a positive climate and making it normal to have positive and constructive conversations about difficult topics. By embracing these ideals, your business will be more successful, and you will be modeling behavior that can positively impact those outside your business and even our country.

As for employees, doing your part and using the braver conversation skills can go a long way toward making your workplace experience better—and you will also be doing a service for our United States!

We finish this chapter by summarizing these ways to create stronger relationships with family, friends, and colleagues:

- Look for the humanity in the other person.
- Set boundaries as necessary.
- Look for ways to talk openly about areas of difference, applying braver conversation skills in those situations.
- Think ahead about how you might engage with family members who take on various roles.
- Be a positive role model for children when it comes to facing difficult conversations.
- Model respectful behavior and good listening skills when political topics come up at work.

## FOR FURTHER THOUGHT

- Are you avoiding conversations in ways that may undermine relationships, and what might you do differently?
- What skills would help you better engage with those have strongly held political opinions that are different from yours?
- If you have lost friends or family relationships due to politics, what steps might you consider trying to re-engage?
- What might be some helpful ways to engage with friends who you know have different political views from yours?
- What steps can you take to positively and proactively converse with work colleagues whose political views are different from your own?

Chapter 15

# LEADING OTHERS FOR A BETTER AMERICA

> *"I think leadership's always been about two main things: imagination and courage."*—Paul Keating

Moving into a leadership role is not required for you to have better relationships or to make our country better. The most important part of leadership is self-leadership—striving to understand and live by your values; becoming more open to differing viewpoints; and embracing your heart in everyday interactions and conversations with family, friends, colleagues, and others.

But if you want to do more, please step up! Our country needs as many of us as possible to be willing to lead others to help diminish the politics of contempt.

Perhaps you want to use your leadership influence to organize your friends or neighbors to go beyond their political bubbles, like Beth has done with her community discussion groups. Perhaps you can promote a less politically polarized culture in an organization where you already have connections, such as a church, synagogue, mosque, book club, or civic group. Or maybe there is an important civic renewal project in your community that you are willing to help lead as a civic entrepreneur. Perhaps you are ready to step into a more active leadership role with a group such as Braver Angels.

## FORMAL VS. INFORMAL LEADERSHIP

*"Leadership isn't something that anyone can give you—you have to earn it and claim it for yourself."—Travis Bradberry*

There are many books about leading others, most focusing on formal leadership—when someone is officially recognized with a title. This could be someone at work such as a CEO, manager, or supervisor. It could also be a sports coach or someone in a volunteer role such as the Lions Club president or head of the Parent Teacher Association (PTA). Elected officials can also be considered formal leaders, although they certainly don't have supervisory authority over their constituents.

Informal leadership is also very important, maybe even more so than the formal kind. By informal leadership, we mean acting without having a leadership title or official role. Informal leaders apply their talents as people who are respected and appreciated by those who are willing to listen to their ideas and may be willing to follow them to address a community need.

Formal leaders lead by title and official authority and, if they are truly effective, also by their personal influence. Informal leaders lead by influence and their ability to attract and inspire others to their causes. Most often, we think of formal leaders in paid roles, but there can also be formal leaders in volunteer roles. For example, Doug serves as New England regional leader with Braver Angels. Beth has served in volunteer leadership roles as vice president for education and president of her local Toastmasters public speaking group and as co-moderator of Common Ground Nashville. Becky has been a volunteer in her church and with Girls on the Run.

We think of formal leaders in business, government agencies, or nonprofits, but informal leaders operate within these structures as well. Think of work colleagues who are respected by others. They may not have direct supervisory authority, but people are influenced by their ideas and behavior. Informal leaders can also operate outside of any formal structure, such as when someone convinces neighbors to attend a government meeting or a Braver Angels workshop.

While the distinction between formal and informal leadership can be important, most of the leadership principles outlined in this chapter apply to both types of roles.

A key point is that you cannot lead others effectively without leading yourself first. Leadership starts with positive role modeling, embracing your values, and acting in ways you expect others to act. People are less successful in informal and formal leadership when they fail to embrace self-leadership.

## LEADERSHIP FROM THE DEEPEST PART OF OURSELVES

*"At the heart of great leadership is a curious mind, heart, and spirit."*
—Chip Conley

The most effective type of leadership is driven by "inner game" qualities connected to the deepest parts of ourselves and have more to do with character, courage, and conviction than with skills or competencies. According to the authors of *Mastering Leadership*, "If you lead from a deep sense of purpose, translate that into clear vision, and build alignment among key stakeholders (teamwork) in the realization of that vision, you are highly likely (.94 correlation) to be an effective leader."[1]

Research shows that how a formal leader acts explains, more than any other variable, whether people feel engaged in their work.[2] Furthermore, the most effective leaders bring out two to three times more staff talent than do the least effective leaders, and businesses and organizations with the best leaders are the highest performing. Building change in our country necessitates leaders who apply these same principles to working with citizens and volunteers.

Those in leadership positions who lack these key personal qualities are also less effective in developing new leaders, a key aspect of successful leadership.[3] The polarization crisis requires us to build a deep bench of leaders who can collectively create change.

How we act influences others, either positively or negatively. Positive leadership is contagious, be it in the workplace or in volunteer situations. A key place to start is building relationships that go deeper than the common what's-in-it-for-me perspective. Too many relationships are transactional. The most effective leaders invest time to build connections and get to know their colleagues and teammates. Others will follow you if you lead with authenticity, self-awareness, and positive energy.

Stephen M. R. Covey, son of the famous author, observed that people don't want to be managed; they want to be led and inspired. Leaders, he said, need to "be efficient with things and effective with people." He added that "with people, fast is slow and slow is fast."[4]

That last phrase is especially brilliant. When we interact quickly or superficially with people, we have little influence and make minimal impact. But when we take the time to get to know them and build relationships, we build trust and can have a more significant influence. This ties directly to our definition of leadership: actions and behaviors that influence the actions and behaviors of others. These kinds of connections can help overcome the impact of conflict entrepreneurs on our country.

Start with applying the key aspects of self-leadership and then build out from there. Remember, with people, fast is slow and slow is fast. Looking inward at your actions and changing your behaviors are critical steps toward making it more likely that you will positively influence others.

## THE POWER OF TEAMWORK

*"Alone we can do so little, together we can do so much."—Helen Keller*

While individuals can sometimes accomplish great things, people working together almost always accomplish more. The power of synergy—that one plus one can add up to so much more than two—is exemplified by effective teamwork. We need teams with deep commitments to build positive change across these United States. Too often, however, teams operate with suboptimal effectiveness because members are underutilized or frustrated.

Great teamwork doesn't happen by accident; it requires formal or informal leadership that proactively creates team cohesion and a positive climate, with members who clearly understand their roles and what it means to be an effective team member. The ability to create and sustain successful teams starts with having a clear and well-communicated purpose. Knowing your people and their talents is vital, as is putting together the team in a way that aligns purpose and people. Establish clear expectations that are proactively communicated, and manage conflicts when they arise. Be sure to acknowledge achievements, monitor progress, and sustain team morale. And, of course, be prepared to make any adjustments as new situations arise.

As noted earlier, conflicts are not necessarily bad, but they need to be appropriately managed to hold ego and emotion in check. The extremes are fight versus flight, and a need to win versus a willingness to minimize. Much better is finding the sweet spot where candor and curiosity are in balance. Effective team members need skills in both areas, including the ability to clearly state a position, explain the whys, inquire to understand others, and listen. Leaders help shape the direction of the discourse toward learning, progress, and growth.

And what about the role of a team member who is not designated as the leader? Each person has an obligation to be fully present and engaged in the work of the team. Respect for other team members, even when there is serious disagreement, is vital. Further, nearly all of us can build trust by improving our listening skills— learning to listen better to understand, rather than to simply respond.

Building this kind of positive team culture can help drive change across our nation, moving us "from I to we."

## APPLYING LEADERSHIP SKILLS IN EVERYDAY LIFE

*"Find small ways to add value to others' lives."—Adam Grant*

Of course, most of our daily interactions with people are quick, transactional, and soon forgotten. But passing on kindness and acknowledging others doesn't take that much effort, and the effect can be lasting. When a person is influencing you in a positive way, we encourage you to do the same—pass it on.

> **From Doug**  Three qualities of effective leaders that I emphasize in my training workshops are positive energy, authenticity, and self-awareness (including understanding how our behaviors impact others). I try to embrace these in my everyday actions and recognize them in others as well. During contact with store clerks, flight attendants, and other people, it can be difficult to assess authenticity and self-awareness, but positive energy is often easy to recognize. When I interact with someone who looks me in the eye with a seemingly authentic smile (or who says "How are you?" or "Have a nice day" beyond the usual I-am-obligated-to-say-that), I try to give positive feedback. It feels good to acknowledge someone who seems attentive, helpful, and friendly.

Practicing everyday kindness skills can make them seem more natural and easier to apply as you build a team of people who want to see our country be less divisive.

In his book *This Is Day One: A Practical Guide to Leadership That Matters,* Drew Dudley describes observing an efficient grocery line cashier, telling her how much he appreciates her work, and receiving a grateful response.[5] Some may not think of a cashier as a leader, but doing your job well and being a good role model are both important leadership traits, asserts Dudley. He asks each of us to consider: "What have I done today to recognize someone else's leadership?"

*She is just doing her job,* might be a counterargument to offering praise, but acknowledging good work can provide many benefits. Simple heartfelt statements, such as, "I appreciate the way you do your job," or "You are a good role model," are easy to say when you mean them, and these kinds of actions can be contagious, reinforcing a positive culture in everyday situations!

Be an unsung hero, on the lookout for small ways to help (and lead) others.

Don't underestimate how these kinds of interactions can contribute to addressing our national divide. A person may inquire about your Braver

Angels pin or there may be an opportunity to share about your commitment to depolarization. You might see them again later and strike up another conversation. They might even join your efforts to better our country!

*From Becky* — Working with a closely connected team, I've seen the value in building close and trusting relationships. We aim to start every meeting with connection, which helps us get to know and appreciate our colleagues beyond our work relationships. I've noticed that it's easier to talk about difficult issues with a strong relational foundation in place. One of our colleagues has been highly engaged with volunteering in her community during elections and with her party's state committees. She's been recognized and awarded for her contributions and service. As I was building a relationship with her, I didn't know about her politics. I got to know and admire her as a leader first, including how she showed up with people. The strong relationship and trust she built with me slowly caused me to turn to her for guidance in understanding how to get more involved politically. I think others would feel comfortable approaching her, too, even if they don't share her views. I certainly consider her to be a leader and role model who has a positive influence during her everyday interactions.

## APPLYING LEADERSHIP SKILLS TO THE POLARIZATION CRISIS

*"The challenge of our time is to mobilize great masses of people to make change without dehumanizing one another. Not just because it's morally right but because it works."—Amanda Ripley*

Leadership during challenging times requires heightened perspective and skills. This requires us to go deeper and apply our talents in potentially new ways.

**From Doug** US Ambassador Alex Laskaris demonstrated an array of key crisis leadership traits while supporting and encouraging our team in Guinea during the Ebola epidemic. He remained positive and avoided panic and fear, focusing on facts to understand the reality of the situation. This ambassador engaged others, assembled the best talent, and listened to their advice to develop an effective response. He worked to understand the culture and the reality on the ground while embracing transparency and openness to reduce rumors and confusion. He also communicated regularly, sharing what he knew. In this positive environment, I was able to inspire my staff to lead an important community education effort.

---

Building trust is critical. If people lack confidence in their leader, their involvement will invariably be less successful. Leaders who project a positive, engaging approach will be more effective in rallying people to a cause.

As we've mentioned before, Doug was in Ukraine when that country was first invaded by Russia in 2014. The current situation in the United States is not exactly a crisis like the war in Ukraine or Ebola in West Africa, but we can't help but think of the word *crisis* as we face the deep political divide in our country. The leadership challenge is a big one—but it can be met by applying practical steps, including these:

1. Be informed, ensuring that the news you consume is as unbiased as possible.
2. Identify your available time, money, and energy resources for getting involved in a way that best works for you to make a positive impact and change our country for the better.

3. Research local groups or organizations and inquire about volunteer opportunities, looking for opportunities to build relationships while using your strengths and gifts.
4. Show up to serve others, listening to engage and understand their perspectives.
5. Lead by example, with authenticity, humility, and empathy for others.

Yes, these are challenging times, but please don't be intimidated. If you are willing to learn and lead, please believe that you can make a difference!

## DEVELOP A PERSONAL LEADERSHIP PLAN

*"Take care of each moment, and it will lead into the next one."*
—Kristen LaRue

Mobilizing masses is not an easy task, but it requires that we are willing to step out of our comfort zones. Our country needs your help. Touch one person, then another, and they touch others—and the next thing you know, we have mobilized many. Maybe even masses!

To help guide you through this process, write down a few thoughts that will help you develop a personal leadership plan. Here are a few ideas to help get your started, and we also include a checklist in the appendix.

**Review what we have shared.** Consider the self-leadership skills described earlier, as well as those for having courageous conversations, promoting critical thinking, and engaging in positive interactions with family, friends, and colleagues. What points resonate with you? What might you want to do? Start with what you are good at, but don't feel like you have to be limited by that. A more important question is what would you like to do to better your life and relationships? What efforts might you be willing to lead that would feel impactful for you? Then think about what it might take to move you in that direction.

**What do you want to learn?** What would help you move toward what you want to do? Focus on two or three areas that would help you increase your leadership skills and effectiveness at reducing polarization, and make a plan to gain the knowledge you will need.

**Seek advice and feedback.** Identify people who can help you, and reach out to them for ideas and suggestions. These might be trusted individuals or people in an organization such as Braver Angels.

**Make connections.** This could be closely aligned with the last point. What people or organizations can you work with to apply your leadership talents in bridge building? Reach out to multiple people and expand your pool of helpful contacts.

**Find a home.** Your connections might lead you to an organization or to a community group where you want to focus your efforts. Consider your options and decide to move where your intuition tells you it would be best.

**Feel free to say no.** Be sure your plan helps you achieve your goals, and don't get overwhelmed with requests and ideas from others. Stay focused on what you think is most important and what you actually *want* to do.

**Bring it together.** Take all the information you have collected and decide specifically what you will do. Do you want a formal or informal leadership role? Are you aligning with an organization or operating outside of any formal structure? Are you focused on a civic renewal project in your community or civics education in schools? The possibilities are endless, so take the time to narrow your options down and decide what you believe will work best for you.

**Make it happen.** Then take your plan and make it happen. Yes, there will be setbacks, but this is always the case with any challenging endeavor. Just know that what you are doing is important and move ahead step by step.

**Reassess from time to time.** Making periodic adjustments is inevitable with any project. Use your connections for feedback and advice, and modify the plan as needed. Don't be discouraged—this is hard work for sure—but keep the faith that you will contribute to ending our nation's division.

A recent Gallup survey identified hope and trust as the two most important qualities people seek in their leaders, followed by compassion and stability. Hope was highest by far and exactly what we strive to deliver to our beautiful country.[6]

We each have an extraordinary opportunity to make a difference in people's lives, including our own. Please don't underestimate your leadership potential to build hope and better our great nation! To paraphrase our Braver Angels friend Bill Doherty, hope is the choice that we all need to make, because the alternatives are so much worse.

### FOR FURTHER THOUGHT

- What could make you ready to step into a leadership role to help our country overcome the politics of contempt?
- How might you best apply your talents and influence toward leading others?
- What steps could you take to improve your leadership skills?
- What can you do to develop trust, promote a climate of purpose and connection, and attract others to the cause?
- What would help you create and implement a personal leadership plan?

# SECTION V

# YOU WILL MAKE OUR COUNTRY BETTER

*"Act as if what you do makes a difference. It does."* —William James

Chapter 16

# FIND YOUR PATH— THINK GLOBAL, ACT LOCAL

> *"If people live in accordance with norms they abhor, the circumstances are right for sudden change. People can be unleashed."*
> —Cass Sunstein

Author Cass Sunstein's book is titled *How Change Happens.*[1] In another book with the same title, author Leslie Crutchfield argues that winning movements lead with messages that "connect with people at their human core."[2] She quotes Bill Novelli, who led the Campaign for Tobacco-Free Kids, who said that movements need to "change people's minds about what is acceptable, about what is normal."[3] Significant societal shifts do not occur at random, but require sustained advocacy by a large network of individuals and organizations who persistently campaign in the face of almost endless obstacles.

Crutchfield describes six key patterns that drive change:

1. Motivating grassroot support to change social norms
2. Strategic vision that aligns the movement's many parts
3. Social marketing strategies and campaigns that change people's hearts
4. Enticing appeals that offer something better than the current system
5. Engaging with businesses to get their support
6. Strong leaders who let go of their egos to deeply listen and understand differing views

On the last point, Crutchfield states: "Successful leaders don't so much create movements out of thin air as tap into energy that percolates around them. They give that energy shape, channeling it toward a common cause." These leaders "give voice to grievances and concerns that many people have, but who may not possess the conviction, courage, or capability to speak out publicly and personally initiate change."[4]

So, how might you contribute your talents and skills to focus on one or more of these six priority areas? Do you think you could help move the hearts and minds of others? Or help create a vision for change in your community? What about working with the business community? Or using social marketing to counter conflict entrepreneurs and become a civic entrepreneur?

Let's get more specific about applying these ideas to your situation and interests.

Some years ago, we first heard the powerful phrase "think global, act local." Someone got the idea to turn it into a bumper sticker, changing the adjectives to adverbs. "Think globally, act locally" may be more grammatically correct, but it seemed to diminish the simple message. We prefer the first version!

The wonderful idea, of course, is to think big while acting in small ways that contribute to the larger purpose. To act local means to function within your personal sphere of influence, such as thinking in a new way, interacting with one other person, or perhaps taking on a community project in the spirit of civic renewal. The key idea is that small actions can contribute to a larger purpose.

So, how might we envision thinking global and acting local in this time of deep division? Think about a journey for our country and its citizens, evolving from the present situation toward a better future. This is how we describe, in a single sentence, the current situation:

*Political polarization and distrust are dividing Americans in ways that foster dysfunctional governance and threaten the future of our nation.*

What would a better future look like? How about this:

*American political institutions operate in the spirit of citizenship and common purpose, with vigorous policy debates and people treating each other with dignity and respect, even if they disagree.*

Of course, there is also the possibility that things could decline. We describe this possibility as:

*Political polarization, bitterness, and rancor build to the point of social unrest, violence, and civil war.*

So, we have *three scenarios:* the present situation (aka the status quo) and two possible futures, one better and one worse. We obviously believe that the first future option is desirable, so we refer to that in positive terms. We recognize that some conflict entrepreneurs might consider a future with social unrest, violence, and civil war as "positive," but we clearly have a contrary perspective!

## HOW TO BEST CONFRONT THE POLARIZATION CHALLENGE

The goal is to move the status quo vertical line in the center to the right, toward a better future.

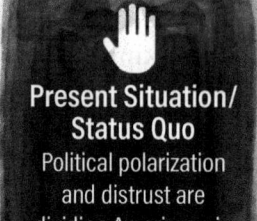

**A Worse Future**
Political polarization, bitterness, and rancor build to the point of social unrest, violence, and civil war.

**Present Situation/ Status Quo**
Political polarization and distrust are dividing Americans in ways that foster dysfunctional governance and threaten the future of our nation.

**A Better Future**
American political institutions operate in the spirit of citizenship and common purpose, with vigorous policy debates and people treating each other with dignity and respect, even if they disagree.

**Forces Pushing for Positive Change**

- Exhausted majority dissatisfied (but disconnected)
- Citizens embrace more kindness and empathy
- Political leaders may be dissatisfied (but fear diverging from the party line)
- There is more common ground than believed
- Skills in engaging with others
- Civics education in schools
- Advocates for reduced use of social media
- Citizen leaders want change
- Braver Angels

**Forces Pushing for Negative Change**

- Influence of conflict entrepreneurs
- Social media algorithms
- Discourteous behavior amid declining interpersonal and listening skills
- Binary thinking and identity politics
- Political and government dysfunction (including politicians rewarded by bad behavior)
- Financial insecurity and wealth disparities
- Educational disparities/dominance by elites
- Sorting and siloing
- Citizen apathy

### Forces Pushing for Positive Change

- Other organizations (see list in appendix)
- Add other factors that you think could help create a better future:
  _____
  _____
  _____
  _____
  _____

### Forces Pushing for Negative Change

- Disconnection, loneliness, and distrust (including declines in social capital)
- Changes in the media environment and information overloads
- Misinformation, disinformation campaigns and foreign propaganda
- Decline of civics education
- Historical changes
- Discord across generations
- Fear
- Widespread distrust of governmental institutions
- Segmentation of our citizenry: urban vs. rural, college graduates vs. high school educated, elites vs. working class
- Threatening and canceling
- Compromise, once considered positive, seen negatively by many
- Primary elections favor candidates on the extremes
- Money in politics
- Gerrymandering
- Add other factors that you think are contributing to the problem:
  _____
  _____
  _____
  _____

- Which of the positive forces can we magnify?
- What other positive forces could we add?
- Which of the negative forces can we diminish through our collective actions?

Now, consider the various factors (or forces) that are contributing to the present situation and what could "push" circumstances to make things better or worse. Both the positive and negative factors are summarized in the graphic on the previous page that uses force-field analysis (FFA), a framework first developed by social psychologist Kurt Lewin.[5] The FFA model helps us understand the factors that influence our situation. This includes both *positive forces* driving toward a better future and *negative forces* holding us back (and potentially making the situation worse than what we are experiencing today).

This framework is useful for considering how we might influence the various positive and negative factors in ways that could help build a better country. While the situation can feel chaotic and even hopeless at times, this approach helps us focus on what we can control or at least influence.

We do not need to accept the status quo (or worse) as inevitable. Yes, sometimes we are tempted to sink into malaise and feelings of hopelessness. But we can proactively move our country toward a better future by acting in ways that augment the positive factors and diminish the negative ones.

To be more specific, consider the graphic on the previous page. We can move our country from the present situation (represented by the vertical center line) toward a better future (represented by the right side of the graphic). How? By *increasing* the factors pushing for positive change and *diminishing* those pushing for negative change. Of course, not all forces have the same impact, and some situations will be harder to impact than others, but the FFA approach gives us a useful framework.

## YOUR EVERYDAY ACTIONS CAN MOVE THE NEEDLE

*"Peace begins with a smile."*—Mother Teresa

*Interesting graphic,* you may say, but where to start? Consider these questions: Which of the positive and negative factors do you think are the most influential? Which factors might be the easiest to influence? What approaches and actions might be effective in helping to move the center line to the right? Which factors are most interesting to you personally? Where might you be willing to invest your time and energy?

Your everyday actions can move the needle on these positive forces from the graphic:

- Citizens embrace more kindness and empathy
- Skills in engaging with others

*Really?* you say. *How does that change the country?*

When you demonstrate these actions, you lead by example—even if your intention is not to lead others. When you act in a way that shows someone with whom you disagree that you respect them, that can move them to do the same. Your simple actions can touch others who, in turn, touch others, and thus have a positive ripple effect! What about the negative forces that could be reduced? Consider these:

- Disconnection, loneliness, and distrust (including declines in social capital)
- Discourteous behavior amid declining interpersonal and listening skills
- Sorting and siloing
- Threatening and canceling

Disconnection, loneliness, and distrust, including declines in social capital, can be addressed by connecting with others. Applying your listening and interpersonal skills is a powerful way to expand your impact. Could you join the local Rotary Club, library guild, food pantry, book club, faith group, or other organizations in your community? Many organizations are looking for volunteers, and this a great way to make positive connections. In the process of working together on a project with people who may be different from ourselves (different races, religions, political leanings), we can get out of our bubbles and strengthen the fabric of our nation. Expanding connections with others can also add to your personal health and well-being. Our experiences with Braver Angels have greatly expanded our connections in very meaningful ways.

Also, express in a respectful way that you are concerned about discourteous behavior and practices such as threatening and canceling. It may seem like a stretch to think that you, as one person, can have a major impact on diminishing polarization, but, at a minimum, you will be contributing. Even if you don't want to do more, please know that how you act and see others in everyday life can make an important contribution. You never know when other people in your circle might become interested in your perspective or in broadening their viewpoints, and you can be an influential resource.

## APPLYING YOUR TALENTS TO ADDRESS OTHER FACTORS

*"Impossible is just a big word thrown around by small men who find it easier to live in the world they've been given than to explore the power they have to change it."—Muhammad Ali*

Taking on these big challenges will be hard to do on your own, so find others to work with. These could be community organizations or those who have a specific commitment to address the polarization challenge. Take on this challenge with a long-term view in the spirit of this wonderful thought by Dora Akunyili: "A society grows great when old men plant trees whose shade they know they shall never sit in."[6]

Reviewing the various forces in the graphic above, some will be more challenging to budge than others. On the tougher side, we would put financial insecurity and wealth disparities, distrust of governmental institutions, and segmentation among citizenry (urban versus rural, college graduates versus high school educated, elites versus working class). These are important areas we need to grapple with as a country, but they could also be starting places for individuals working to reduce the politics of contempt.

Another challenging area would be structural reforms such as money in politics, gerrymandering, and primary elections favoring candidates on the extremes. These topics need serious debate and consideration, but they will be difficult to affect unless we first find ways to have better conversations about politics.

Promoting civics education in schools might be on the "easy" side (although none of these are really easy). Getting involved with your school board or lobbying the state board of education or the state legislature could create a positive force for change. The goal could be to ensure that every high school student gets solid instruction on the rights and responsibilities of citizenship, how to vote, the different branches of government, and more.

Of course, people with different political perspectives will have different ideas as to what the program should look like, so nothing is ever simple. But with hope, hard work, and strong communication skills, it can be possible to find common ground on a shared approach and civics curriculum. This is one way a group of concerned citizens could have a big impact in their community.

Here are a few other areas where you might consider applying your talents to decrease negative influences or increase the positive forces. We combined a few of the factors into the clusters described below.

**Conflict entrepreneurs.** It is going to be hard to eliminate conflict entrepreneurs, but a potential way to diminish their influence would be to help yourself and others better understand how they operate and play on our fears. Creating well-designed educational campaigns could be a potentially impactful approach. Start with your personal commitment to applying critical thinking, and then find ways to share with others how we are being divided. While it is not always easy to differentiate, foreign influence is a big contributor. Who among us wants to be guided by the leadership of foreign countries that take advantage of social media to divide Americans? This could be a powerful way to drive positive change.

It is also possible to think in terms of channeling the conflict entrepreneur model into a more productive venture. Could profit and influence be achieved by depolarizing others? Could seeking social change be rechanneled in a way that results in respecting the dignity of all individuals? Could it be possible to create and promote civic entrepreneurs (including maybe yourself!) who work to create a more hopeful future?

**Healthier use of social media.** This cluster includes the negative impacts of social media algorithms and changes in the media environment alongside the positive force of those advocating for revisiting the use of social media. Changing the social media algorithms is obviously a big reach, but consider your personal use of social media. How much time do you spend each day and are you posting or commenting about politics or making negative comments about people who may disagree with you? There is a growing body of research that indicates that the widespread use of social media can be unhealthy for children and adults alike. In an interview, Princeton sociologist Zeynep Tufekci observed:

> "But if I weren't studying [social media], I would spend a lot less time on it because it is designed to waste your time. It is very specifically designed to draw you in and waste your time and it distorts your thinking. Social media is tribalizing. It's an in-group, out-group pushing environment—just trying to keep you there. It creates distortions in your thinking. If I were not also studying these things, I would limit my time on social media purely because I think it would make my thinking less useful. It would mislead me. It would distort my thinking and my emotions. Even when I'm studying it—because I need to understand something—I feel 'oh gosh, I have to take a break,' because I am a person too. I start having certain inaccurate impressions about the world that I know are just coming from social media."[7]

We can promote healthy use of social media, understanding of how the algorithms work, and how different media appeal to targeted groups. We won't easily change the media, but we can increase public awareness of how it operates. Encouraging people to spend less time on their cell phones can also be impactful.

Of course, social media can be used in positive and healthy ways if managed carefully. As Becky noted earlier, this includes expanding the reach of positive messages, such as promoting the ideas in this book through our *Together Across Differences* newsletter. We can make a positive difference when we choose to share our thoughts and expertise through social media posts with encouraging, helpful, and useful content.

**Empowering our American identity.** This cluster includes several factors. On the positive side:

- The exhausted majority is dissatisfied
- There is more common ground than believed
- Citizen leaders want change
- The power of the US Constitution

And on the negative side:

- Binary thinking and identity politics
- Citizen apathy

In *American Covenant: How the Constitution Unified Our Nation—and Could Again,* author Yuval Levin makes the argument that the US Constitution has exceptional power to help facilitate disagreements in a healthy way, enabling us to resolve disputes and help forge unity despite our deep divisions.[8] The Constitution enshrines our history and moves us forward together toward a more perfect union. Promoting a vision of a national identity on what it means to be American could be a powerful approach to this national challenge.

**Better politicians.** We noted the positive factor that many political leaders may be dissatisfied (but fear diverging from the party line), as well as these negative forces:

- Primary elections favor candidates on the extremes.
- Compromise, once considered positive, is seen negatively by many.
- Politicians rewarded by bad behavior.

We believe there is potential to work with candidates and elected officials to temper the national discord that is infecting our country. How often do we communicate with our elected officials when they do something right? Or speak up when we see them pandering to bullies or contributing to polarization?

We are heartened by feedback from elected state representatives after Braver Angels workshops in the New Hampshire House of Representatives, including these observations: "We can work together if we only will listen to the opposing view," "There is hope," "A wonderful way to find collaboration despite our differences," and "I was inspired by our collaboration and wish our constituents could see us." With the right approaches and relationships, efforts like these can be expanded across the country.

**Social skills and connections** is another cluster. Be creative and find the best path for you. Consider how you might take those ideas and up your game to more actively engage with others. Organizations such as Braver Angels offer a community of people eager to work on the issues that concern you.

To recap, carefully consider the possibilities and, if you want to step up, select the best path for you. Think global and then act local in the spirit of these powerful words from Lao Tzu:

*"The journey of a thousand miles begins with one step."*

## FOR FURTHER THOUGHT

- How might thinking global while acting local reduce our national division?
- In what ways do you want to apply your everyday actions and behaviors to the polarization problem?
- Which of the positive and negative factors driving political division do you think could be most easily influenced to reduce the politics of contempt?
- What path might you be ready to follow to help move our country in a positive direction?
- Are you willing to help lead others to address these challenges and, if so, how do you want to start?

Chapter 17

# EMBRACE THE COURAGE TO CHANGE AND GROW

> *"Whatever you can do, or dream you can, begin it. Boldness has genius, power, and magic in it!"*
> *—Johann Wolfgang von Goethe*

As you've realized by now, we encourage you to dig deep within yourself, embrace hope, and consider leading others to help better our country. We suggest finding ways to "rebuke the vilification of political opponents"[1]—pushing back when people on your side make derogatory comments about "those people" on the other side.

Then again, maybe "rebuke" is too strong a word if you are trying to convince people (including yourself) to see things in a different way. "Resist" might be a better word choice when you think of managing your own thoughts, and perhaps "oppose" works better when you engage in healthy conversations with others. But to be as effective as possible, please oppose others' ideas in a skillful way that includes listening and acknowledging before you move on to pivoting and offering your perspective.

This is hardly easy, but by embracing personal change, we can grow and develop the skills and confidence to make a difference in our own and other people's lives.

## ADOPTING PERSONAL CHANGE

*"A ship in harbor is safe—but that is not what ships are built for."*
*—John Shedd*

Change is a fundamental aspect of growing as a person, and embracing the ideas in this book may require you to think and act in new ways.

We hope you welcome this, but we recognize that changing ourselves is easier said than done—even if we really want to do it.

**From Doug** I love the cartoon of a man at a podium asking, "Who wants change?" with the assembled crowd enthusiastically raising their hands in response. But when the speaker asks, "Who wants *to* change?" they quietly look down at their feet.

We all—or at least most of us in the exhausted majority—want to see our country change in a way that embraces more kindness and respect for others. At the same time, it is human nature to want others to do the changing rather than us. But, like it or not, it needs to start with you and me.

We are all creatures of habit, so initiating personal change takes time and commitment. This is true even for simple changes. For example, about five years ago, I realized I had been tying my shoes incorrectly for many years. No wonder they kept coming untied! But even when I committed to changing, it took a conscious effort not to fall back on old habits.

Now, I finally get it mostly right.

If simple adjustments like how to tie a pair of shoes differently take that much effort, what about more significant changes—like really listening to those with different ideas or helping to better our country?

Change is hard, but on the other hand, who wants stagnation? Besides, even when we see ourselves as static, change is happening whether we plan for it or not. So, it is better to embrace change with a positive spirit! Understanding this can create space for personal growth. Jim Kouzes and Barry Posner observe: "You can't expect to become better at leadership, or anything else for that matter, without doing something different than you are currently doing."[2]

Three key aspects stand out for successfully implementing change: vision, planning, and discipline. Having a clear vision of what you want to achieve, and why you want to do it, is essential. This is also very helpful when the going gets tough, as it invariably does. Second is sound planning, which is a process of working through all the required steps. Plans are always subject to modification, of course, but it is important to embrace the five P's: prior planning prevents poor performance. Third is the discipline to carry through on implementation.

This is not a simple, straightforward process. It is important to continuously experiment, assess, and adjust your efforts. To sustain change, we need to adapt as we go along (which we could have included as a fourth step). "With each tweak and tinker, we learn, improve, and hone our next version—all while keeping our motivation alive," explains Kyra Bobinet, author of *Unstoppable Brain*.[3]

An even tougher challenge than changing ourselves is encouraging and inspiring others to change, including how they think about people with whom they disagree. Start with modeling the positive changes you want to see, which can benefit both those on your side of politics as well as others who see things differently. If we want "those people" to act more like "us," we better make sure "us" is a more attractive and better alternative!

We can inspire others to change by presenting a compelling vision for the future.[4] A kinder country will be pretty attractive for most people. As you go forward, keep in mind that change is a process that requires ongoing commitment and the discipline to stay with it. And it also requires courage.

## THE POWER OF MORAL COURAGE

*"Screw your courage to the sticking place and we'll not fail."—William Shakespeare*

Moral courage is the ability to act when facing popular opposition, indignity, or risk to personal reputation. It is being brave and confident enough to do what you believe is right. While we all admire courage in theory, enthusiasm may diminish when we actually need to apply it. After all, courage is risky!

Some fear is natural, especially when taking on as daunting a challenge as political polarization. Courage is not so much the absence of fear, but rather the ability to manage a situation despite having fear. One good strategy is to focus on your values instead of your fears.

**From Beth:** During the COVID pandemic, I remember being on a work call where my colleagues were voicing their frustrations about patients who weren't getting vaccinated. I understood where they were coming from. My colleagues were exhausted, and our ICU beds were filled to capacity. However, I saw things differently. I decided to speak up and share my viewpoint that people had lots of reasons for declining the vaccine. I suggested that we might want to ask people what their concerns were and address whatever it was that they brought up in plain language, such as the safety and effectiveness of the vaccines. It was scary, because who was I, a neurology sleep specialist, to bring up my opinion with ICU specialists and infectious disease doctors on the front lines of the pandemic? Fortunately, one of our institutional leaders jumped in and said that he agreed with me about being compassionate to patients who had questions. I really appreciated his support.

There are many forces that push to keep us divided and disincentivize us to speak up. People who fight for change may be ostracized or even lose their jobs. But when people manage the process well, they often see their reputations improve and their prominence rise.[5] Brené Brown describes the deep connection between courage and vulnerability, adding that daring leaders who live their values "are never silent about hard things."[6]

Unfortunately, courage can be challenging to fully internalize. It's not the sort of thing you can easily pick up in a book or at a workshop. Like many kinds of changes that help us grow, embracing courage requires an ongoing commitment. But we can choose to be courageous, focusing on meaningful connections with others and becoming more thoughtful and reflective. Addressing the polarization challenge involves connecting with others with authenticity and being true to your values.

Lady Macbeth goaded her husband to screw his courage to the sticking place in Shakespeare's famous play. While generally sound advice, it is not always simple or straightforward. A reckless approach can lead to overconfidence and poor decision-making, as happened to Mr. Macbeth. Winston Churchill once offered this powerful advice: "Courage is what it takes to stand up and speak; courage is also what it takes to sit down and listen."[7] Courage, too, includes expressing your opinion when you know it won't be popular, as well as admitting to both yourself and others when you make a mistake.

## RESILIENCY WHEN THE GOING GETS TOUGH

*"Life is always a tightrope or a feather bed. Give me the tightrope."*
*—Edith Wharton*

Resiliency is about both change and courage and amplifying them both over the long term. We know this work is challenging—that conflict entrepreneurs will push hard against positive change and will do all they can to keep us divided.

**From Becky** — Everyday life offers so many opportunities for resiliency. As a business owner, the COVID pandemic created so many disruptions to my plans. Nearly as soon as the world shut down, we lost one of our biggest clients, representing 10 percent of our annual income. I had a contract to buy and renovate a building as office space for my (then mostly local) team. Instead, I canceled the contract and gave up most of my leased office space. In order to preserve our employee team, we cut some contract staff. We worked on initiatives to serve our community during uncertain times, embarking on a daily webinar series, *Daily Connection,* that we produced for free to bring people together to discuss positive and uplifting topics. While we fell far short of where we hoped to be as a company, those stressful situations brought our team closer together.

---

A key to resiliency is having previously done the work of identifying your purpose and defining what is truly most important for you to do and achieve. Once you are clear about your plan for adopting change that will improve your life, your relationships, and our country, you will move forward in ways you truly embrace and believe in.

We love the poem "To Be of Use" by Marge Piercy, because it describes the people we want to be and the people we want to connect with. She describes people "who strain in the mud and the muck to move things forward" and "do what has to be done, again and again."[8] What has to be done, of course, is much more than paid employment; it incorporates all aspects of daily life, including health, family, friendships, and community involvement. This includes striving to demonstrate our key values and important personal characteristics such as kindness, authenticity, courage, wisdom, and treating others with dignity and respect.

There are many obstacles pushing against positive changes. Moving our country toward a better future will require resiliency. Please join the fight, but do so in the spirit that this will be a hard road with disappointments and setbacks—but also successes!

## WHAT ABOUT RISK?

*"It's a shallow life that doesn't give a person a few scars."*
*—Garrison Keillor*

You may be wondering: *What if I go all in and push back against the messages of conflict entrepreneurs and others fostering division? Identities around politics can run strong, and when they are threatened, however justly, there can be pushback.*

Physical courage—bravery in the face of pain, hardship, or threat of death—is obviously required of the military, police, firefighters, and some other workers. But should everyday people who strive to end polarization and national division need the same type of courage? Hopefully not, but we recognize there is some risk in this work, although hopefully not the physical kind. If people are upset with our message, we may lose friends, family members, or maybe even our reputation. No matter how positively we act, some people may feel threatened by this effort and could even be egged on by conflict entrepreneurs. The good news, if this happens, is that you are being effective. You are a change agent. Good for you!

**From Becky:** I find it risky as a business owner to let people know where I stand, unless I know where they stand already. For example, I often have potential clients with faith-related content. While it's easy for me to pass as an evangelical, it feels awkward because even though I can speak the language, I no longer fully live in that world. I am worried that if I speak openly about my beliefs, I'll lose business. It's similar to the way I felt in 2016 when most of my business connections lamented the presidential election results, and I felt the need to hide that I had voted Republican. It's far easier in 2024 to admit that I voted Republican in 2016 because I can follow up by saying I changed my mind.

---

If you are risk-averse and want to still make a difference, start small. Have a one-on-one conversation with someone you disagree with about politics or public policy. Maybe start with one family member or friend. And if the conversation doesn't go swimmingly, take a step back and talk about sports, or cooking, or whatever you have in common. Focus first on building the relationship and trust with the other person.

Psychologists Jamil Zaki and Luiza Santos offer this perspective:

"If you're like most people, you belong to an exhausted majority. You probably want greater cooperation, peace and freedom. You also might think that the people you disagree with want the opposite, and that political disaster is inevitable. Scientists like us treat this despair not by lying to people, but by telling them the truth. As long as we let conflict entrepreneurs guide us, we will loathe each other, escalate and give up on anything better. If we instead follow the data, we can realize that the great majority of Americans want something better. A more hopeful future can come into focus."[9]

Take courage and consider this thought from Ralph Waldo Emerson: "The purpose of life is not to be happy. It is to be useful, to be honorable, to be compassionate, to have it make some difference that you have lived and lived well."

## WHAT ABOUT YOUR HEALTH?

*"We cannot hope to experience peace in the world, if we do not have peace in our life."—Headspace meditation*

We have been writing about changing our country for the better and building positive relationships, which are both incredibly important goals. There is another aspect of this that is even more significant. And that is personal health, especially mental health. People with the strongest opinions about politics may be at risk of undermining their health and well-being which can negatively impact relationships with others. Not only do we not want to endanger our health, but it is difficult to positively influence others if we are not in a healthy place ourselves.

**From Doug** I can easily get upset about national and world events, such as the war in Ukraine, where I once lived. At the same time, I have come to understand that getting overly upset can lead to reduced sleep and undermine my health. One special aspect of writing this book is that it has given me a way to take meaningful action. I need to keep reminding myself to avoid getting distracted by other things, especially what I cannot control or influence. I have chosen my path, and I strive to stay focused and mindful, which helps me feel better.

How are you reacting to events in our country? Are you happy about the results of the 2024 election? If so, maybe your health is in a good place. Or, if you are gloating at those on the losing side with a zeal that provokes and upsets others, maybe not so much. Are you honoring the dignity of others and expressing respect for others in healthy ways?

What if your candidate was on the losing side? Are you acting angrier or more upset than before the election? Are you sometimes yelling at the television when certain politicians appear? Have your feelings impacted other aspects of your life, such as relationships with family, friends, or coworkers? Has your reaction made you irritable or changed the way you approach common tasks unrelated to politics, such as waiting in line or sitting in traffic?

We can be quick to blame others for our emotional state: It is all Donald Trump's or Joe Biden's fault. This tendency to blame is more likely if we are operating in a bubble of people with the same opinions and reactions. We can fall into a pattern of validating the opinions of others who agree with us, and they may do the same with respect to us. This kind of back-and-forth may be attractive in a superficial way, but it can agitate us further.

There is a benefit to having our beliefs scrutinized and challenged. It's an opportunity to explore and even solidify our own values, which are bound to shift with time and experience. Avoid viewing this process as a threat but instead as an opportunity for self-inquiry. Are you acting in alignment with your values and with understanding that the values of others may be different from yours? This perspective can help improve your state of mind.

We see activism such as participating in peaceful protests, writing letters to the editor, supporting political campaigns, and running for office as generally positive steps—if they are done in the spirit of treating others with dignity and respect. Name-calling, shaming others, and angry outbursts fall into the kinds of negative behaviors that could potentially undermine your health. And you probably won't win any people over to your side either.

We don't control the actions of others; we only control our responses. How would responding versus reacting impact your sense of well-being? What do you gain from each experience, and what do you lose? We need to take responsibility for our behaviors and reactions, starting from a place of how we see and think about others. It is so much easier to blame others for our own bad behavior.

We each need to own our reactions to events, especially when they veer into unhealthy feelings and actions. This includes embracing mindfulness and stepping back to reflect on what we could do better. Getting help from others (such as a therapist) can also be helpful.

## YOU WILL MAKE OUR COUNTRY BETTER!

*"What is it you plan to do with your one wild and precious life?"*
*—Mary Oliver*

One possible answer to this question from Oliver's poem "The Summer Day" comes from author Carlos Castaneda:

> "For me there is only the traveling on the paths that have a heart, on any path that may have a heart. There I travel, and the only worthwhile challenge for me is to traverse its full length. And there I travel—looking, looking, breathlessly."[10]

To preserve our Union, we must drive in the direction of Hope (and later maybe we can take a nice hot Bath!). (Maine state highway photo by Doug Teschner.)

Our path with a heart is connecting with people across the political divide to strengthen relationships and diminish the polarization that threatens the future of our nation. Of course, it is presumptuous for us to think this goal is a high priority for your one precious life. Still, you have read this book to the end, so we take that as a sign that you are interested—even if maybe not breathlessly! How might you help better our troubled country?

We found inspiration listening to the *On Being* podcast describing ways to overcome conflict and build trust. Host Krista Tippett and her guest Amanda Ripley talked about spiritual work that can bring hope, dignity, faith, joy, and wonder to situations where there is intolerance of others.[11]

On another *On Being* podcast episode, Mary Catherine Bateson offered this perspective:

> "I like to think of men and women as artists of their own lives, working with what comes to hand through accident or talent to compose and recompose a pattern in time that expresses who they are and what they believe in, making meaning even as they are studying and working and raising children, creating and recreating themselves."[12]

Robert Putnam adds that we're not going to fix polarization or other big problems until we start feeling that we have an obligation to care for other people.[13] After all, the bottom line in life is the quality of our relationships and connections with others: how we touch and influence people and how they touch and influence us. The rest is just details.

Are you ready to make a personal plan to take the ideas in this book and move forward as the artist of your life? You can paint a picture of a special future for you and those close to you as well as for our special country.

## MAKE A PERSONAL PLAN, THEN IMPLEMENT IT

*"The first place to look for leadership is within yourself." —Jim Kouzes and Barry Posner*

Creating a personal plan starts with consideration of what interests and excites you, what your talents are, and what you would like to learn. In the appendix there is a checklist with the key ideas in this book. The checklist includes Looking Inward areas, where you might best develop and improve yourself, as well as Acting Outward categories where you can take positive action with others. Take some time to review that list and identify a few areas where you want to focus.

As part of this process, you might want to get input from friends, family, and other trusted people. Go back to the relevant chapters or seek out other resources to break your plan into manageable steps. By the end of this process (which you might want to do over several days or even weeks), you will hopefully have a clearer idea of how to improve your health and well-being, build positive relationships, and strengthen our country.

Then, move forward in the spirit of doing something bigger than yourself, with resolve and confidence. Periodically reassess your plan and make adjustments, reaching out to others for help. Be sure to check back on items you are hesitant to make happen in the spirit of this thought from Scott Mautz: "Many of the things in life that we hope for, dream for, long for, never come to fruition because of invisible barriers that we put up ourselves."[14]

## IT'S GOING TO GET BETTER, BUT WE NEED TO START NOW

*"For there is always light, if only we're brave enough to see it, if only we're brave enough to be it."—Amanda Gorman*

A favorite book is *The Man Who Planted Trees,* a powerful fable about a man who spent his life planting one hundred acorns each day in a barren area of southern France.[15] As a result, the landscape was transformed over time from devoid of life to a vibrant nature with much happier inhabitants.

OK, maybe some find this a bit Pollyanna-ish, but we believe that everyday people can plant seeds of change that will grow and flourish, transforming our lives and country for the better. Yes, the cynics will raise their eyebrows, but we offer a positive vision in the spirit of these words from Mahatma

Gandhi: "A small body of determined spirits, fired by an unquenchable faith in their mission, can alter the course of history."[16]

---

**From Doug** I took a day off from writing for an October hike up Mount Osceola in the New Hampshire White Mountains. While driving to the trailhead through beautiful foliage and inspiring views of snow-capped peaks, I pulled out an old Genesis CD—a long-ago gift from my son who remembered as a young child hearing these same songs on my pickup truck cassette player.

I hadn't listened to Genesis in a while and was struck by the inspiring energy in the final track "It's Gonna Get Better." The 1983 lyrics seem so relevant to today's challenges, calling me to shout out and reach up with my hands in the air and keep hoping that things will get better. The song goes on that making things better can start with a feeling and will take time. But we need to start, because we know it's time for change.[17]

---

Will you join us? Please reach out with your hands in the air!

*"Savor your existence. Live every moment. Do not waste a breath."*
*—Nando Parrado*

## FOR FURTHER THOUGHT

- What do you want to do next in your one wild and precious life?
- How might you want to change and grow, and what would help you get started?
- How can you be more courageous and resilient when facing opposition, threats, or risk to personal reputation?
- What is your path with a heart and what seeds of change are you willing to plant?
- What can help you develop and implement a personal plan to strengthen your health and well-being, build relationships, and help change our country for the better?

Now that you have finished reading this book, what are you going to do first? Here is one final thought:

Perhaps the most important first step in helping change our country for the better is to build a new relationship with one person who voted on the other side of the political divide. Reach out and have coffee. Learn about their family, childhood and school experiences, work and career, hobbies, and other interests. Be curious and respectful, ask questions, and learn about that person's life experiences and why they vote and think the way they do. And, of course, share your story. Your lives can be enriched, as will our nation. Positive change, starting two people at a time.

APPENDIX

# ADDITIONAL RESOURCES AND INFORMATION

> *"May our children and our children's children to a thousand generations, continue to enjoy the benefits conferred upon us by a united country."*
> —Abraham Lincoln

**Together Across Differences.** For updated information on the ideas on this book, please subscribe to the free *Together Across Differences* newsletter at https://togethernow.substack.com/. The authors and other thought leaders use this platform to update information in the book and share much more on how we can contribute to building a nation of kindness, dignity, and respect.

**Voter stories.** After the 2024 election, we interviewed a variety of people across the country with a range of political perspectives. You can find these interesting stories on the *Beyond the Politics of Contempt* book website (beyondthepoliticsofcontempt.com).

**Hope in action: Braver Politics in a state legislature.** Throughout the book, we shared stories of our volunteer work with Braver Angels, including workshops and the creation of a bipartisan caucus in the New Hampshire House of Representatives. More details on this Braver Politics effort are included on the Together Across Differences Substack at togethernow.substack.com.

In the following pages, you will find these additional sections:

- **A Checklist for Changing Yourself and Our Country**—A summary of the key points in this book
- **Braver Angels**—Information on this leading national organization working to bridge the political divide and diminish polarization
- **Other Organizations**—A sample of additional groups that are working to address these issues

# A CHECKLIST FOR CHANGING YOURSELF AND OUR COUNTRY (A SUMMARY OF THE KEY POINTS IN THIS BOOK)

*"Nothing good happens by accident."*—Ken Blanchard

Below we summarize the key ideas and suggestions in this book in the form of a checklist. Please go through and pick what seems most relevant to you and where you think you can make a difference. Initially, think broadly: check areas where you are comfortable, but also consider stretching to learn and try new things that could be impactful.

You can put a question mark next to an idea if you are not sure, use double X's for highest priorities, rate items from 1 to 3—whatever works best for you!

We divided this checklist into categories under two major headings: Looking Inward and Acting Outward.

First, prioritize the Looking Inward areas where you think you can best develop and improve yourself. Consider one to three areas you think are most important to work on first, and perhaps mark other items that could be in your phase 2 plan. We realize that there is some overlap across the listed items so feel free to combine or edit if this feels helpful for you.

Second, try to prioritize three to five areas in the Acting Outward categories. Maybe mark others for the future.

While it might be tempting to do all the Inward items before taking on the Outward list, we believe you can work on both at the same time. Just resist getting in too far on the more challenging second list items until you are confident you have a good grasp on the most relevant items in the first list. Good luck!

## LOOKING INWARD
## Thinking and Seeing Differently

_____ Consider how you might be more kind in daily life, including avoiding making assumptions about other people.

_____ Review how often you think in terms of "us versus them" or find yourself speaking with disdain toward those on the other side of the political divide. How might you see others differently?

_____ Consider situations when you may have criticized others without a heart to help and how you might want to act differently in the future.

_____ Take proactive steps to expand your recognition of the positive work of others.

_____ Internalize a mindset of dignity and respect for those with different political beliefs.

_____ Embrace more openness and curiosity about those who have different ideas and opinions.

_____ Consider how you can separate advocating for policy positions from disparaging people who have contrary opinions.

_____ Identify your top values, reflect on how consistently you apply them, and consider what you might do differently to narrow any gap.

_____ Consider ways to increase empathy, authenticity, vulnerability, and gratitude in your daily life.

## Increase Your Knowledge and Understanding of the Forces Driving Polarization

_____   Clearly understand the difference between healthy and unhealthy conflict.

_____   Increase your awareness of factors creating unhealthy conflict and division, and especially how they may be influencing you.

_____   Consider where you might fit on the Hidden Tribes spectrum, focusing on whether you are in a wing group or the exhausted majority and whether you might want to change.

_____   Review how social change happens and consider how your talents might apply.

## Reflect on How You Are Being Influenced in Unhealthy Ways

_____   Identify forces driving division that are most influential in your daily life.

_____   Consider whether you may be contributing to the polarization problem and, if so, what might you do differently.

_____   Reflect on your use of media and social media, how these are influencing you, and whether you might want to make changes.

_____   Consider the extent to which you may be influenced by misinformation or disinformation and if you are experiencing barriers to critical thinking.

_____   Consider whether you fall into behavior of shaming others or encouraging/admiring those who shame others.

_____   Reflect on whether the political divide is negatively impacting your health and what steps you could take to become healthier.

_____   Consider whether politics is negatively impacting your relationships with family, friends, or others, and what steps you could take to improve these relationships.

## Build on Your Life History

_____ Reflect on the decisions that shaped who you are today and actions you took that impacted others.

_____ Reviewing your personal history and life experiences, identify future steps where you might contribute to positive change.

_____ Consider the needs of your community and how you could promote citizen-led solutions and perhaps become a civic entrepreneur.

_____ Decide to invest more time and energy in personal self-development.

_____ Review the forces (both positive and negative) impacting our country and identify areas where you might best build on past life experiences to help reduce polarization.

## Embrace the Courage to Change and Grow

_____ Consider how you could contribute to a moral reawakening in our country.

_____ Identify why and how you might want to change, and what would help you get started.

_____ Examine how your willingness to change aligns with your personal goals and values.

_____ Consider how you can be more courageous and resilient when there may be risk or setbacks.

_____ Identify and implement steps to embrace more moral courage when facing popular opposition, indignity, or risk to personal reputation.

## ACTING OUTWARD
### Develop Key Skills

_____ Raise up your self-leadership skills and model positive behaviors that can influence others.

_____ Improve your ability to engage in courageous conversations using LAPP skills: listening, acknowledgment, pivot, and perspective.

_____ Strengthen your critical thinking skills to address the polarization challenge.

_____ Develop your capacity and skills for effectively leading others.

_____ Develop confidence and practice in standing up to people on your own political side when facing pushback for engaging with those with different political viewpoints.

### Apply New Skills for Both Impact and Self-Improvement

_____ Seek opportunities to connect rather than engaging in fight, flight, or avoidance when facing difficult conversations.

_____ Apply the braver conversation skills in interactions with family, friends, neighbors, and strangers.

_____ Seek out and engage with people who have political opinions different from yours.

_____ Positively engage with work colleagues whose political views are different from your own.

_____ Think global and act local to develop a personal path to help address the polarization challenge.

_____ If you are inclined toward political activism, integrate a bridge-building component.

## Offer Your Leadership Talents

_____ Consider how you might apply vision, relationship building, and persistence to build a positive result in your community or state.

_____ Model behavior as a change leader that will inspire others to act in ways that will better our country.

_____ Make a plan to develop trust, promote a climate of purpose and connection, and attract others to the cause.

_____ Listen and empathize with both allies and adversaries, giving voice to grievances and concerns.

_____ Lead change by communicating emotional, visceral messages to move hearts and minds, offering more enticing appeals than those of conflict entrepreneurs.

_____ Proactively reach out to individuals and organizations, advocating in a positive way in the face of potential obstacles.

_____ Work with businesses to elicit their support to actively help bridge the national divide.

_____ Publicly challenge the messages of conflict entrepreneurs or apply their methods in a more positive way to become a civic entrepreneur.

## Join Organizations and Groups Addressing the Polarization Challenge

_____ Embrace the concept that people who join organizations can foster a moral reawakening in our country.

_____ Educate yourself about Braver Angels and other organizations that are addressing the polarization challenge.

_____ Find your niche within an organization. For example, in Braver Angels, there are countless opportunities, including being an ambassador, organizer, workshop moderator, leader of a local alliance, and more.

# BRAVER ANGELS

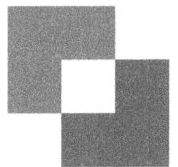

Braver Angels (https://braverangels.org/) was founded in 2016 by David Blankenhorn, Bill Doherty, and David Lapp. A national citizens' movement, it brings Americans together to bridge the partisan divide and strengthen our democratic republic. This nonprofit organization envisions an America with a respectful embrace of political disagreements, where civic friendship flourishes and competing perspectives strengthen our nation. Embracing values of respect, humility, honesty, and responsible citizenship, the goal is not to change people's views of issues, but to change their views of each other.

Braver Angels leadership is structured to ensure balance among people who lean red, blue, and purple. Key principles are described in "The Braver Angels Way":

- We state our views freely and fully, without fear.
- We treat people who disagree with us with honesty, dignity, and respect.
- We welcome opportunities to engage those with whom we disagree.
- We believe all of us have blind spots and none of us are not worth talking to.
- We seek to disagree accurately, avoiding exaggeration and stereotypes.
- We look for common ground where it exists and, if possible, find ways to work together.

Braver Angels offers free debates, structured one-on-one conversations, and a variety of workshops (both in-person and online) on topics such as "Skills for Disagreeing Better" and "Families and Politics." These include practical ways to better manage conversations with family, friends, and work colleagues. For example, the "Depolarizing Within" workshop focuses on:

- Becoming more aware of your own inner polarizer and finding ways to counteract that impulse.
- Learning how to be critical without stereotyping, dismissing, ridiculing, or showing contempt.
- Building skills for intervening in a constructive way in social conversations that veer into contempt and ridicule for people who hold other political views.

There is also a shorter forty-minute online version.

Braver Angels has volunteer-led chapters (called alliances) throughout the country and offers diverse initiatives that support citizens, schools and universities, elected officials, and churches and faith organizations. The Braver Network initiative brings organizations from across the country together to help grow and spread a social movement for bridging the partisan divide.

To learn more or join Braver Angels, please scan this QR Code:

https://bit.ly/bpocbook

# OTHER ORGANIZATIONS

There are many organizations across the country working on the ideas in this book from a variety of perspectives. A significant number are aligned with Braver Angels as members of the Braver Network (see https://braverangels.org/braver-network/). The list below is a small sample and not intended to be comprehensive. We anticipate that additional organizations will be created after the publication of this book.

**BridgeUSA** empowers young people to engage in constructive dialogue and disagreement to improve the quality of politics. With college and high school chapters throughout the country, this group champions understanding, empathy, open-mindedness, and a willingness to engage those who are different from oneself (https://bridgeusa.org/).

**Builders** (formerly Starts with Us) works to equip citizens to overcome toxic polarization and solve our toughest problems together. Its approach is to reach and teach people at scale, equip them with new skills and innovative tools, and mobilize grassroots civics to hold political leaders accountable (https://buildersmovement.org/).

**Civity** supports leaders and community organizations through in-person and online trainings and in-depth coaching sessions focused on intentionality, authenticity, story-sharing, and putting differences on the table. They recognize first-hand the need for creating a culture and building institutions in which everyone has what they need to thrive (https://www.civity.org/).

**Living Room Conversations** connects people within communities and across differences to build trust and understanding. Its conversational model is designed to create a welcoming environment where people can respectfully discuss important issues. The model creates opportunities that allow everyone to feel seen and heard while celebrating the differences that make us all unique (https://livingroomconversations.org/).

**More in Common** works to address the underlying drivers of fracturing and polarization and build more united, resilient, and inclusive societies in which people believe that what they have in common is stronger than what divides them. Focusing on several priority countries, the group's work starts with collecting data about experiences, values, fears, and hopes, engaging people through surveys, interviews, focus groups, community conversations, and expert interviews. Its groundbreaking Hidden Tribes report is often cited in this book (https://www.moreincommon.com/).

**More Like Us** works to correct dangerous political misperceptions of each other at scale. It targets the information environment to change how Americans see and feel about each other across politics, providing guidance and resources to sectors including education, journalism, and the arts (https://www.morelikeus.org/).

**National Institute for Civil Discourse** is a University of Arizona initiative founded in 2011 after the Tucson shooting that killed six people and injured former Congresswoman Gabrielle Giffords. The group has a focus on studying and supporting efforts to improve the quality of civil conversation (https://nicd.arizona.edu/).

**No Labels** is a national organization of Democrats, Republicans, and independents working to bring American leaders together to solve the nation's problems. No Labels believes that America's "commonsense majority" needs to work together to ensure elected officials hear the voice of the middle ground. No Labels supported creation of the Problem Solvers Caucus in the U.S. House of Representatives (https://nolabels.org/).

**The Dignity Index** is designed to prevent violence, ease divisions, and solve problems by drawing our attention away from the biases of partisan politics and toward the power we each have to heal our country and each other. The index scores distinct phrases along an eight-point scale from contempt to dignity. Lower scores (1 to 4) reflect divisive language while higher scores (5 to 8) reflect language grounded in dignity. In its pilot season, a trained group of students scored selections from candidate speeches, debates, fundraising outreach, social media posts, and campaign ads (https://www.dignity.us/).

**The People** gathers and enables everyday Americans to find common ground and take action together to create a government that is truly of, by, and for the people. For example, its New Hampshire Together initiative brought citizens together to develop election and legislative reform proposals (https://www.thepeople.org/).

**The Village Square** is dedicated to bridging divides through discussion and spirited disagreement. The organization spearheads a variety of programming centered around civility and community-building, both locally in Florida and through assisting communities nationally to support civility efforts (https://tlh.villagesquare.us/).

**The Listen First Project** is the backbone organization for the movement to bridge divides in America. It supports a coalition of more than 500 organizations bringing Americans together across divides to build understanding, trust, relationships, and solutions to turn down the heat and find a way forward together. Seeing an escalating crisis of toxic polarization and believing the best way to turn the tide is by working together, four bridging organizations (Listen First Project, Village Square, Living Room Conversations, and National Institute for Civil Discourse) created the #ListenFirst Coalition in 2017 to aggregate, align, and amplify many diffuse bridging efforts (https://www.listenfirstproject.org/).

# Endnotes

## INTRODUCTION

1. "New Hampshire Community Profiles," New Hampshire Employment Security, Economic & Labor Market Information Bureau, accessed May 4, 2025, https://www.nhes.nh.gov/elmi/products/cp/.
2. Becky Robinson, *Reach: Create the Biggest Possible Audience for Your Message, Book, or Cause* (Berrett-Koehler Publishers, 2022).
3. "The Hidden Tribes of America: A Year-Long Project of More in Common Launched in October 2018," *Hidden Tribes,* accessed May 4, 2025, https://hiddentribes.us/.
4. "Mahatma Ghandi," Wikiquote, accessed April 30, 2025, https://en.wikiquote.org/wiki/Mahatma_Gandhi.

## CHAPTER 1

1. Frank Bruni, *The Age of Grievance* (Avid Reader Press/Simon & Schuster, 2024).
2. Jacob Hess, "If You Could Escape All the Anger About Politics, Would You Want To?" *Deseret News,* October 15, 2024, https://bit.ly/43ZYhlr.
3. Gary Fields and Linley Sanders, "Americans Agree That the 2024 Election Will Be Pivotal for Democracy, but for Different Reasons," *AP News,* modified December 15, 2023, https://apnews.com/article/democracy-2024-election-trump-biden-poll-39309519c8473175c25ab5a305e629ba.
4. "2024 Presidential Election: Biden Two Percentage Points Over Trump, but Conventional Wisdom Comes Into Question," Marist Poll, April 3, 2024, https://maristpoll.marist.edu/polls/april-2024-presidential-election/.
5. Andrew Prokop, "Here's how many Republicans don't want their kids to marry Democrats," *Vox,* September 23, 2014, https://www.vox.com/xpress/2014/9/23/6828715/heres-how-many-republicans-dont-want-their-kids-to-marry-democrats.
6. *Merriam-Webster Dictionary,* "2024 Word of the Year: Polarization," December 9, 2024, https://www.merriam-webster.com/wordplay/word-of-the-year.

7. As we use the term *polarization* in this book, we are focused primarily on affective polarization. *Toxic polarization* is another term that aligns closely with affective polarization. For more information on the distinction between ideological and affective polarization, see Shanto Iyengar, et al., "The Origins and Consequences of Affective Polarization in the United States," *Annual Review of Political Science* 22, no. 1 (2019): 129–146, https://.doi:10.1146/annurev-polisci-051117-073034.
8. Mónica Guzmán, *I Never Thought of it That Way: How to Have Fearlessly Curious Conversations in Dangerously Divided Times* (BenBella Books, 2022), xxii.
9. Brittany Longsdorf, panelist, Maine Calling radio show, "Finding a Sense of Hope When the News all Around Us Is Bleak," July 15, 2022, 50 min., 24 sec., https://www.mainepublic.org/show/maine-calling/2022-07-15/finding-a-sense-of-hope-when-the-news-all-around-us-is-bleak.
10. Rhitu Chatterjee, "Stressed About Politics? Here Are 5 Ways to Take Care of Your Mental Health," *Health News,* NPR.org, July 19, 2024, https://www.npr.org/sections/shots-health-news/2024/07/18/nx-s1-5041980/politics-election-anxiety-mental- health-tips.
11. "2024 Presidential Election," Marist Poll.
12. Doris Kearns Goodwin, "Our Last Great Adventure," *Atlantic,* May 2024, https://bit.ly/3SBJF5n.
13. Thomas Friedman, "Optimism in Tough Times," *New York Times,* September 25, 2005.
14. Krista Tippett, "On Hope," *Orion* magazine, March 2, 2020, https://orionmagazine.org/article/on-hope/.
15. Yuval Levin, "Online Conversation: Is There an American Covenant? With Yuval Levin," conversation with Cherie Harder, The Trinity Forum, YouTube video and transcript, 55 min., 53 sec., November 1, 2024, https://ttf.org/portfolios/online-conversation-american-covenant-with-yuval-levin/.

## CHAPTER 2

1. Peggy Noonan, "We Are Starting to Enjoy Hatred: The Country Has Long Been Divided, but Estrangement Has Become Alluring in the Age of Biden and Trump," *Wall Street Journal,* May 30, 2024, https://www.wsj.com/opinion/we-are-starting-to-enjoy-hatred-c3005b05.
2. David Brooks, "How America Got Mean: In a Culture Devoid of Moral Education, Generations Are Growing Up in a Morally Inarticulate, Self-referential World," *Atlantic,* August 14, 2023.

3. Laura Kwerel, "A Woman Undergoing Chemotherapy Gets a Special Message from a Stranger," NPR.org, June 11, 2024, https://www.npr.org/2024/06/11/nx-s1-4996500/chemotherapy-cancer-stranger-unsung-hero-good-news.
4. Laura Kwerel, "She Was Terrified Waiting for Surgery. Then Her Anesthesiologist Began to Sing," My Unsung Hero, NPR.org, October 22, 2024, https://www.npr.org/2024/10/21/nx-s1-5159740/anesthesiologist-surgery-good-news-kindness.
5. Ian Lenahan, "Bowl-O-Rama Manager Takes on 'Rude,' 'Abusive' Customers," *NH Business Review*, September 10, 2021, https://read.nhbr.com/nh-business-review/2021/09/10/#?article=3865927.
6. Miss Manners, "Miss Manners: Are People Oblivious or Just Plain Rude When It Comes to Sports Etiquette?," NJ.com, February 19, 2024, https://www.nj.com/advice/2024/02/miss-manners-are-people-oblivious-or-just-plain-rude-when-it-comes-to-sports-etiquette.html.
7. Peter D'Auria, "Final Reading: Health Care Workers Still Face Threats and Attacks in Vermont's Hospitals, Advocates Say," *VTDigger,* March 12, 2025, https://vtdigger.org/2025/03/12/final-reading-health-care-workers-still-face-threats-and-attacks-in-vermonts-hospitals-advocates-say/.
8. Ronald Bourque, "The Discordant Epidemic: Collaboration Is So Much Better and More Productive than Fighting," *NH Business Review,* Dec. 15, 2023.
9. "We Just Disagree," Dave Mason, *Let It Flow,* Columbia, 1977.
10. Arthur C. Brooks, *Love Your Enemies; How Decent People Can Save America from the Culture of Contempt* (Broadside Books, 2019), 13.
11. James Heffernan, "There's a Difference Between Intifada and Genocide" *Valley News,* December 16, 2023.
12. Mónica Guzmán, *I Never Thought of it That Way: How to Have Fearlessly Curious Conversations in Dangerously Divided Times* (BenBella Books, 2022), 45.
13. Kelly Corrigan, "Going Deep with Judd Apatow on Women, Collaboration and How Funny Works," *Kelly Corrigan Wonders* podcast, September 3, 2024, https://play.prx.org/listen?ge=prx_338_4642f2a5-21d5-48b4-b415-8e7653e26ee2&uf=https%3A%2F%2Ffeeds.feedburner.com%2FKellyCorriganWonders.

## CHAPTER 3

1. Derek Black's story is the subject of Pulitzer Prize-winning journalist Eli Saslow's 2018 book, *Rising Out of Hatred* (Doubleday, 2018).
2. "Center for Politics Study: Partisan Desires Override Support for Constitutional Freedoms and American Values," The Center for Politics, October 18, 2023,

https://centerforpolitics.org/crystalball/center-for-politics-study-indicates-many-americans-favor-actions-that-challenge-constitutional- bounds-to-serve-partisan-aims/.
3. Paige Sutherland and Meghna Chakrabarti, "How Can Politicians Better Serve the American People? Senator Andy Kim Has Some Ideas," interview with Andy Kim, *On Point* (radio show), WBUR, December 17, 2024, https://www.wbur.org/onpoint/2024/12/17/senator-andy-kim-politicians-new-jersey.
4. Mark M. Beckwith, *Seeing the Unseen: Beyond Prejudices, Paradigms, and Party Lines* (Morehouse Publishing, 2022), 55.
5. Beckwith, *Seeing the Unseen*, 59.
6. German Lopez, "George W. Bush in Dallas: 'Too often we judge other groups by their worst examples,'" *Vox*, July 12, 2016, https://www.vox.com/2016/7/12/12164176/george-bush-dallas-shooting-speech-video.
7. Beth's story is referenced in more detail in the following article: Mónica Guzmán, "Confronting Our COVID Condescension," September 20, 2021, https://braverangels.org/confronting-our-covid-condescension/.
8. Asia Tabb, "Braver Angels: How to Prepare for the Election," interview including Nita Landis, Mónica Guzmán, and Chris Hausner, *The Spark*, WITF, October 4, 2024. https://www.witf.org/2024/10/04/braver-angels-how-to-prepare-for-the-election/.
9. David Keen, "Personal and Political Shaming Is Running Hot, Yet It Doesn't Work," *Psyche*, February 8, 2024, https://psyche.co/ideas/personal-and-political-shaming-is-running-hot-yet-it-doesnt-work.
10. Ellie Lisitsa, "The Four Horsemen: Contempt," *Gottman Relationship* Blog, Gottman Institute, last modified Dec 11, 2024, https://www.gottman.com/blog/the-four-horsemen-contempt/.

## CHAPTER 4

1. Alejandra O'Connell-Domench, "Politics Are Increasingly Becoming a Dating Dealbreaker—Especially for Women," *The Hill*, March 25, 2023, https://thehill.com/changing-america/enrichment/arts-culture/3917348-politics-are-increasingly-a-dating-dealbreaker-especially-for-women/.
2. David Brooks, "America is Having a Moral Convulsion," *Atlantic*, October 5, 2020, https://www.theatlantic.com/ideas/archive/2020/10/collapsing-levels-trust-are-devastating-america/616581/.
3. Amanda Ripley, *High Conflict: Why We Get Trapped and How We Get Out* (Simon & Schuster, 2021).
4. Ripley, *High Conflict*, 279.

5. Ripley, *High Conflict,* xi.
6. Ira Glass, host, *This American Life* podcast, episode 478, 26:39, "Red State Blue State," November 2, 2012, WBEZ Chicago, https://www.thisamericanlife.org/November 2, 2012.
7. "Bringing Brave Spaces to Higher Education," Dartmouth College, September 26, 2024, https://home.dartmouth.edu/news/2024/09/bringing-brave-spaces-higher-education.
8. David Blankenhorn, *In Search of Braver Angels: Getting Along Together in Troubled Times* (Braver Angels, 2022), 10–4.
9. Governor Spencer Cox, "How to Disagree with Respect—Not Hate," TED Talk, Vancouver, Canada, April 2024, 12 min., 16 sec., https://www.ted.com/talks/spencer_j_cox_how_to_disagree_with_respect_not_hate?utm_campaign=tedspread& utm_medium=referral&utm_source=tedcomshare.
10. Jason Swensen, "Eager to Cool the Political Heat? It's Possible, Say University of Utah Researchers and Others," *Deseret News,* November 5, 2024, https://www.deseret.com/utah/2024/11/05/elections-university-of-utah-politics-toxic-stanford-research-misperceptions/.
11. Governor Spencer Cox, delegation speech, Utah Republican State Convention, Salt Lake City, Utah, April 27, 2024.
12. Don Bacon, "The Other Party Isn't the Enemy," *Wall Street Journal,* opinion, September 9, 2024, https://www.wsj.com/opinion/the-other-party-isnt-the-enemy-rep-don-bacon-american-before-republican-8104de0f.
13. Ripley, *High Conflict,* 73.
14. Andru Volinsky, "Fear of Political Reprisal and Updates on School Funding Litigation," *A Book, an Idea, and a Goat Substack,* September 25, 2024, https://andruvolinsky.substack.com/p/fear-of-political-reprisal-and-updates?utm_source=post-email.
15. *Merriam-Webster Dictionary,* "activism," accessed April 20, 2025, https://bit.ly/43Zha86.

## CHAPTER 5

1. Jonathan Haidt, *The Righteous Mind: Why Good People Are Divided by Politics and Religion* (Vintage Books, 2012), xxiii.
2. Ezra Klein, *Why We're Polarized* (Avid Reader Press/Simon & Schuster, 2020), xiv.
3. News Editor, "New Data Show How the Pandemic Affected Learning Across Whole Communities," *Harvard Graduate School of Education News,* May 11, 2023, https://bit.ly/455T4K1.

4. Rakesh Kochhar, "The State of the American Middle Class: Who Is in It and Key Trends from 1970 to 2023," Pew Research Center, May 31, 2024, https://www.pewresearch.org/race-and-ethnicity/2024/05/31/the-state-of-the-american-middle-class/.
5. Board of Governors of the Federal Reserve System, *Economic Well-Being of U.S. Households in 2023* (Washington, DC: Board of Governors, 2024), https://www.federalreserve.gov/publications/files/2023-report-economic-well-being-us-households-202405.pdf.
6. Bureau of Labor Statistics, U.S. Department of Labor, *The Economics Daily*, "Median Weekly Earnings $946 for Workers with High School Diploma, $1533 for Bachelor's Degree," accessed November 25, 2025, https://www.bls.gov/opub/ted/2024/median-weekly-earnings-946-for-workers-with-high-school-diploma-1533-for-bachelors-degree.htm.
7. US Census Bureau, "Census Bureau Releases New Educational Attainment Data," news release, February 16, 2023, https://www.census.gov/newsroom/press-releases/2023/educational-attainment-data.html.
8. Peggy Noonan, "Trump and the Rise of the Unprotected: Why Political Professionals are Struggling to Make Sense of the World They Created," *Wall Street Journal*, February 25, 2016, https://www.wsj.com/articles/trump-and-the-rise-of-the-unprotected-1456448550.
9. Emily Schmidt, "Reading the Numbers: 130 Million American Adults Have Low Literacy Skills, but Funding Differs Drastically by State," APM Research Lab, March 16, 2022, https://www.apmresearchlab.org/10x-adult-literacy.
10. Mónica Guzmán, *I Never Thought of it That Way: How to Have Fearlessly Curious Conversations in Dangerously Divided Times* (BenBella Books, 2022), 31.
11. Beth Saulnier, "Exploring the Widening Chasm Between Urban and Rural Voters," Cornellians, Cornell University, January 27, 2022, https://alumni.cornell.edu/cornellians/urban-rural-voters/.
12. Seth Kaplan (sethkaplan28), LinkedIn post, April 30, 2024, https://www.linkedin.com/posts/sethkaplan28_neighborhoods-local-society-activity-7191066294870245376-1vp4/.
13. Ron Johnston, David Manley, Kelvyn Jones, and Ryne Rohla, "The Geographical Polarization of the American Electorate: A Country of Increasing Electoral Landslides?," *GeoJournal* 85, no. 2 (2020): 187–204, https://research-information.bris.ac.uk/ws/portalfiles/portal/177976591/ChangingLandslidesNov19F_1.pdf.
14. Guzmán, *Never Thought*, 32.
15. Gillian Sandstrom, "Relationships 2.0: The Power of Tiny Interactions," Hidden Brain podcast, *Hidden Brain Media*, April 14, 2025, 1:34:50, https://hiddenbrain.org/podcast/relationships-2-0-the-power-of-tiny-interactions/.

16. Office of the US Surgeon General, *Our Epidemic of Loneliness and Isolation: The U.S. Surgeon General's Advisory on the Healing Effects of Social Connection and Community* (Washington, DC, US Department of Health and Human Services, 2023), https://www.hhs.gov/sites/default/files/surgeon-general-social-connection-advisory.pdf.
17. Robert Putnam, *Bowling Alone: The Collapse and Revival of American Community* (Touchstone Books, Simon & Schuster, 2001). See also the 2023 documentary film *Join or Die*, directed and produced by Rebecca Davis and Pete Davis based on Putnam's later book, written with Shaylyn Romney Garrett, *The Upswing: How America Came Together a Century Ago and How We Can Do It Again* (Simon & Schuster, 2020).
18. Braver Angels founder Dr. Bill Doherty, email to Doug Teschner, November 24, 2021.
19. Amanda Ripley, *High Conflict: Why We Get Trapped and How We Get Out* (Simon & Schuster, 2021), 123.
20. See a summary at Bailey Schott, "Strengthening Civic Health in New Hampshire: The Power of Community Connection," Casey School of Public Policy (blog), University of New Hampshire, October 14, 2024, https://carsey.unh.edu/blog/2024/10/strengthening-civic-health-new-hampshire.
21. Seth Kaplan, LinkedIn post, April 30, 2024.
22. Stephen Covey, *The 7 Habits of Highly Effective People: Powerful Lessons in Personal Change*, 25th anniversary edition (Simon & Schuster, 1989/2013), 247–272.
23. Jonathan Rauch, "The Cancel Culture Checklist," JonathanRauch.com, August 6, 2020, https://www.jonathanrauch.com/jrauch_articles/2020/08/the-cancel-culture-checklist.html.
24. April Lawson, "Why We Cancel: Understanding the Logic Behind Today's Social Capital Punishment," *Comment*, February 29, 2024, https://comment.org/why-we-cancel/.
25. Najaf Imran, "The Unsettling Reality of Social Media Algorithms," *Medium*, December 10, 2024, https://medium.com/contentalogist/the-unsettling-reality-of-social-media-algorithms-4b97305dd1e1.
26. Claire E. Robertson, Kareena del Rosario, and Jay J Van Bavel, "Inside the Funhouse Mirror Factory: How Social Media Distorts Perceptions of Norms," *ScienceDirect*, December 2024, https://www.sciencedirect.com/science/article/abs/pii/S2352250X24001313.
27. Joshua Brown, "Talking with Zeynep Tufekci," *UVM News*, University of Vermont, March 1, 2024, https://www.uvm.edu/uvmnews/news/talking-zeynep-tufekci.

28. Klein, *Why We're Polarized,* 149.
29. Klein, *Why We're Polarized,* 163.
30. Daniel Kahneman, *Thinking, Fast and Slow,* (Farrar, Straus and Giroux, 2013).
31. US Department of State, *Weapons of Mass Distraction: Foreign State-Sponsored Disinformation in the Digital Age,* Christina Nemr and William Gangware (Park Advisors, www.Park-Advisors.com, 2019), https://www.state.gov/wp-content/uploads/2019/05/Weapons-of-Mass-Distraction-Foreign-State-Sponsored-Disinformation-in-the-Digital-Age.pdf.
32. Nate Ostiller and The Kyiv Independent News Desk, "Microsoft says Russian Disinformation Campaign Targeting US Election Has Begun," *The Kyiv Independent,* April 18, 2024, https://kyivindependent.com/microsoft-says-russian-disinformation-campaign-targeting-us-election-has-begun/.
33. Julianna Frieman, "'We Are Being Manipulated': Professor Explains How China Is Spreading Pro-Hamas Sentiment on College Campuses," *Daily Caller,* April 23, 2024, https://dailycaller.com/2024/04/23/nyu-professor-explain-china-spread-pro-hamas-sentiment-college-campus-msnbc/.
34. Marc Ambinder, "The Outrage Industrial Complex," *Atlantic,* February 20, 2009, https://www.theatlantic.com/politics/archive/2009/02/the-outrage-industrial-complex/845/.
35. John Fensterwald, "Latest National Test Results Underscore Declining Knowledge of U.S. History and Civics," *EdSource,* May 3, 2023, https://edsource.org/2023/latest-test-results-underscore-declining-knowledge-of-u-s-history-and-civics/689766.
36. "About Us," Constructive Dialogue Institute, accessed May 2, 2025, https://constructivedialogue.org/about/.
37 David Blankenhorn, *In Search of Braver Angels: Getting Along Together in Troubled Times* (Braver Angels, 2022), 32.
38. Julian Adorney, "Living Out of Our False Identities (Part 1)," *Heal the West Substack,* March 21, 2024, https://www.healthewest.org/p/living-out-of-our-false-identities?link_id=2&can_id=a56f8ac3f07f9a4692530b818e1833cc&source=email-three-ways-to-diffuse-the-tension-8&email_referrer=email_2287612&email_subject=can-we-reduce-our-fear-around-the-election.

## CHAPTER 6

1. Amanda Ripley, *High Conflict: Why We Get Trapped and How We Get Out* (Simon & Schuster, 2021), 137–8.

2. Fabio Duarte, "Time Spent Using Smartphones (2025 Statistics)," *Exploding Topics* blog, modified April 24, 2025, https://explodingtopics.com/blog/smartphone-usage-stats.
3. Paul Frysh, "How to Break Your Phone Habit," WebMD, medically reviewed by Shruthi N, MD, on May 24, 2022, https://www.webmd.com/balance/ss/slideshow-break-phone-habit?ecd=wnl_spr_022624&ctr=wnl-spr022624_supportTop_title_2&mb=GPzL98een%40NHWt92%40sKgS8LePTvD8f%40B97sAafT23s8%3d.
4. Stephen Hawkins, Daniel Yudkin, Míriam Juan-Torres, and Tim Dixon, *Hidden Tribes: A Study of America's Polarized Landscape,* ResearchGate, October 2018, https://www.researchgate.net/publication/360792060_Hidden_Tribes_A_Study_of_America's_Polarized_Landscape.
5. "Combating Conflict Entrepreneurs," Carnegie Endowment for International Peace, February 7, 2002, https://carnegieendowment.org/events/2002/02/combating-conflict-entrepreneurs?lang=en.
6. Jonathan Haidt, *The Anxious Generation: How the Great Rewiring of Childhood Is Causing an Epidemic of Mental Illness* (Penguin Press, 2024).
7. Jonathan Haidt, "Why the Past 10 Years of American Life Have Been Uniquely Stupid," *Atlantic*, May 2022, https://www.theatlantic.com/magazine/archive/2022/05/social-media-democracy-trust-babel/629369/.
8. Ripley, *High Conflict,* 95.
9. William Vaillancourt, "Alex Jones Raked in $165 Million Over Three Years Selling Supplements and Prepper Gear," *Rolling Stone,* January 7, 2022, https://www.rollingstone.com/politics/politics-news/alex-jones-infowars-store-165-million-1281059/.
10. Lisa Hagen and Chris Haxel, *No Compromise* podcast, 8 episodes, NPR, 2021, https://www.npr.org/podcasts/510356/no-compromise.
11. Mark Lynas, "GMOs Are Green: How an Environmentalist Changed His Mind About Biotechnology," Heuermann Lectures, posted October 10, 2016, by Institute of Agriculture and Natural Resources, University of Nebraska-Lincoln, YouTube, 68 min., 56 sec., https://heuermannlectures.unl.edu/gmos-and-biotechnology-gmos-are-green-how-environmentalist-changed-his-mind-about-biotechnology/.
12. "A Few Elected Officials Spend Time Creating Conflict, and It's a Problem for Democracy," Polarization Research Lab, posted on August 12, 2024, https://polarizationresearchlab.org/2024/08/12/news-americas-political-pulse-elected-official-data-and-dashboard-launch/.
13. The Dignity Index, https://www.dignity.us/.

14. Ezra Klein, *Why We're Polarized* (Avid Reader Press/Simon & Schuster, 2020), xix.
15. James Barragan, "No Time for Apathy: Why the American Public Must Fully Engage in Democracy," Bernard D. Nossiter '47 Lecture, May 1, 2024, The Rockefeller Center at Dartmouth, YouTube, 58:54, https://www.youtube.com/watch?v=sQgdDeVFTyU.
16. David Brooks, "How America Got Mean: In a Culture Devoid of Moral Education, Generations Are Growing Up in a Morally Inarticulate, Self-Referential World," *Atlantic,* August 14, 2023, https://www.theatlantic.com/magazine/archive/2023/09/us-culture-moral-education-formation/674765/.
17. Robert Putnam and Shaylyn Romney Garrett, *The Upswing: How America Came Together a Century Ago and How We Can Do It Again* (Simon & Schuster, 2020).
18. *Join or Die,* directed by Pete Davis (Delevan Street Films, 2023), https://www.joinordiefilm.com/.

## CHAPTER 7

1. Stephen Hawkins, et al., *Hidden Tribes: A Study of America's Polarized Landscape* (More in Common, July 2018/electronic preprint available August 21, 2019), https://www.researchgate.net/publication/360792060_Hidden_Tribes_A_Study_of_America's_Polarized_Landscape.
2. "Tracking Political Opinions of U.S. Citizens," Polarization Research Lab, September 2024, https://americaspoliticalpulse.com/citizens/.
3. Hawkins, et al., *Hidden Tribes.*
4. Karl Vick, "The Growing Evidence That Americans Are Less Divided Than You May Think," *Time,* July 2, 2024, https://time.com/6990721/us-politics-polarization-myth/?utm_source=Klaviyo&utm_medium=campaign&utm_campaign=07112024&utm_content=mvt1&_kx=YMC8_6b1yNU6iLksg4B_VSgHsUAuI1AleGmTZdFXFd-ceIRndE3O-JYCPc04PpCmy.TAzfUF.
5. "Voter Perspective," New Hampshire Together, The People New Hampshire, accessed May 3, 2025, https://www.thepeople.org/newhampshire.
6. Yanna Krupnikov, "US 2.0: Not at the Dinner Table," *Hidden Brain* podcast, Hidden Brain Media, February 19, 2024, https://hiddenbrain.org/podcast/not-at-the-dinner-table/.
7. Ezra Klein, *Why We're Polarized* (Avid Reader Press/Simon & Schuster, 2020), 17.

8. Wayne Gerson, "American Grandeur, in Both Landscape and Spirit," *Valley News,* June 15, 2024.
9. Francis S. Barry, *Back Roads and Better Angels: A Journey into the Heart of American Democracy,* (Steerforth, 2024).
10. Stacey Lindsay, "Can We Truly Move Beyond the Vitriol to a Better Place? Former NIH Director Francis S. Collins Shows Us How," *Maria Shriver's Sunday Paper,* October 5, 2024, https://www.mariashriversundaypaper.com/former-nih-director-francis-collins-road-to-wisdom/.
11. Hawkins, et al., *Hidden Tribes.*
12. Manu Meel, host, The Hopeful Majority podcast, episode 71, "2024 Election: There is a New Divide ft. Tim Urban," interview with Tim Urban, November 5, 2024, https://www.thehopefulmajority.com/episodes/ep-71-2024-election-there-is-a-new-divide-ft-tim-urban.
13. BridgeUSA is a youth movement for better politics; see more at https://www.bridgeusa.org/.
14. Hawkins, et al., *Hidden Tribes.*
15. Sami Sage and Emily Amick, "How Positive Engagement Can Bring the Exhausted Majority Back into Politics," *Newsweek* magazine, June 25, 2024, https://www.newsweek.com/2024/07/05/how-positive-engagement-can-bring-exhausted-majority-back-politics-1915355.html.

## CHAPTER 8

1. James M. Kouzes and Barry Z. Posner, *Learning Leadership: The Five Fundamentals of Becoming an Exemplary Leader* (Wiley, 2016).
2. Brené Brown, Dare to Lead: Brave Work. *Tough Conversations.* Whole Hearts (Random House, 2018), 186.
3. Scott Mautz, *Lead On!* blog post received by author, June 19, 2024. Mautz has a tool to help identify your values in his book *The Mentally Strong Leader: Build the Habits to Productively Regulate Your Emotions, Thoughts, and Behaviors* (Peakpoint Press, 2024).
4. Ken Burns, keynote address, (Brandeis University's 73rd Commencement Exercises, Waltham, Massachusetts), May 19, 2024.
5. Viktor E. Frankl, *Man's Search for Meaning* (Beacon Press, 2006), 66.
6. Kelly Corrigan, host, *Kelly Corrigan Wonders* podcast, "Going Deep with David Byrne and Judy Woodruff on Staying Positive," season 1, episode 217, interview with Judy Woodruff, November 5, 2024, https://podcasts.apple.com/gb/podcast/going-deep-with-david-byrne-judy-woodruff-on-staying/id1532951390?i=1000675725432.

## CHAPTER 9

1. C. Sreechinth, *Einstein Wisdom: Quotes from an Extraordinary Brain* (UB Tech, 2016), 170.

## CHAPTER 10

1. Stephen Hawkins, et al., *Hidden Tribes: A Study of America's Polarized Landscape* (More in Common, July 2018/electronic preprint available August 21, 2019), https://www.researchgate.net/publication/360792060_Hidden_Tribes_A_Study_of_America's_Polarized_Landscape.
2. Beth A. Malow, et al., "Bridging the Divide on Climate Solutions: Development, Implementation, and Evaluation of an Online Workshop for Climate Volunteers," *Journal of Climate Change and Health 7* (August 2022), https://www.sciencedirect.com/science/article/pii/S2667278222000669?via%3Dihub.
3. "How Can Granite Staters Participate?," *New Hampshire Together: A Project of the People,* accessed May 3, 2025, https://newhampshiretogether.us/participate/.
4. Hawkins, et al., *Hidden Tribes.*
5. Ezra Klein, *Why We're Polarized* (Avid Reader Press/Simon & Schuster, 2020), 63.
6. Hawkins, et al., *Hidden Tribes.*
7. Gary Fields and Amelia Thomson-Deveaux, "Yes, We're Divided. But New AP–NORC Poll Shows Americans Still Agree on Most Core American Values," Associated Press, April 3, 2024, https://apnews.com/article/ap-poll-democracy-rights-freedoms-election-b1047da72551e13554a3959487e5181a.
8. Arthur Brooks, *Love Your Enemies* (Broadside Books, 2019), 61–66.
9. Harry C. Boyte, *Commonwealth: A Return to Citizen Politics* (Free Press, 1989), 4.
10. Susan Clark and Woden Teachout, *Slow Democracy: Rediscovering Community, Bringing Decision Making Back Home* (Chelsea Green Publishing, 2012).
11. Peter Levine, "On Civic Renewal on the Threshold of 2021," *A Blog for Civic Renewal: Defining Civic Engagement, Democracy, Civic Renewal, and Related Terms,* December 18, 2020, https://peterlevine.ws/?s=civic+renewal.
12. Charles Heckscher, *Introduction to Citizen-Led Solutions: A Playbook for Braver Angels Field Units,* (Braver Angels, June 13, 2024), https://docs.google.com/document/d/13abjKFJYV4E9piDtEFRxI3zNae2OF-vV-j8hsTdN9K0/edit?tab=t.0.

13. Anthony Simon Laden, *Taking the Engagement in Civic Engagement Seriously* (Institute for Policy and Civic Engagement, University of Illinois at Chicago, May 2012), https://ipce.red.uic.edu/wp-content/uploads/sites/41/2018/10/TakingCivicEngagementSeriouslyFinalFY12.pdf.
14. California State Legislature, *Senate Bill No. 328, Chapter 868: Pupil Attendance: School Start Time,* approved October 13, 2019, https://leginfo.legislature.ca.gov/faces/billTextClient.xhtml?bill_id=201920200SB328.
15. Florida Senate, *Bill Summary: CS/HB 733—Middle School and High School Start Times,* 2023 Regular Session, https://www.flsenate.gov/Committees/Bill-Summaries/2023/html/3139.
16. Eric Turer, email message to author Teschner, Feb 19, 2024. Turer is the current co-chair of the Braver Angels-inspired bipartisan caucus, the Granite Bridge Legislative Alliance.
17. Douglass P. Teschner, "Beating Ebola: Peace Corps' Untold Story of Fighting the Virus in Guinea," *WorldView,* National Peace Corps Association, Summer 2019, Peacecorpsconnect.org/beating-ebola/.
18. Braver Angels, *Citizen-Led Solutions.*

## CHAPTER 11

1. Stephen Hawkins, et. al, *Hidden Tribes: A Study of America's Polarized Landscape* (More in Common, July 2018/electronic preprint available August 21, 2019), https://www.researchgate.net/publication/360792060_Hidden_Tribes_A_Study_of_America's_Polarized_Landscape.
2. Drew Dudley, "Everyday Leadership," TEDx Toronto, September 2010, 6 min., https://www.ted.com/talks/drew_dudley_everyday_leadership.
3. James M. Kouzes and Barry Z. Posner, *Learning Leadership* (Wiley, 2016), 57.
4. "What is Self-Leadership?," Andrew Bryant, Self-Leadership International, accessed May 3, 2025, https://www.selfleadership.com/what-is-self-leadership.
5. Stephen R. Covey, *The 7 Habits of Highly Effective People* (Simon and Schuster, 2013), 297–319. (Habit 7 is "Sharpen the Saw.")
6. Tom Brady, interview by Oprah Winfrey, *Super Soul Sunday,* OWN Network, June 17–18, 2018, video segment, 55 sec., https://www.oprah.com/own-supersoulsessions/tom-brady-on-life-after-football-i-think-about-it-more-now.
7. Tal Ben-Shahar, *Happier: Learn the Secrets to Daily Joy and Lasting Fulfillment* (McGraw Hill, 2007).
8. "15 Ways to be Happier," WebMD, medically reviewed on June 1, 2024, https://www.webmd.com/balance/ss/slideshow-be-happier.

9. Brené Brown, "I Don't Have to Chase Extraordinary Moments to Find Happiness: It's Right in Front of Me," interview by Gretchen Rubin, *Forbes,* July 15, 2011, https://www.forbes.com/sites/gretchenrubin/2011/07/15/i-dont-have-to-chase-extraordinary-moments-to-find-hapiness-its-right-in-front-of-me/.
10. Corey Keyes, *Hidden Brain* podcast, "Why You Feel Empty," Hidden Brain Media, June 10, 2024, https://hiddenbrain.org/podcast/why-you-feel-empty/.
11. Justin Bariso, "13 Signs of High Emotional Intelligence," Inc., February 28, 2018, https://www.inc.com/justin-bariso/13-things-emotionally-intelligent-people-do.html.
12. Jonathan Haidt, *Righteous Mind: Why Good People Are Divided by Politics and Religion* (Vintage, 2013), 56.
13. Covey, *7 Habits,* 154.
14. Covey, *7 Habits,* 29.
15. Denise McClain and Ryan Pendell, "Why Trust in Leaders Is Faltering and How to Gain it Back," *Gallup Workplace,* April 17, 2023, https://www.gallup.com/workplace/473738/why-trust-leaders-faltering-gain-back.aspx.
16. Ryan McCostlin, "The Trust Wager," *My Notebook* blog, April 23, https://www.ryanmccostlin.com/blog/trust-wager.
17. Roger Fisher and William L. Ury, *Getting to Yes: Negotiating Agreement Without Giving In,* (Penguin Books, 1991), 17–39.
18. Fisher and Ury, *Getting to Yes,* 73.
19. "Mindfulness Meditation: Psychologists Have Found That Mindfulness Meditation Changes our Brain and Biology in Positive Ways, Improving our Mental and Physical Health," American Psychological Association, October 30, 2019, https://bit.ly/43vvOE6.

## CHAPTER 12

1. Mark Beckwith, "The Different Layers of Campus Anger," *Seeing the Unseen: Beyond Prejudices, Paradigms, and Party Lines* (blog), accessed May 4, 2025, https://www.markbeckwith.net/2024/05/08/the-different-layers-of-campus-anger/#:~:text=Anger%20shows%20up%20whenever%20the,%2C%20their%20language%2C%20their%20principles.
2. Peggy Prichard, *Braver Angels Newsletter,* received by Doug Teschner, June 5, 2024.
3. Mark Beckwith, email message to Doug Teschner, May 5, 2025.
4. This is also one of the key habits described by Stephen Covey in his classic *The 7 Habits of Highly Effective People.*

5. Jon White and Alexandra Taketa, *What You Don't Know About Listening Could Fill a Book, Leadership Edition* (Jon White Consulting, 2014).
6. Guy Itzchakov and Avraham N. Kluger, "The Power of Listening in Helping People Change," *Harvard Business Review*, May 17, 2018, https://hbr.org/2018/05/the-power-of-listening-in-helping-people-change.
7. Amanda Ripley, "The Protest Trap," *Unraveled* (Substack newsletter), June 24, 2024, https://amandaripley.substack.com/p/the-protest-trap.
8. Guy Itzchakov and Avraham N. Kluger, "The Power of Listening in Helping People Change."
9. Adam Grant, "'Your Ideas Are Not Your Identity': Adam Grant on How to Get Better at Changing Your Mind," https://behavioralscientist.org/your-ideas-are-not-your-identity-adam-grant-on-how-to-get-better-at-changing-your-mind/.
10. Todd E. Pressman, PhD, *Deconstructing Anxiety: The Journey from Fear to Fulfillment* (Rowman & Littlefield Publishers, 2019).
11. Scott Mautz, "The Mentally Strong Leader: Build the Habits to Productively Regulate Your Emotions, Thoughts, and Behaviors, *Lead On!* blog, April 8, 2023.
12. Jim Kouzes, "The Five Practices of Exemplary Leadership," Sponsored by the Association of California School Administrators, Region 8, https://regions.acsa.org/wp-content/blogs.dir/9/files/2014/08/ACSA_Kouzes_08.01.14.v2.pdf
13. Scott Mautz, "Mentally Strong Leader."
14. James Detert, "Words and Phrases to Avoid in a Difficult Conversation," *Harvard Business Review*, June 21, 2021, https://hbr.org/2021/06/words-and-phrases-to-avoid-in-a-difficult-conversation.

## CHAPTER 13

1. Dolly Parton, "Dolly Parton Sings and Gets COVID Vaccine Shot," posted by Associated Press, March 3, 2021, YouTube, 3:54, https://www.youtube.com/watch?v=OjbSWebA3Ko.
2. "Vanderbilt Kennedy Center Produces Videos on COVID-19 Vaccine and Individuals with Intellectual Disability," MyVU News, Vanderbilt University, December 19, 2021, https://news.vanderbilt.edu/2021/12/19/vanderbilt-_kennedy-center-produces-videos-on-covid-19-vaccine-and-individuals-with-intellectual-disability/.
3. "Misinformation and Disinformation," American Psychological Association, accessed May 4, 2025, https://www.apa.org/topics/journalism-facts/misinformation-disinformation.

4. Audrey Nguyen, "To Combat Misinformation, Start with Connection, Not Correction," NPR, September 30, 2024, https://www.npr.org/2024/09/30/g-s1-24711/to-combat-misinformation-start-with-connection-not-correction.
5. Nguyen, "Combat Misinformation."
6. David Blankenhorn, "My Debate with Dialogue," *The American Interest*, January 16, 2020, https://www.the-american-interest.com/2018/01/10/my-debate-with-dialogue/.
7. Beth A. Malow, "The Art of Communicating Science," TEDx Vanderbilt University, April 10, 2022, posted on July 5, 2022, 11 min., 6 sec., https://www.youtube.com/watch?v=oTvRlbIOMzg.
8. Nicholas Whaley, *Open Rhetoric: A Collaborative History of Rhetorical Theory and Practice* (Pressbooks digital self-publishing), Part III, https://pressbooks.pub/openrhetoric/chapter/aristotles-rhetorical-appeals/.
9. For more about the Braver Angels Truth and Trust Project, see https://braverangels.org/truth-and-trust/.
10. Dan M. Kahan et al., "The Polarizing Impact of Science Literacy and Numeracy on Perceived Climate Change Risks," *Nature Climate Change*, no. 2 (May 27, 2012), https://www.nature.com/articles/nclimate1547.
11. Francis S. Collins, *The Road to Wisdom: On Truth, Science, Faith, and Trust* (Little, Brown and Company, 2024), 50–51.
12. Daryl Van Tongeren, "The Curious Joy of Being Wrong: Intellectual Humility Means Being Open to New Information and Willing to Change Your Mind," *The Conversation*, December 26, 2023, https://theconversation.com/the-curious-joy-of-being-wrong-intellectual-humility-means-being-open-to-new-information-and-willing-to-change-your-mind-216126.
13. "Ex NIH-Director and Truck Driver Explore How to Bridge Divisions Deepened by the Pandemic," *PBS News Hour*, hosted by Judy Woodruff, produced by Frank Carlson, featuring Francis S. Collins and Wilk Wilkinson, March 26, 2025, https://www.pbs.org/newshour/show/ex-nih-director-and-truck-driver-explore-how-to-bridge-divisions-deepened-by-the-pandemic.
14. Jonathan Rauch, "The Constitution of Knowledge," *Persuasion* (Substack newsletter), June 28, 2021, https://www.persuasion.community/p/jonathan-rauch-the-constitution-of.
15. Beth Malow, "Tools to Evaluate Media," Medium, November 30, 2023, https://medium.com/p/f4ed487936a8. Also "Intro to Speech Communication: Evaluate Sources," Lake Land College Library, LibGuides, accessed May 4, 2025, https://lakeland.libguides.com/c.php?g=696344&p=5309611.

16. For additional media literacy resources, consult NewseumED at https://newseumed.org.
17. Adam Dick, "New Medical Study: Your Face Mask Is Not Protecting You," *Peace and Prosperity* blog, Ron Paul Institute for Peace and Prosperity, November 18, 2020, https://archive.is/ySMZ5.
18. Daniel Horowitz, "Massive Danish Study on Surgical Masks Found That Recommendation to Wear Masks Did Not Provide Statistically Significant Reduction in Infection Rates Among Mask Wearers," *Blaze News,* Blaze Media, November 18, 2020, https://www.theblaze.com/column/opinion/horowitz-massive-danish-study-no-reduction-infection-rates.
19. Henning Bundgaard et al., "Effectiveness of Adding a Mask Recommendation to Other Public Health Measures to Prevent SARS-CoV-2 Infection in Danish Mask Wearers: A Randomized Controlled Trial," *Annals of Internal Medicine* 174, no. 3 (November 28, 2020), https://www.acpjournals.org/doi/10.7326/M20-6817.
20. Jessica McDonald, "Danish Study Doesn't Prove Masks Don't Work Against the Coronavirus," FactCheck.org: A Project of the Annenberg Public Policy Center, November 25, 2020, https://www.factcheck.org/2020/11/danish-study-doesnt-prove-masks-dont-work-against-the-coronavirus/.
21. Horowitz, "Massive Danish Study."
22. Horowitz, "Massive Danish Study."
23. See All Sides, https://www.allsides.com/unbiased-balanced-news.
24. See The Flip Side, https://www.theflipside.io/.
25. See Tangle, https://www.readtangle.com/.
26. See Ground News, https://ground.news/.
27. "AllSides Media Bias Chart," AllSides, accessed May 4, 2025, https://www.allsides.com/media-bias/media-bias-chart.

## CHAPTER 14

1. David Brooks, *How to Know a Person: The Art of Seeing Others Deeply and Being Deeply Seen* (Random House, 2023), 9.
2. "The Paradox of TikTok," *Hidden Brain* Substack newsletter, August 29, 2024, https://news.hiddenbrain.org/p/the-paradox-of-tiktok.
3. Jud Caswell, "The Great Divide," Alderdown Songs, released as a single in 2020, https://judcaswell.com/track/3671704/the-great-divide.
4. Amanda Ripley, *High Conflict: Why We Get Trapped and How We Get Out* (Simon & Schuster, 2021), xii.

5. Cara Goodwin, "How to Raise Empathetic Children," *Psychology Today*, September 11, 2024, https://www.psychologytoday.com/us/blog/parenting-translator/202408/new-research-on-raising-empathetic-children.
6. Katelyn Hedrick and Lydia Saad, "Talking Politics at Work: A Double-Edged Sword," *Gallup Workplace*, August 22, 2024, https://www.gallup.com/workplace/648581/talking-politics-work-double-edged-sword.aspx.
7. Ryan Pendell, "Respect at Work Returns to a Record Low," *Gallup Workplace*, January 13, 2025, https://www.gallup.com/workplace/655040/respect-work-returns-record-low.aspx.
8. Hedrick and Saad, "Talking Politics."
9. Mary-Frances Winters and Mareisha N. Reese, *We Can't Talk about That at Work! How to Talk about Race, Religion, Politics, and Other Polarizing Topics* (Berrett-Koehler Publishers, 2024).

## CHAPTER 15

1. Robert J. Anderson and William A. Adams, *Mastering Leadership: An Integrated Framework for Breakthrough Performance and Extraordinary Business Results* (Wiley, 2015), 222.
2. James M. Kouzes and Barry Z. Posner, *Learning Leadership: The Five Fundamentals of Becoming an Exemplary Leader* (Wiley, 2016), 133.
3. Robert J. Anderson and William A. Adams, *Scaling Leadership: Building Organizational Capability and Capacity to Create Outcomes That Matter Most* (Wiley, 2019).
4. "6 Powerful Lessons from Stephen R. Covey and Hyrum Smith," Franklin-Covey, September 22, 2021, https://www.franklincovey.de/en/2021/09/22/6-powerful-lessons-from-stephen-r-covey-and-hyrum-smith/#:~:text=It%20requires%20us%20to%20slow%20down%2C%20take,fast%20is%20slow%20and%20slow%20is%20fast.%E2%80%9D.
5. Drew Dudley, *This Is Day One: A Practical Guide to Leadership That Matters* (Grand Central Publishing, 2018).
6. John Clifton and Benedict Vigers, "What Do People Need Most from Leaders? New Gallup Research Spotlight Four Needs of Followers Worldwide," *Gallup Workplace*, February 11, 2025, https://www.gallup.com/workplace/655817/people-need-leaders.aspx#:~:text=Hope%20stands%20out%20as%20the,nine%20positive%20leadership%20traits%20mentioned.

## CHAPTER 16

1. Cass R. Sunstein, *How Change Happens* (MIT Press, 2019).
2. Leslie Crutchfield, *How Change Happens: Why Some Social Movements Succeed While Others Don't* (Wiley, 2018), 13.
3. Crutchfield, *How Change Happens,* 79.
4. Crutchfield, *How Change Happens,* 145.
5. Kurt Lewin, "Defining the Field at a Given Time,'" *Psychological Review* 50, no. 3 (1943): 292–310, republished in Resolving Social Conflicts & Field Theory in Social Science (Washington, D.C. American Psychological Association, 1997).
6. "Dora Akunyili," Wikiquote, accessed May 25, 2025, https://en.wikiquote.org/wiki/Dora_Akunyili.
7. Joshua Brown, "Talking with Zeynep Tufekci," UVM News, University of Vermont, March 1, 2024, https://www.uvm.edu/uvmnews/news/talking-zeynep-tufekci.
8. Yuval Levin, *American Covenant: How the Constitution Unified Our Nation—and Could Again* (Basic Books, 2024).

## CHAPTER 17

1. James Barragan, "No Time for Apathy: Why the American Public Must Fully Engage in Democracy," Bernard D. Nossiter '47 Lecture, May 1, 2024, The Rockefeller Center at Dartmouth, YouTube, 58:54, https://www.youtube.com/watch?v=sQgdDeVFTyU.
2. James M. Kouzes and Barry Z. Posner, *Learning Leadership: The Five Fundamentals of Becoming an Exemplary Leader* (Wiley, 2016), 133.
3. Kyra Bobinet, "How Permanent Behavior Change Really Works: Iteration Is the Key to Sustainable Behavior Change," *Psychology Today,* May 29, 2024, https://www.psychologytoday.com/us/blog/unstoppable-brain/202405/how-permanent-behavior-change-really-works.
4. Morgan Galbraith, "To Get Employees on Board with Change, Tell Them How They Benefit," *Harvard Business Review,* December 14, 2018, https://hbr.org/tip/2018/12/to-get-employees-on-board-with-change-tell-them-how-they-benefit.
5. James R. Detert, "Cultivating Everyday Courage: The Right Way to Speak Truth to Power," *Harvard Business Review,* November–December 2018, https://hbr.org/2018/11/cultivating-everyday-courage.

6. Brené Brown, *Dare to Lead: Brave Work. Tough Conversations. Whole Hearts* (Random House, 2018), 194.
7. Terry R. Vergon, *A Journey of Epiphanies: Learning Leadership,* (Sapient Services, 2013), 211. https://www.google.com/books/edition/A_Journey_of_Epiphanies_Learning_Leaders/9b9pBQAAQBAJ?hl=en&gbpv=0.
8. Marge Piercy, "To Be of Use," *Poems and Resilience,* Poetry Foundation, May 22, 2017, https://www.poetryfoundation.org/poems/57673/to-be-of-use.
9. Jamil Zaki and Luiza Santos, "How the Psychology of Political Division Could Lead Us Out of It," *Washington Post,* September 10, 2024, https://www.washingtonpost.com/opinions/2024/09/10/cognitive-therapy-heal-political-division/.
10. Carlos Castaneda, "The Words of Don Juan (Juan Matus), His Teachers, and Members of His Warrior's Party, on the Warrior's Way," Internet Archive, accessed May 4, 2025, https://archive.org/stream/CarlosCastanedaTheWordsOfDonJuanMatus/Carlos%20Castaneda-The%20Words%20Of%20Don%20Juan%20Matus_djvu.txt.
11. Krista Tippett, host, *On Being* podcast, "Stepping out of 'the Zombie Dance' We're in and into 'Good Conflict' That Is, in Fact, Life-Giving," interview with Amanda Ripley, February 9, 2023, https://onbeing.org/programs/amanda-ripley-stepping-out-of-the-zombie-dance-were-in-and-into-good-conflict-that-is-in-fact-life-giving/.
12. Krista Tippett, host, *On Being* podcast, "Living as an Improvisational Art," quoting writing by guest Mary Catherine Bateson, December 31, 2020, https://onbeing.org/programs/mary-catherine-bateson-living-as-an-improvisational-art/. This quote is from Bateson's book, Composing a Further Life: The Age of Active Wisdom (Knopf, 2010).
13. Lulu Garcia-Navarro, "'The Interview': Robert Putnam Knows Why You're Lonely," *New York Times,* July 13, 2024, https://www.nytimes.com/2024/07/13/magazine/robert-putnam-interview.html?unlocked_article_code=1.IU4.Z-Vb.MKiJYVvAm1Uk&smid=url-share.
14. Scott Mautz, "On the Power of Acting As If," *Lead On!* blog, July 17, 2024, https://www.linkedin.com/pulse/issue-159-special-edition-power-acting-scott-mautz-tk4bc/.
15. Jean Giono, *The Man Who Planted Trees,* 20th Anniversary edition (Chelsea Green, 2007).
16. Anil Dutt Misra, *Inspiring Thoughts of Mahatma Gandhi* (Concept Publishing Company, 2008), 36.
17. "It's Gonna Get Better," by Genesis, track 5 on *Genesis,* Atlantic Records, 1983, compact disc.

# Index

## A

ableism, 177
abortion debate, 45
abusive behavior, increase in, 29–30
acceptance, importance of, 174
acknowledge, in LAPP implementation steps, 151
Acting Outward areas, in checklist for change, 231, 235–236
action(s). *See also* decisions shaping life and values; positive change, contributing to; thinking global, acting local
  as blunting power of conflict entrepreneurs, 84–86
  everyday, impact of, 204–206
  overcoming divide through, 98–99
  role in civic renewal, 124–126
activism
  and bridge building, 59–60
  positive, 222
  positive changes for, 120, 121
Adams, William A., 187
adapting as we go along, importance of, 215
advice, in personal leadership plan, 194
advocacy, 114, 120
affective polarization, 21. *See also* polarization
*The Age of Grievance* (Bruni), 19
agency, 163
aggressive behavior in medical settings, 30–32
Akunyili, Dora, 206
Alda, Alan, 162
Ali, Muhammad, 206
Ambinder, Marc, 72–73
*American Covenant* (Levin), 209

American identity
  embracing, 123–124
  empowering, 209
American politics. *See* exhausted majority; polarization; politics of contempt; "us vs. them," moving beyond
Amick, Emily, 99
Anderson, Robert J., 187
angel, being, 35–37
Angelou, Maya, 28
anger, in fight mode, 147. *See also* politics of contempt
apathy, citizen, 74. *See also* exhausted majority
Apatow, Judd, 36
Aristotle, 162–163
"The Art of Communicating Science" (Malow), 162–163
artist of our own lives, being, 224
associations, local, 68
assumptions
  making, 43
  resisting, 140
audience, in ESCAPE tool, 167
authenticity
  and braver conversations, 148–149
  in leaders, 190
  as personal value, 111, 113
  in self-leadership, 138
avoidance mode, 147–148

## B

*Back to the Future* film, 107
Bacon, Don, 58
Barragan, James, 84
Barry, Francis, 96

Bateson, Mary Catherine, 224
Beckwith, Mark, 33, 44, 147, 148
believing in yourself, 136–137
belligerent behavior, increase in, 29–30. *See also* politics of contempt
Ben-Shahar, Tal, 137
*Beyond the Politics of Contempt* book website, 229
binary (zero-sum) thinking, 57, 63–64. *See also* polarization; politics of contempt; "us vs. them," moving beyond
Black, Derek, 39–40, 45
Blanchard, Ken, 84, 231
Blankenhorn, David, 57, 74, 162
Bobinet, Kyra, 215
*A Book, an Idea and a Goat* newsletter, 59
boundaries
   establishing with family, 174–175
   setting for braver conversations, 154
Bourque, Ron, 32
*Bowling Alone* (Putnam), 67
Boyte, Harry, 124
Bradberry, Travis, 186
Brady, Tom, 136–137
Braver Angels
   braver conversation skills, 149–152
   Braver Politics effort, 6, 230
   contributing to positive change, 121–122
   debate on abortion, 45
   and effective communication, 162
   "Family and Politics" workshop, 175
   finding common ground, 24
   impact of workshops on politicians, 210
   joining, 236
   as model for finding hope, 16–18
   overview, 5, 230, 237–238
   promotion of civic renewal, 124–126, 127–128
   "Red/Blue" workshops, 17
   "Skills for Bridging the Divide" workshop, 127–128
   "Skills for Disagreeing Better" workshop, 150–152
   Truth and Trust Project, 163
Braver Angels Action Team within CCL, 121
braver conversations
   applying in daily life, 156–157
   and critical thinking, 169
   versus fight, flight, or avoidance, 146–148
   key principles for, 150
   LAPP implementation steps, 150–152
   and moral courage, 217
   and openness to change, 154–155
   overview, 145–146
   positive engagement through, 172
   questions for further thought, 158
   on social media, 153–154
   starting small with, 220
   values and mindset, importance of, 148–149
Braver Network initiative, 238
Braver Politics effort, 6, 230
Brentwood, New Hampshire, 127–128
bridge building, 39–40, 59–60. *See also* braver conversations; hope; positive change, contributing to; positive engagement with others; "us vs. them," moving beyond
BridgeUSA, 239
Brooks, Arthur, 35, 123–124
Brooks, David, 27–28, 53, 63, 84, 171
Brooks, Jim, 171
Brown, Brené, 101–102, 138, 175, 217
Bruni, Frank, 19
Bryant, Andrew, 135–136
Budd, Courtenay, 99
Builders (formerly Starts with Us), 239
Burns, Ken, 105
Bush, George W., 46
business leaders modeling positive behavior, 181–182
bystander role, 175

C

cancel culture, 70, 206
candidates
   bettering, 210
   as conflict entrepreneurs, 82–83
   positive changes from, 120, 121
Carnegie Foundation, 121

Castaneda, Carlos, 223
Caswell, Jud, 174
CCL (Citizens' Climate Lobby), 121
change. *See also* checklist for change; personal change; positive change, contributing to
   beginning with ourselves, 21
   embracing positive, 24
   encouraging and inspiring others to, 215–216
   openness to, and braver conversations, 154–155
   patterns driving, 199–200
checklist for change
   Acting Outward areas, 235–236
   Looking Inward areas, 232–234
   overview, 230, 231
children, demonstrating positive engagement to, 176–177
Churchill, Winston, 217
citizen apathy, 74. *See also* exhausted majority
citizen-led solutions, 124–129
*Citizen-Led Solutions Playbook* (Braver Angels), 125
Citizens' Climate Lobby (CCL), 121
civic engagement, 126
civic renewal, 124–129
civics education
   decline of, 73–74
   promoting, 207
civil discourse, 114
Civity, 239
Clark, Susan, 124
climate issues, 20, 60, 121, 155
cognitive biases, 163–164
Cold War, 74
colleagues
   braver conversations with, 156–157
   managing political conflict with, 179–183
collectively blunting power of conflict entrepreneurs, 84–86
college protests, 56–57
Collins, Francis, 96, 164
Collins, Jim, 140

common ground, finding, 24, 93–94, 98–99. *See also* exhausted majority
Common Ground Nashville civil discourse group, 24
commonwealth, defining, 124
communication, science, 162–163
community involvement, disengagement from, 67, 68
community problems, solving, 124–129
"Complicating the Narrative" discussion group, 93–94
conflict. *See also* braver conversations; polarization; politics of contempt; positive engagement with others
   and activism, 59–60
   engaging across, 9
   healthy vs. unhealthy, 7, 53–57
   moving from unhealthy to healthy, 57–59
   questions for further thought, 61
   recognizing ourselves as enablers of, 103–106
   role of leaders in managing, 189
   stages or approaches to, 57
conflict entrepreneurs
   diminishing influence of, 207–208
   as force driving politics of contempt, 72–73
   identifying, 81–84
   need to collectively blunt power of, 84–86
   overview, 77–81
   questions for further thought, 86
   and unhealthy conflict, 54
Congress, conflict entrepreneurs in, 83
Conley, Chip, 187
connections. *See also* positive engagement with others; relationships
   applying talents to address, 210
   expanding, 205–206
   in personal leadership plan, 194
   role in building hope, 23–24
Constitution, US, 209
*The Constitution of Knowledge* (Rauch), 165
constructive engagement. *See* positive engagement with others
contagious nature of hate, 32–33

contempt, politics of. *See* polarization; politics of contempt; "us vs. them," moving beyond
context, in ESCAPE tool, 167
control, focusing on what we can, 104
conversations, overcoming divide through, 98–99. *See also* braver conversations; positive engagement with others
Cormen, Tom, 95
Corrigan, Kelly, 36, 131
courage
   and braver conversations, 148–149
   on checklist for change, 234
   moral, power of, 216–217
   as personal value, 113
   physical, 219
Covey, Stephen, 69, 136, 139, 140
Covey, Stephen M. R., 188
COVID pandemic
   aggressive patient behavior during, 31
   critical thinking and, 159–160, 161–163, 165–168
   and forces driving politics of contempt, 64, 68–69
   lack of kindness during, 29
   mask-wearing during, 29, 31, 46–47, 165–170
   and power of moral courage, 216
   and resiliency, 218
   scars left by, 19
   vaccination during, 159–160, 162, 216
Cox, Spencer, 57–58
creative artists, positive changes from, 121
critical thinking
   barriers to, 163–164
   Beth's reflections on COVID pandemic, 161–163
   overview, 159–161
   practicing in relation to polarization, 165–168, 170
   questions for further thought, 170
   sharing your process with others, 169–170
Crutchfield, Leslie, 199–200
culture, effects of politics of contempt on, 18–20, 27–28

curiosity
   and braver conversations, 148–149
   in intellectual humility, 164
   in self-leadership, 139

D

*Daily Connection* webinar series, 218
daily life, applying braver conversation skills in, 156–158
Dalai Lama (Tenzin Gyatso), 27, 178
*Dare to Lead* (Brown), 101–102
decisions shaping life and values
   Becky's reflections on, 115–116
   Beth's reflections on, 112–114
   on checklist for change, 234
   Doug's reflections on, 108–112
   overview, 107–108
   self-reflection on, 116–117
defender role, 175
democracy, slow, 124
Democrats, 19–20. *See also* polarization; politics of contempt
depolarization, 57, 120
"Depolarizing Within" workshop (Braver Angels), 237–238
derogatory terms, 42, 46–47. *See also* polarization; politics of contempt
despair
   caused by politics of contempt, 15–16
   finding hope amid, 21–25
dialogue. *See* braver conversations; positive engagement with others
dignity. *See also* kindness
   embracing, 35
   power of to bridge differences, 39–40
   seeing everyone as deserving of, 41–44
   versus shaming others, 46–47
Dignity Index, 83, 241
diplomacy, 102, 113
"Disagreeing Better" campaign, 57–58
disagreement. *See also* braver conversations; positive engagement with others
   better ways of, 98–99
   engaging across, 9
discipline, role in implementing change, 215

disconnection, social
  as force driving politics of contempt, 67–69
  reducing, 205–206
discourteous behavior
  as force driving politics of contempt, 69–70
  reducing, 206
disdain, politics of. See hate; politics of contempt; "us vs. them," moving beyond
disinformation, 72, 160–161. See also critical thinking
distancing ourselves from others, 171, 172
distrust, reducing, 205–206. See also politics of contempt; "us vs. them," moving beyond
diversity, equity, and inclusion practices, 44–45
division, political. See polarization; politics of contempt; "us vs. them," moving beyond
Dixon, Tim. See Hidden Tribes
Doherty, Bill, 16, 149–150, 175, 195
dominance by elites, 66
Drucker, Peter, 1
Dudley, Drew, 133

E
Ebola pandemic in Guinea, 19, 128, 192
echo chambers. See siloing
educational disparities, 66
Einstein, Albert, 113
elites, dominance by, 66
Emerson, Ralph Waldo, 161, 220
empathy
  and braver conversations, 148–149
  impact of parental modeling of, 176–177
  in self-leadership, 139
*The Empire Strikes Back* film, 81
engagement, civic, 126
engager role, 175
ESCAPE (Evidence, Source, Context, Audience, Purpose, and Execution) tool, 165–168
Esther 4:14, 112

everyday actions, impact of, 204–206
everyday life, applying leadership skills in, 189–191
everyone, as deserving of dignity and respect, 41–44
evidence, in ESCAPE tool, 166
example, leading by, 205
execution, in ESCAPE tool, 168
exhausted majority
  and civic renewal, 124–125
  overview, 7–8, 91–94
  path forward for, 98–99
  perspectives on, 94–98
  questions for further thought, 100
external impacts of life decisions, 110–111

F
Facebook, 79, 173. See also social media
fact-checking, 161. See also critical thinking
FactCheck.org, 167
"Family and Politics" workshop, 175
family political conflict, navigating, 174–176
fast thinking, 72
fear. See also politics of contempt
  as force driving politics of contempt, 74
  and power of moral courage, 216
  as reason for flight or avoidance, 148
feedback, in personal leadership plan, 194
fight mode, 146–147
financial insecurity, 65–66
Fisher, Roger, 141
flight mode, 147, 148
*The Flip Side,* 168
force-field analysis (FFA), 202–204
forces driving politics of contempt
  binary thinking and identity politics, 63–64
  citizen apathy, 74
  civics education, decline of, 73–74
  conflict entrepreneurs, 72–73
  declining social capital, 67–69
  deteriorating social dynamic, 69–70
  educational disparities and dominance by elites, 66
  fear, 74

forces driving politics of contempt *(continued)*
  financial insecurity and wealth disparities, 65–66
  historical changes, 74
  media environment and information overload, 71–72
  misinformation and disinformation, 72
  overview, 63
  political and government dysfunction, 64–65
  questions for further thought, 75
  social media algorithms, 70–71
  sorting and siloing, 66–67
foreign influence, 72, 207
formal leadership, 186–187. *See also* leadership
Fowler, Susan, 133
Frank, Anne, 107
Frankl, Viktor E., 101, 105
Freud, Anna, 135
Friedman, Thomas, 22
friends. *See also* braver conversations; relationships
  skills for managing conflicts with, 178–179
  on social media, 173

G
Gandhi, Mahatma, 8, 153, 225–226
Garrett, Shaylyn Romney, 85, 86
generalization, 57
Genesis, 226
geographic siloing, 3
geographical sorting, 67
Gerson, Wayne, 96
Getschman, Ted, 122
*Getting to Yes* (Fisher and Ury), 141
Gingrich, Newt, 83
Giono, Jean, 225
*Gladiator* film, 107–108
gladiator role, 175
global thinking. *See* thinking global, acting local
Goethe, Johann Wolfgang von, 156, 213
Gonzalez, Laurence, 163

*Good to Great* (Collins), 140
Goodwin, Doris Kearns, 22
Gorman, Amanda, 225
Gottman, John, 47
Gottman, Julie, 47
government dysfunction, 64–65
grace value, 102
grandiose language, in fight mode, 147
Granite Bridge Legislative Alliance (New Hampshire), 6, 122
Grant, Adam, 154, 189
gratitude, 137–138
"The Great Divide" (Caswell), 174
Greatest Generation, 74
Grinch, the, 27, 36
*Ground News,* 168
groups addressing polarization challenge, joining, 236
growing value, 102
growth mindset, embracing, 138
Guinea, Ebola epidemic in, 19, 128, 192
Gun Owners of America, 82
Guzmán, Mónica, 21, 36, 47, 59, 94

H
Haidt, Jonathan, 63–64, 80, 139, 172
*Happier* (Ben-Shahar), 137
happiness, gratitude as key to, 137–138
Haskins, Henry Stanley, 146
hate. *See also* politics of contempt; "us vs. them," moving beyond
  confronting, 44–46
  enjoyment of, 27
  increase in, 32–33
"Hate Has No Home Here" signs, 44
Haverhill, New Hampshire, 2–3
Hawkins, Stephen. *See* Hidden Tribes
health, and personal change, 221–223
healthy conflict
  and activism, 59–60
  moving from unhealthy conflict to, 57–59
  questions for further thought, 61
  vs. unhealthy conflict, 7, 53–57
heart, inward reflection on, 105
Heffernan, James, 35–36

Hemingway, Ernest, 145
*Hidden Brain* podcast, 172
*Hidden Tribes* (Hawkins, Yudkin, Juan-Torres, and Dixon)
   American political tribes, 92
   American views of leadership, 133
   differing perspectives on exhausted majority, 94–95, 96–97
   exhausted majority description, 7–8
   intolerance in current political climate, 93
   need for national identity, 123
   overcoming political divide, 98–99
   polarization as business model, 78
   positive changes mentioned in, 120–121
high conflict. See unhealthy conflict
high rung thinking, 98–99
Hodge-Williams, Samantha, 28
hope
   Braver Angels as model for finding, 16–18
   embracing in self-leadership, 138
   finding amid despair, 21–25
   overview, 7
   role in leadership, 195
   turning politics of contempt into politics of, 1
*Hopeful Majority* podcast, 98
Horowitz, Daniel, 166, 167
"How America Got Mean" (Brooks), 27–28
*How Change Happens* (Crutchfield), 199–200
*How Change Happens* (Sunstein), 199
"How Positive Engagement Can Bring the Exhausted Majority Back Into Politics" (Sage and Amick), 99
How to Know a Person (Brooks), 171
humility
   and critical thinking, 164
   vs. humiliation, 33
   in self-leadership, 139

I

identity
   embracing national, 123–124
   empowering American, 209

identity politics, 63–64. *See also* politics of contempt
ideological polarization, 21
immigration, 93–94
important activities, leaving time for, 139–140
*In Search of Braver Angels* (Blankenhorn), 57
individualism, 86
influence on others, as type of leadership, 133–135
influencers, political, 82
informal leadership, 133–135, 186–187. *See also* leadership; self-leadership
information overload, 71–72
in-groups. See siloing
intellectual humility, 164
interpersonal skills, declining, 69–70
intolerance, politics of. See politics of contempt
inward reflection, importance of, 101–106, 116–117. *See also* decisions shaping life and values; Looking Inward areas, checklist for change
Israel, conflict in, 56
issues, focusing on underlying, 141
I-statements, 151
*It's a Wonderful Life* film, 107
"It's Gonna Get Better" (Genesis), 226

J

James, William, 159, 197
Jefferson, Thomas, 171
Johnson, Samuel, 165
Jones, Alex, 82
journalists, as conflict entrepreneurs, 82
Juan-Torres, Míriam. See Hidden Tribes
judging others, resisting, 140
Jung, Carl, 154

K

Kahneman, Daniel, 72
Kaplan, Seth, 67, 68, 124
Keating, Paul, 185
Keen, David, 47
Keillor, Garrison, 219
Keller, Helen, 108, 188

Kennedy, Robert, 98
Kim, Andy, 43–44
kindness
   being kinder, 33–34
   bridging differences with, 39–40
   in leaders, 189–190
   power of, 28
   reduction in, 28–30
   seeing everyone as deserving of, 41–44
   as value, 102
King, Martin Luther, Jr., 46
Klein, Ezra, 39, 64, 71–72, 83–84, 95
Kouzes, Jim, 134, 155, 215, 224
Krupnikov, Yanna, 95

L

La Rochefoucauld, François de, 30
Laden, Anthony Simon, 126
landslide counties, 67
Lao Tzu, 210
LAPP (Listen, Acknowledge, Pivot, and Perspective) steps, 150–152, 169
LaRue, Kristen, 193
Laskaris, Alex, 192
Lawson, April, 70
leadership. *See also* self-leadership
   on checklist for change, 236
   developing personal leadership plan, 193–195
   Doug's approach to, 110–111
   driving change, 200
   everyday life, applying skills in, 189–191
   by example, 205
   formal vs. informal, 186–187
   key personal qualities related to, 187–188
   modeling positive behavior, 181–182
   overview, 133–135, 185
   polarization crisis, applying skills to, 191–193
   and power of teamwork, 188–189
   questions for further thought, 195
learning
   from children, 177
   in personal leadership plan, 194
Lebanon, New Hampshire, 3

Levin, Yuval, 23, 209
Levine, Peter, 124
Lewin, Kurt, 204
life story. *See* decisions shaping life and values
Lincoln, Abraham, 13, 35, 99, 148, 229
Listen, Acknowledge, Pivot, and Perspective (LAPP) steps, 150–152, 169
listening skills
   declining, 69–70
   improving, 23–24
Living Room Conversations, 239–240
local, acting. *See* thinking global, acting local
local associations, 68
local politics, 82–83
loneliness
   as force driving politics of contempt, 67–69
   reducing, 205–206
Looking Inward areas, checklist for change, 231, 232–234
*Love Your Enemies* (Brooks), 35
Luke 6:27, 35
Lutz, Robert, 169
Lynas, Mark, 82
Lyons, Mary Fran, 28

M

Maclaren, Ian, 33
Maher, Bill, 91
majority, exhausted. *See* exhausted majority
Malow, Beth
   on activism, 60
   on aggression in medical settings, 32
   background and reasons for writing book, 5
   on being kinder, 34
   and Braver Angels, 17, 18
   on braver conversation skills, 155
   on confronting hatred, 45
   on contributing to positive change, 121, 122, 126–127
   on critical thinking and COVID pandemic, 159–160, 161–163

on decisions shaping life and values, 112–114
and effects of politics of contempt on relationships, 16
on exhausted majority, 93–94, 98
on forces driving politics of contempt, 64, 65, 68, 69, 71, 73
on leadership, 134
on listening to others, 23–24
on personal change, 216
reasons for self-publishing book, 7
on reduction in kindness, 29
on seeing everyone as deserving of dignity and respect, 42
on self-leadership, 138, 140, 141
on shaming others, 46–47
"Tools to Evaluate Media" blog post, 165
values of, 102
*The Man Who Planted Trees* (Giono), 225
"Managing Difficult Conversations with Colleagues" workshop, 150
Mandela, Nelson, 44
*Man's Search for Meaning* (Frankl), 105
mask-wearing, during COVID pandemic, 29, 31, 46–47, 165–170
Mason, Dave, 32
*Mastering Leadership* (Anderson and Adams), 187
Mautz, Scott, 104–105, 154, 157, 225
MaxVoting, 122
Mead, Margaret, 119
meaning, living with, 137
mean-spirited behavior. See politics of contempt; "us vs. them," moving beyond
media. *See also* social media
   as force driving politics of contempt, 71–72
   positive changes from, 121
medical emergencies, national, 19
medical settings, aggressive behavior in, 30–32
Meel, Manu, 98
mental health
   and personal change, 221–223
   taking care of, 22
Meta, 79, 81, 173. *See also* social media
Middle East conflict, 56
Miller, Todd, 91–92
mindfulness, 141
mindset, and braver conversations, 148–149
misinformation, 72, 160–161. *See also* critical thinking
moral awakening, contributing to. See positive change, contributing to
moral courage, power of, 216–217
More in Common, 240. *See also* Hidden Tribes
More Like Us, 240
Mother Teresa, 204
Murthy, Vivek H., 67
*My Unsung Hero* podcast, 28, 111

## N

name-calling, in fight mode, 147
National Governors Association, 57–58
national identity
   embracing, 123–124
   empowering, 209
National Institute for Civil Discourse, 240
national medical emergencies, 19
national moral awakening, contributing to. See positive change, contributing to
national politics, 83. *See also* polarization; politics of contempt; "us vs. them," moving beyond
negative forces
   in force-field analysis, 202–204
   reducing, 205–206, 207–210
New Hampshire
   contributing to positive change in, 121–122
   Doug's work in state legislature, 55–56, 65
   exhausted majority in, 95
   geographic siloing in, 2–3
   Granite Bridge Legislative Alliance, 6, 122
   impact of workshops on politicians in, 210

"Skills for Bridging the Divide" workshop in, 127–128
social disconnection in, 68
"New Medical Study: Your Face Mask is Not Protecting You" blog post (Ron Paul Institute for Peace and Prosperity), 165–168
news sources, as conflict entrepreneurs, 82
Newton, Isaac, 51
Nguyen, Sarah, 160–161
*No Compromise* podcast, 82
No Labels, 240
Noonan, Peggy, 66
Nouwen, Henri, 176
Novelli, Bill, 199
nuance, seeing, 64

## O
Oliver, Mary, 223
*On Being* podcast, 224
O'Neill, Tip, 82
open-ended questions, 150–151
open-mindedness, in intellectual humility, 164
openness to change, 154–155
optimism, 22–23
organizations addressing polarization challenge, 236, 237–241. *See also* Braver Angels
"The Other Party Isn't the Enemy" (Bacon), 58
Outrage-Industrial Complex, 72–73

## P
pain caused by politics of contempt, 4
Palestine, conflict in, 56
parenting, demonstrating positive engagement in, 176–177
Parrado, Nando, 226
Parton, Dolly, 159–160
Paul, Ron, 166
peacekeeper role, 175
The People, 241
People's New Hampshire Together citizens' assembly, 122

personal actions. *See also* decisions shaping life and values; positive change, contributing to; thinking global, acting local
as blunting power of conflict entrepreneurs, 84–86
overcoming divide through, 98–99
personal change. *See also* checklist for change
adopting, 214–216
and health, 221–223
important first step in, 227
influence on country, 223–224
making and implementing plan for, 224–225
moral courage, power of, 216–217
need to start immediately, 225–226
overview, 213–227
questions for further thought, 227
resiliency, 217–219
and risk, 219–220
personal identity, politics and, 53
personal leadership plan, developing, 193–195
personal reflection, 101–106, 116–117. *See also* decisions shaping life and values; Looking Inward areas, checklist for change
perspective, in LAPP implementation steps, 151–152
pessimism, 23
philanthropists, 121–122
physical courage, 219
Piercy, Marge, 218
Pirsig, Robert, 89
pivot, in LAPP implementation steps, 151
planning, role in implementing change, 215
polarization. *See also* conflict entrepreneurs; forces driving politics of contempt; politics of contempt
applying leadership skills to, 191–193
as business model, 78
checklist for change, 233, 236

confronting by thinking global, acting local, 201–204
critical thinking, practicing in relation to, 165–168, 170
and politics of contempt, 21
recognizing if we are part of problem, 103–106
Polarization Research Lab, 83, 93
political candidates
  bettering, 210
  as conflict entrepreneurs, 82–83
  positive changes from, 120, 121
political conversations. See braver conversations; positive engagement with others
political dysfunction, 64–65
political influencers, 82
political parties, 83–84
political posts on social media, 172–173
political reforms, suggested, 122–123
political tribalism, 19, 92. *See also* siloing
politicians
  bettering, 210
  as conflict entrepreneurs, 82–83
politics of contempt. *See also* conflict entrepreneurs; forces driving politics of contempt; "us vs. them," moving beyond
  applying leadership skills to, 191–193
  book overview, 7–9
  bridging differences through dignity and respect, 39–40
  choice to self-publish book, 7
  confronting by thinking global, acting local, 201–204
  confronting hatred, 44–46
  effects on American society and culture, 18–20
  and healthy vs. unhealthy conflict, 53–57
  moving from unhealthy to healthy conflict, 57–59
  negative effects on relationships, 15–16
  and other wide-ranging challenges, 20–21
  pain caused by, 4
  polarization caused by, 21

post-inauguration reflection on, 2–4
practical approach in book, 4
questions for further thought, 9–10, 48, 75
reasons for book, 5–6
recognizing if we are part of problem, 103–106
and seeing everyone as deserving of dignity and respect, 41–42
shaming others, 46–47
turning into politics of hope, 1
positive change, contributing to
  citizen-led solutions, 124–129
  embracing national identity, 123–124
  overview, 119–123
  questions for further thought, 129
positive energy, in leaders, 190
positive engagement with others
  demonstrating for children, 176–177
  family political conflict, navigating, 174–176
  friends, managing conflicts with, 178–179
  overview, 171–172, 182
  questions for further thought, 183
  social media, managing relationships on, 172–173
  work, managing political conflict at, 179–182
positive forces
  in force-field analysis, 202–204
  moving needle on, 205, 207–210
Posner, Barry, 134, 215, 224
prejudices, increasing openness about, 70
present, being, 141
Prichard, Peggy, 147
propaganda, foreign, 72
"The Protest Trap" (Ripley), 152
Proverbs 29:18, 116
purpose
  in ESCAPE tool, 167–168
  living with, 137
Putin, Vladimir, 41
Putnam, Robert, 67, 85–86, 224

## Q

Quadrant I (urgent/important), 139, 140
Quadrant II (not urgent/important), 139, 140
Quadrant III (urgent/not important), 139
qualities related to leadership, 187–188, 190
"Question Authority" bumper sticker, 20

## R

Rauch, Jonathan, 70, 165
realism, in intellectual humility, 164
reassessing personal leadership plan, 195
"Red State Blue State" podcast, 56
"Red/Blue" workshops (Braver Angels), 17
Reese, Mareisha N., 181
Reeve, Cristopher, 14
reflection, importance of inward, 101–106, 116–117. *See also* decisions shaping life and values; Looking Inward areas, checklist for change
reforms, suggested political, 122–123
relationships. *See also* positive engagement with others
  and braver conversations, 152
  building of by leaders, 187–188, 191
  building with someone on opposite side, 227
  managing on social media, 172–173
  negative effects of politics of contempt on, 15–16
  in personal leadership plan, 194
  role in civic renewal, 124–129
Republicans, 19–20. *See also* polarization; politics of contempt
resiliency, 217–219
resources, 229–230
respect. *See also* kindness
  embracing, 35
  and family political conflict, 175–176
  lack of at work, 180
  power of to bridge differences, 39–40
  seeing everyone as deserving of, 41–44
  vs. shaming others, 46–47
Ripley, Amanda
  on acceptance, 174
  *On Being* podcast, 224
  on conflict entrepreneurs, 77
  on leadership, 191
  on need to matter, 68
  on positive use of social media, 80
  on relationships, 152
  on unhealthy conflict, 53, 54, 58
risk, and personal change, 219–220
Robinson, Becky
  background and reasons for writing book, 5–6
  on braver conversation skills, 145
  on contributing to positive change, 119–120
  on decisions shaping life and values, 115–116
  on exhausted majority, 97
  on leadership, 191
  on personal change, 218, 219–220
  on positive engagement with others, 174–175, 177, 179–180
  on positive use of social media, 80–81
  reasons for self-publishing book, 7
  values of, 103
Ron Paul Institute for Peace and Prosperity, 165–168
Roosevelt, Eleanor, 41
Roosevelt, Theodore, 22
rudeness, 29–30
Rumi, xii
rural areas, geographical sorting in, 67
Russia, disinformation campaigns by, 72
Rwanda, genocide in, 18–19

## S

Sage, Sami, 99
Salmansohn, Karen, 32
Santos, Luiza, 220
school start times, 126–127
Schweitzer, Albert, 179
science communication, 162–163
self-awareness, 138, 190
self-development, dedicating time to, 136
self-leadership
  authenticity and self-awareness, 138

believing in yourself, 136–137
empathy, curiosity, and humility, 139
gratitude, embracing as key to happiness, 137–138
hope and growth mindset, embracing, 138
living with meaning and purpose, 137
mindfulness and presence, 141
as most important part of leadership, 185, 187
overview, 135–136
questions for further thought, 143
resisting assumptions and judging others, 140
time, using wisely, 139–140
trustworthiness, 140–141
win-win thinking, 141
working toward, 142
self-reflection, importance of, 101–106, 116–117. *See also* decisions shaping life and values
Serenity Prayer, 104
Shakespeare, William, 216, 217
shaming others, 46–47
sharing critical thinking process with others, 169–170
Shedd, John, 214
shutting people out, 171, 172
silence, going beyond, 99
siloing. *See also* polarization
   as force driving politics of contempt, 66–67
   geographic, 3
   questioning, 9
   on social media, 173
   stepping out of political silos, 36
"Skills for Bridging the Divide" workshop (Braver Angels), 127–128
"Skills for Disagreeing Better" workshop (Braver Angels), 150–152
slow democracy, 124
slow thinking, 72
small steps, taking toward positive change, 119–120
smartphones. *See also* social media

and success of conflict entrepreneurs, 77
use and misuse of, 78
sniper role, 175
social capital, declining, 67–69
social disconnection
   as force driving politics of contempt, 67–69
   reducing, 205–206
social dynamic, deteriorating, 69–70
social media
   braver conversations on, 153–154
   as force driving politics of contempt, 70–71
   healthier use of, 208–209
   managing relationships on, 172–173
   potential to fuel positive use of, 80–81
   and success of conflict entrepreneurs, 77–80, 81
   use and misuse of, 78
social skills, applying talents to address, 210
sorting, 66–67
sources
   in ESCAPE tool, 166–167
   presenting both sides of stories, 168
Stanford Polarization and Social Change Lab, 57
Starts with Us (now Builders), 239
"The Summer Day" (Oliver), 223
Sunstein, Cass, 199
supportiveness, contagious nature of, 134
Swire-Thompson, Briony, 161
synergy, power of, 188–189

T
*Tangle*, 168
Taylor-Klaus, David, 116
teachableness, in intellectual humility, 164
Teachout, Woden, 124
teamwork, power of, 188–189, 191
technology companies
   as conflict entrepreneurs, 81
   positive changes from, 121
teen sleep biology, 126–127
Tenzin Gyatso (Dalai Lama), 27, 178

Teschner, Doug
  on aggression in medical settings, 31
  background and reasons for writing book, 6
  and Braver Angels, 16–18
  on braver conversation skills, 149, 153
  on conflict entrepreneurs, 78
  on contributing to positive change, 122, 128
  on decisions shaping life and values, 108–112
  on effects of politics of contempt on relationships, 15–16
  on exhausted majority, 91, 94–95
  on forces driving politics of contempt, 65
  on healthy vs. unhealthy conflict, 55–56
  on humility vs. humiliation, 33
  on leadership, 135, 190, 192
  on personal change, 214, 221, 226
  on polarization as business model, 77
  on positive engagement with others, 173, 174
  post-inauguration reflection, 2–4
  reasons for self-publishing book, 7
  on reduction in kindness, 29
  on seeing everyone as deserving of dignity and respect, 41, 43
  on self-leadership, 137, 142
  values of, 102
therapy, 137
*Thinking, Fast and Slow* (Kahneman), 72
thinking global, acting local
  areas to apply talents, 206–210
  confronting polarization challenge by, 201–204
  everyday actions, impact of, 204–206
  overview, 199–201
  questions for further thought, 211
*This American Life* podcast, 56
*This Is Day One* (Dudley), 190
thoughts, recognizing gap between values and, 103–106
threatening
  culture of, 70
  reducing, 206

time, using wisely, 139–140
Tippett, Krista, 22–23, 224
"To Be of Use" (Piercy), 218
*Together Across Differences* newsletter, 81, 229
"Tools to Evaluate Media" blog post (Malow), 165
toxic polarization. See polarization
tribalism, political, 19, 92. *See also* polarization; siloing
trust, 79, 140–141, 192
Truth and Trust Project (Braver Angels), 163
Tufekci, Zeynep, 208
Turer, Eric, 127–128

U

*An Unfinished Love Story* (Goodwin), 22
unhealthy conflict. *See also* polarization; politics of contempt
  and activism, 59–60
  vs. healthy conflict, 7, 53–57
  moving to healthy conflict from, 57–59
  questions for further thought, 61
unhealthy influences, on checklist for change, 233
*The Upswing* (Putnam and Garrett), 85
Urban, Tim, 98
urban areas, geographical sorting in, 67
urgent/important matrix, 139–140
Ury, William L., 141
US Constitution, 209
"us vs. them," moving beyond
  and aggressive behavior in medical settings, 30–32
  being an angel, 35–36
  being kinder, 33–34
  bridging differences by, 39–40
  confronting hatred, 44–46
  embracing dignity and respect, 35
  and healthy vs. unhealthy conflict, 53–57
  and increase in hate, 32–33
  moving from unhealthy to healthy conflict, 57–59
  overview, 7, 27–28, 213

questions for further thought, 35–36, 48
recognizing gap between thoughts and values, 103–106
and reduction in kindness, 28–30
seeing everyone as deserving of dignity and respect, 41–44
vs. shaming others, 46–47

## V

vaccine, COVID, 159–160, 162, 216
*Valley News* column (Gerson), 96
values. *See also* decisions shaping life and values
  and braver conversations, 148–149
  making list of, 101–103
  recognizing gap between thoughts and, 103–106
Van Tongeren, Daryl, 164
Vick, Karl, 94
The Village Square, 241
violence, in medical settings, 30–32
vision, role in implementing change, 215
Volinsky, Andru, 59
Vonnegut, Kurt, 27
voter stories, 229
voting methods, positive changes for, 122
vulnerability
  and braver conversations, 148–149
  connection between courage and, 217

## W

*We Can't Talk about That at Work!* (Winters and Reese), 181

"We Just Disagree" (Mason), 32
wealth disparities, 65–66
WebMD, 78, 138
website for book, 229
well-being, and personal change, 221–223
Wharton, Edith, 217
white nationalism, Derek Black's renunciation of, 39–40
Wilkinson, Wilk, 164
Williamson County, Tennessee, 126–127
Winters, Mary-Frances, 181
win-win thinking, 141
Woodruff, Judy, 105
work
  braver conversations in, 156–157
  managing political conflict at, 179–183

## X

X, 81. *See also* social media

## Y

Yarrow, Peter, 16–17
Yudkin, Daniel. See Hidden Tribes

## Z

Zaki, Jamil, 220
zero-sum (binary) thinking, 57, 63–64. *See also* polarization; politics of contempt; "us vs. them," moving beyond

# ACKNOWLEDGMENTS

Bringing a book into the world is a daunting task. So many people helped make this book possible, and we are incredibly grateful.

The Weaving Influence team has been amazing in their production, publishing, and marketing efforts. Thank you to Lori Weidert, Rachel Royer, Sydney Spencer, Wendy Haan, Molly Kellie, Amy Driehorst, Keri Hales, Kelly Edmiston, Stephanie Jordan, Laura Finch, Isabel Thornton, Kurt Menard, and Russ Hawkins.

Braver Angels volunteers and staff have been incredibly supportive and inspiring, including David Blankenhorn, Mónica Guzmán, and Rev. Mark Beckwith (who all endorsed the book), as well as Bill Doherty, David Lapp, Barbara Thomas, Maury Giles, Elizabeth Doll, Gabbi Timmis, Courtenay Budd, Craig Diamond, Kira Barone, John Kerr, Sabrina Pedersen, Sharmin Banu, Rob Hanson, Donna Murphy, Jay Wilgus, Bruce and Kathy Morlan, Maryanne Colter, Connie Shortes, and so many others.

We offer an extra loud shout-out to three extraordinary Braver Angels volunteers: Gary Holland (who also wrote an endorsement), Steve Saltwick (who also critiqued the citizen-led solutions chapter), and Catherine Clark (who provided valuable feedback on the entire book and researched and edited footnotes). Gary, Steve, and Catherine went so far above and beyond in supporting this book. We cannot thank them enough.

Special thanks to the others who provided endorsements: Hon. Sherman Packard, Susan Clark, Stephen Hawkins, Scott Mautz, Shaylyn Romney Garrett, Lenny Mirra, Hon. David Scanlan, Steve Driehaus, and Seth Gillihan.

We received invaluable feedback from those who invested the time to review and comment on full drafts or selected chapters: Pamela Hertzog, Hilary Hodge, Sue Lani Madsen, Travis Tripodi, Leslie Lopato, Jet Vertz, Ben Teschner, and James McKim.

Thank you to podcast hosts Martha Engber of Vigilant Positivity, Richard Davies of How Do We Fix It?, and Wilk Wilkinson of Derate the Hate. We look forward to discussing our book with other podcasters, including Brian MacDonald, as well as On the Other Hand hosts April Chatham-Carpenter and J. Glen White.

So many others helped us in various ways, including Robert Putnam, Bernie Marvin, Aaron Goulette, Terry Pfaff, Olivia Zink, George Zeller, Austin Pert, Hermence Matsotsa, Erica Evans, Timothy MacIntyre, Ken Mello, and James, Jennifer, and Peter Teschner. Thank you all!

We appreciate the efforts of our book ambassadors who wrote reviews and shared about the book on their social networks.

Special thanks to Matt Donahue for his wonderful legal support, which played a critical role in helping launch Together Across Differences LLC.

There are so many others who supported and inspired us. Naming you all would fill another book.

 When I began to write this book in January 2024, I knew success would require a team effort. I am especially grateful that Beth Malow and Becky Robinson joined me as coauthors. When you take on a big project like writing a book, you can only hope to have such amazing partners.

Beth, like me, volunteers with Braver Angels, so we share a deep commitment to and passion for this work. Her energy is boundless, coupled with a deep array of skills that overlap and, in multiple ways, exceed mine. We complement and enrich each other so remarkably well.

Becky added immensely to this effort, bringing a whole new set of skills that enabled us to achieve so much more. While not having Braver Angels experiences like Beth and me, Becky brought new perspectives that greatly enriched and strengthened the text. I cannot thank her enough.

I want to thank Amanda Andrews, Jeff Feingold, and Mike Cote, who published my "Growing Leadership" columns in the NH Business Review over the past seven years. Many of the ideas first articulated in those columns were developed further in this book.

So many readers of those columns and my other ideas and writings (including the monthly Growing Leadership Insights) have been so encouraging and supportive, including Tim Hawley, Ruth and Bill Cioffredi, Todd Miller, Jo Anne Jaworsky, John Schultz, David Teschner (RIP), David Webb, Mal Kircher, Kristen LaRue, Kathy Burnell, Dan Chang, Liese Shewmaker, Bob Wohlfort, Mary K Dennison, Chris Woodside, Laura Waterman, Luke, John, and Juanita Teschner, and so many others. Thank you!

Some special outdoor friends have supported me along life's journey and endured my absence during the book writing, including Tom Johnson, Doug Burnell, Ralph Baldwin, Chris Hawkins, Alton Stone, George Allan, Brian Fowler, and John Skirving.

Lastly, a special shout-out to my wife, who put up with me being so focused and distracted, as well as my two sons and three grandchildren. And to my parents who made it all possible, especially my mom, who raised three sons after my father died so tragically at a young age. I am so grateful and wish you were here to see this.

After reading a few of Doug's chapters and providing input, I was honored when he asked if I would be his coauthor. Being the "leap before I look" person I am, of course I said yes, and I am so glad I did. The last year has been an incredible journey. I am grateful to Doug for trusting me to help him tell this story. He is fully committed to and passionate about the mission of this book and to preserving our democracy for future generations.

I have enjoyed getting to know Becky, and I share Doug's sentiments that she has brought so many strengths to this project. In addition to being a talented writer, she is also an expert in book production and promotion. At every step of the journey, she has guided us about best practices and helped us create a product that we are proud of and that can make a difference for so many.

There are many people to thank. My husband, Steve, deserves top billing, as he generously tolerated my many hours of writing, researching, editing, and responding to beta-reader comments. My sons Austin and Daniel and my brother Brad also encouraged me. My two closest friends from college days, Shari Berkwitz and Linda Becker, were there to enjoy the journey as well.

I'm also grateful to those who shaped me into the bridge-builder I am today, including my co-organizers of Common Ground Nashville (Lynn Heady, Sheila Caruso, and Catherine Clark) and my Braver Angels co-moderator in Vermont, Patricia Higgins. I'm appreciative to Elizabeth Bojsza, Lynne Lamberg, and Terra Ziporyn Snider for their guidance as science communicators.

Like Doug, I wish my mother, Theresa Malow, were alive to read this—she would have been so proud. She was the ultimate bridge-builder—she befriended everyone she met. I'm also grateful to my dad, Monroe Malow, who instilled in me a love of writing (and published his own memoirs), and my brother Robert Malow (who engaged in friendly competitions with me about who had more scientific papers), as they would have loved watching me emerge as a fellow author.

 I'm grateful to have joined Doug Teschner and Beth Malow on this project. Doug has provided helpful encouragement to me for years as a subscriber to my email list. I felt honored to be invited into this project.

I'm in awe of the painstaking work both Doug and Beth did to bring this project to life. My contribution feels minimal in comparison to theirs, and yet they graciously express appreciation for my contributions both in these acknowledgements and every time we talk. I'm most grateful for the friendships we've created through our weekly calls and for the commitment they both show to this important message. I appreciate their willingness to listen to my guidance and for our collaborative work on our Substack publication as well.

Thank you to the supportive communities that surround and support me: our clients (including those who faithfully attend our 4th Friday community, the entire Weaving Influence team, our Team Buzz Builder network and newsletter subscribers, my morning women's group, and my local running friends). You all teach me how to connect with kindness, even across differences.

Thank you to my friends, old and new: Jamie, Sarah N., Sarah D., Lisa, Lindsey, Lesley, Libby, and Michelle. You keep me grounded and inspire me to be better.

Thanks, appreciation, and admiration to Deirdre Honner, whose volunteerism and activism inspires me every day.

Unending love and thanks to my husband and kids. I appreciate your openness and graciousness in allowing me to share our family stories and experiences here, and for my kids' editing suggestions.

# ABOUT THE AUTHORS

## DOUG TESCHNER

I have been incredibly blessed with a good life, including growing up in a loving family in Westborough, Massachusetts. This special community really cared, as was on full display after my father died in a car accident when I was only fourteen years old. I attended church and Sunday school from an early age, which has had a lifelong impact. My mother always communicated to me and my two younger brothers that we could do whatever we wanted in life. She was an amazing influence on my life in so many ways.

I had a good education, earning a BS in forestry and a doctorate (EdD) in administrative leadership at the University of Massachusetts, as well as a master's degree in botany at the University of Vermont where I studied mountain ecology.

I am a mountain lover, hiker, skier, and climber. In my younger days, I had the opportunity to make numerous ascents of major peaks in North America, Europe, and Africa, and once played a role in saving the life of a severely injured man on Mount Washington, New Hampshire, an event that shaped my life in profound ways. I still volunteer with the Appalachian Mountain Club, giv-

Doug on right with former President of Ukraine Leonid Kravchuk. (Photo courtesy of Doug Teschner.)

Doug in California's Sierra Nevada.
(Photo courtesy of Doug Teschner.)

ing naturalist talks and serving as a contributing editor for the *Appalachia* journal.

I have had diverse and satisfying work experiences both in this country and overseas. I served as a Peace Corps Volunteer in Morocco doing forestry projects, and I worked for many years in nonprofits. Inspired by Executive Councilor Ray Burton, I ran for office and was an elected New Hampshire Republican state representative for six terms. I also served as a New Hampshire assistant secretary of state.

Later in my career, I went back overseas, leading US Agency for International Development projects to strengthen the Rwanda and Morocco parliaments and serving as the Peace Corps country director in Burkina Faso, Ukraine, and Guinea. I speak fluent French, intermediate Moroccan Arabic, and some Russian.

When I think about these overseas experiences, I am grateful to have had the opportunity to represent the United States, and I recognize how much these opportunities increased my appreciation for our country when I came back home. I hope that writing this book is an extension of this service to our nation.

Today, I run a small consulting business, Growing Leadership LLC (https://www.growingleadershipllc.com/), but, given concerns about our country, I find myself spending much more time volunteering with Braver Angels and promoting the ideas in this book.

I am blessed to have been married for forty-four years, and we have two wonderful sons and three delightful grandchildren.

Since 2018, I have written the "Growing Leadership" column in the NH Business Review and have increasingly incorporated aspects of this national polarization crisis into my writing. A 2023 column elicited many positive responses, including this one:

> "Your 'Living with Optimism Amid Our Nation's Challenges' article was great. You should be on 60 Minutes to talk about the things you wrote about. I have been saying for several decades that we need thought leaders who can convey a vision of a better future. You are one."

Soon after receiving that message, I decided to write this book.

Some years ago, I developed my why: "*To inspire myself and others to achieve a higher level of personal and professional performance.*" I have brought this spirit to the book, wanting to explore more deeply how each of us can touch hearts and give people hope in these challenging times.

## BETH MALOW

My story shares some commonalities with Doug's, and also differences. I grew up on Long Island, New York, to two Jewish middle-class parents who worked hard to support their children. I will always be grateful for their generosity in supporting my medical school's steep tuition, but even more so for instilling in me a love for learning and a belief that I could accomplish anything I wanted to.

My parents were solid Democrats, although later in life my dad listened to Republican talk show hosts. That baffled me at first, although I now appreciate his being open to listening to diverse viewpoints (as I have worked hard to do as well). My parents, who were married almost seventy years, saw the good in everyone and could get along with anyone. My dad also had a strong love of country and service, and worked as an engineer on the Manhattan Project in Oak Ridge, Tennessee, during World War II.

I feel blessed to have lived in a lot of places, which contributed to my seeing different perspectives. This included medical training in Chicago, New York City, and Boston, where I met my husband. I chose neurology because I was fascinated by how the brain worked and what made people tick.

Work brought us to Ann Arbor, Michigan, where our kids were born, and then to Tennessee. We lived in Williamson County, just south of Nashville, because it was close to work and had strong public schools. It also has a strong Christian conservative community, which I grew to appreciate and admire. I made many close friends who respected my faith, even though it differed from theirs. Nashville was a fabulous city for work (Vanderbilt Medical Center employs both me and my husband, and I currently work remotely) and also for music. I sang in three different choruses and a quartet before COVID put singing on the "high risk" list.

Beth and her husband Steve participating in community theater.

Through music and other activities, I met and befriended many conservatives and progressives, especially after the 2016 election. It was hard to leave the mild weather in that state for New England winters but I've embraced skiing, ice skating, and snowshoeing. Getting outdoors both calms and invigorates me. I've also enjoyed participating with my husband, Steve, in community theater.

Returning to New England has fostered my participation in local civic initiatives. I'm honored to work with energized people in my new state of Vermont, along with those just over the border in New Hampshire. It's a great place to be part of a movement focused on citizen-led solutions.

## BECKY ROBINSON

I am the founder/CEO of Weaving Influence (https://weavinginfluence.com/), a digital marketing agency supporting nonfiction authors since 2012. Our team provides authors, thought leaders, and executives with comprehensive strategic and implementation support, helping them connect with new audiences through their books. Weaving Influence has a strong team of employees and contractors across the United States, working virtually and flexibly to serve our hundreds of clients with excellence.

In the past thirteen years, my team and I have supported more than 235 book launches. I host *The Book Marketing Action Podcast* and teach book marketing strategy through one-on-one sessions and a live course. I am also the award-winning author of *Reach: Create the Biggest Possible Audience for Your Message, Book, or Cause* (Berrett-Koehler Publishers, April 2022).

My husband and I live in Lambertville, Michigan, and have three wonderful young adult kids. I have lived in the Midwest all my adult life. I graduated from Miami University in Ohio in 1992 with a BA in English/creative writing. In 1994, I earned an MA in intercultural studies from Wheaton College Graduate School in Wheaton, Illinois.

I'm always thinking about my next book idea. When Doug Teschner began sharing his vision with me, I immediately recognized the importance of this work for our country at this moment. On the morning after the 2024 national election, I stepped up to join Doug and Beth as coauthor.

www.ingramcontent.com/pod-product-compliance
Lightning Source LLC
Chambersburg PA
CBHW060452030426
42337CB00015B/1562